BOOKS BY GORE VIDAL

NOVELS

Williwaw
In a Yellow Wood
The City and the Pillar
The Season of Comfort
A Search for the King
Dark Green, Bright Red
The Judgment of Paris
Messiah
Julian
Washington, D.C.
Myra Breckinridge
Two Sisters
Burr
Myron
1876
Kalki
Creation
Duluth
Lincoln
Myra Breckinridge and Myron
Empire

SHORT STORIES

A Thirsty Evil

———

PLAYS

An Evening with Richard Nixon
Weekend
Romulus
The Best Man
Visit to a Small Planet

———

ESSAYS

Rocking the Boat
Reflections upon a Sinking Ship
Homage to Daniel Shays
Matters of Fact and of Fiction
The Second American Revolution

# AT HOME

# AT HOME

ESSAYS 1982-1988

# GORE VIDAL

RANDOM HOUSE NEW YORK

PS
3543
I 26
A 89
1988

Originally published in different form in Great Britain by André Deutsch Limited, 1987. Copyright © 1987 by Gore Vidal.

All the essays in this work have previously appeared in *The New York Review of Books, The Nation, Newsweek, Esquire, Vanity Fair, Architectural Digest,* and *The Times* (London) *Literary Supplement.*

Grateful acknowledgment is made to Black Sparrow Press for permission to reprint "Introduction" by Gore Vidal to *Collected Stories of Paul Bowles.* Copyright © 1979 by Gore Vidal. Reprinted by permission of Black Sparrow Press.

Library of Congress Cataloging-in-Publication Data
Vidal, Gore, 1925–
At Home
I. Title.  PS3543.I26A89  1988     814'.54     88-42670
ISBN 0-394-57020-0

Manufactured in the United States of America
Typography and binding design by J. K. Lambert
24689753
First American Edition

# PREFACE

As shadows lengthen now across the greensward, in the immortal Pelham Grenville W.'s eldritch phrase, one's thoughts turn to crepuscular things. Bats flit; bees buzz in bonnets; the millennium, yet again (you can set your clock by it), is at hand, and as the twenty-first century gets ready to welcome us with all manner of good things, let us hope that noisy Armageddon does not intersect too soon our "pale parabola of joy."

Over the years I have noted with what nervousness writers apologize for collections of random pieces that they have written. They seem to think that a collection of essays ought to have a single numinous theme, like dentistry or the writer's own sweet self. Since the second does the binding in any case, why not accept the fact that an essay (from the French *essai,* an attempt) is simply that—an attempt to order one's impressions and reflections on a given subject? These particular essays (1983–1988) are attempts to salvage from lost time people and places that no longer exist as they once were, or at all. I have done this deliberately (which means unconsciously) because I shall never write a formal memoir (I have never been my own subject, a sign of truly sickening narcissism). In any case, as I write of politics, literature, aviation and my father, I do, occasionally, strike a personal note, in order to give some of the geography, if nothing else, of my own life.

As others have remarked, I am obsessed with my own country, whose high imperial noon (1945–1950) coincided with my own high youth, and though I have deplored our military adventures quite as much as my grandfather did in 1898 when he helped lead the anti-imperialists against the forcible annexation of the Philippine islands, I did not expect the general enterprise to become so seedy and corrupt, or our economic and moral collapse to be so swift. But then William James, in a letter to William Dean Howells (1906), struck the note that still resounds: "Exactly that callousness to abstract justice is the sinister feature and, to me, as well as to you, the incomprehensible feature of our U.S. civilization. When the ordinary American hears of cases of injustice he begins to pooh-pooh and minimize them and tone down the thing, and breed excuses from his general fund of optimism and respect for expediency." What James would have made of Ronald Reagan is beyond the imaginable. But he did not live in the age of Reagan. I did. Here's my report.

# Contents

PART II

# PART I

# CHAPTER 1

# AT HOME
# IN WASHINGTON, D.C.

ike so many blind people my grandfather was a passionate sightseer, not
to mention a compulsive guide. One of my first memories is driving
with him to a slum in southeast Washington. "All this," he said,
pointing at the dilapidated red brick buildings, "was once our land." Since
I saw only shabby buildings and could not imagine the land beneath, I was
not impressed.

Years later I saw a map of how the District of Columbia had looked
before the district's invention. Georgetown was a small community on the
Potomac. The rest was farmland, owned by nineteen families. I seem to
remember that the Gore land was next to that of the Notleys—a name
that remains with me since my great-grandfather was called Thomas Not-
ley Gore. (A kind reader tells me that the land-owning Notleys were

located elsewhere in Maryland.) Most of these families were what we continue to call—mistakenly—Scots-Irish. Actually, the Gores were Anglo-Irish from Donegal. They arrived in North America at the end of the seventeenth century and they tended to intermarry with other Anglo-Irish families—particularly in Virginia and Maryland.

George Washington not only presided over the war of separation from Great Britain (*revolution* is much too strong a word for that confused and confusing operation) but he also invented the federal republic whose original constitution reflected his powerful will to create the sort of government which would see to it that the rights of property will be forever revered. He was then congenial, if not controlling, party to the deal that moved the capital of the new republic from the city of Philadelphia to the wilderness not far from his own Virginia estate.

When a grateful nation saw fit to call the capital-to-be Washington City, the great man made no strenuous demur. Had he not already established his modesty and republican virtue by refusing the crown of the new Atlantic nation on the ground that to replace George III with George I did not sound entirely right? Also, and perhaps more to the point, Washington had no children. There would be no Prince of Virginia, ready to ascend the rustic throne at Washington City when the founder of the dynasty was translated to a higher sphere.

Although Washington himself did not have to sell or give up any of his own land, he did buy a couple of lots as speculation. Then he died a year before the city was occupied by its first president-in-residence, John Adams. The families that had been dispossessed to make way for the capital city did not do too badly. The Gores who remained sold lots, built houses and hotels, and became rich. The Gores who went away—my grandfather's branch—moved to the far west, in those days, Mississippi. It was not until my grandfather was elected to the Senate in 1907 that he was able to come home again—never to leave until his death in 1949.

Although foreign diplomats enjoy maintaining that Washington is—or was—a hardship post, the British minister in 1809, one Francis James Jackson, had the good sense to observe: "I have procured two very good saddle horses, and Elizabeth and I have been riding in all directions round the place whenever the weather has been cool enough. The country has a beautifully picturesque appearance, and I have nowhere seen finer scenery than is composed by the Potomac and the woods and hills about it; yet it has a wild and desolated air from being so scantily and rudely cultivated, and from the want of population. . . . So you see we are not fallen into a wilderness,—so far from it that I am surprised no one should before have mentioned the great beauty of the neighborhood. The natives trouble themselves but little about it; their thoughts are chiefly of tobacco, flour, shingles, and the news of the day." *Plus ça change.*

Twenty years ago, that well-known wit and man-about-town, John F. Kennedy, said, "Washington perfectly combines southern efficiency with northern charm." I think that this was certainly true of the era when he and his knights of the Round Table were establishing Camelot amongst the local chiggers. By then too many glass buildings were going up. Too many old houses were being town down or allowed to crumble. Too many slums were metastasizing around Capitol Hill. Also, the prewar decision to make an imperial Roman—literally, Roman—capital out of what had been originally a pleasant Frenchified southern city was, in retrospect, a mistake.

I can remember that when such Roman palaces as the Commerce Department were being built, we used to wonder, rather innocently, how these huge buildings could ever be filled up with people. But a city is an organism like any other and an organism knows its own encodement. Long before the American empire was a reality, the city was turning itself into New Rome. While the basilicas and porticoes were going up, one often had the sense that one was living not in a city that was being built but in a set of ruins. It is curious that even in those pre-nuclear days many of us could imagine the city devastated. Was this, perhaps, some memory of the War of 1812 when the British burned Capitol and White House? Or of the Civil War when southern troops invaded the city, coming down Seventh Street Road?

"At least they will make wonderful ruins," said my grandfather, turning his blind eyes on the Archives Building; he was never a man to spend public money on anything if he could help it. But those Piranesi blocks of marble eventually became real buildings that soon filled up with real bureaucrats, and by the end of the Second World War Washington had a real world empire to go with all those (to my eyes, at least) bogus-Roman sets.

Empires are dangerous possessions, as Pericles was among the first to point out. Since I recall pre-imperial Washington, I am a bit of an old Republican in the Ciceronian mode, given to decrying the corruption of the simpler, saner city of my youth. In the twenties and thirties, Washington was a small town where everyone knew everyone else. When school was out in June, boys took off their shoes and did not put them on again —at least outside the house—until September. The summer heat was— and is—Egyptian. In June, before Congress adjourned, I used to be sent with car and driver to pick up my grandfather at the Capitol and bring him home. In those casual days, there were few guards at the Capitol— and, again, everyone knew everyone else. I would wander on to the floor of the Senate, sit on my grandfather's desk if he wasn't ready to go, experiment with the snuff that was ritually allotted each senator; then I would lead him off the floor. On one occasion, I came down the aisle of the Senate wearing nothing but a bathing suit. This caused a good deal of amusement, to the blind man's bewilderment. Finally, the vice president, Mr. Garner—teeth like tiny black pearls and a breath that was all whisky—came down from the chair and said, "Senator, this boy is nekkid." Afterward I always wore a shirt on the Senate floor—but never shoes.

I date the end of the old republic and the birth of the empire to the invention, in the late thirties, of air conditioning. Before air conditioning, Washington was deserted from mid-June to September. The president— always Franklin Roosevelt—headed up the Hudson and all of Congress went home. The gentry withdrew to the northern resorts. Middle-income people flocked to Rehobeth Beach, Delaware or Virginia Beach, which was slightly more racy. But since air conditioning and the Second World War arrived, more or less at the same time, Congress sits and sits while the presidents and their staffs never stop making mischief at the White House or in "Mr. Mullett's masterpiece," the splendid old State, War and Navy building, now totally absorbed by the minions of President Augustus. The Pentagon—a building everyone hated when it was being built—still gives us no great cause to love either its crude appearance or its function, so like that of a wasp's nest aswarm.

Now our Roman buildings are beginning to darken with time and pigeon droppings while the brutal glass towers of the late twentieth century tend to mask and dwarf them. But here and there in the city one still comes across shaded streets and houses; so many relics of lost time—when men wore white straw hats and suits in summer while huge hats decorated the ladies (hats always got larger just before a war) and one dined at Harvey's Restaurant, where the slow-turning ceiling-fans and tessellated floors made the hottest summer day seem cool even though the air of the street outside was ovenlike and smelled of jasmine and hot tar, while nearby Lafayette Park was a lush tropical jungle where one could see that Civil War hero, Mr. Justice Oliver Wendell Holmes, Jr., stroll, his white moustaches unfurled like fierce battle pennants. At the park's edge our entirely own and perfectly unique Henry Adams held court for decades in a house opposite to that Executive Mansion where grandfather and great-grandfather had reigned over a capital that was little more than a village down whose muddy main street ran a shallow creek that was known to some even then as—what else?—the Tiber.

THE NEW YORK REVIEW OF BOOKS
*April 29, 1982*

# CHAPTER 2

# ON FLYING

1

I was twice footnote to the history of aviation. On July 7, 1929, still on the sunny side of four years old, I flew in the first commercially scheduled airliner (a Ford trimotor) across the United States, from New York to Los Angeles in forty-eight hours. Aviation was now so safe that even a little child could fly in comfort. I remember only two things about the flight: the lurid flames from the exhaust through the window; then a sudden loss of altitude over Los Angeles, during which my eardrums burst. Always the trouper, I was later posed, smiling, for the rotogravure sections of the newspapers, blood trickling from tiny lobes. Among my supporting cast that day were my father, the assistant general manager of the company (Transcontinental Air Transport), his great and good friend, as the never great, never good *Time* magazine would say, Amelia Earhart,

as well as Anne Morrow Lindbergh, whose husband Charles was my pilot.*
Both Lindbergh and Amelia had been hired by the line's promoter, one
C. M. Keys (not even a footnote now but then known as the czar of
aviation), to publicize TAT, popularly known as "The Lindbergh Line."

My second moment of footnotehood occurred in the spring of 1936,
when I was—significantly—on the sunny side of eleven. I was picked up
at St. Albans School in Washington, D.C., by my father, Eugene L. Vidal,
director of the Bureau of Air Commerce (an appointee of one Franklin
D. Roosevelt, himself mere tinkling prelude to Reagan's heavenly choir).
FDR wanted to have a ministry of aviation like the European powers; and
so the Bureau of Air Commerce was created.

On hot spring mornings Washington's streets smelled of melting asphalt,
and everything was a dull tropical green. The city was more like a Virginia
county seat than a world capital. Instead of air conditioning, people used
palmetto fans. As we got into my implausibly handsome father's plausible
Plymouth, he was mysterious, while I was delighted to be liberated from
school. I wore short trousers and polo shirt, the standard costume of those
obliged to pretend that they were children a half-century ago. What was
up? I asked. My father said, You'll see. Since we were now on the familiar
road to Bolling Field, I knew that whatever was up, it was probably going
to be us. Ever since my father—known to all as Gene—had become
director in 1933, we used to fly together nearly every weekend in the
director's Stinson monoplane. Occasionally he'd let me take the controls.
Otherwise, I was navigator. With a filling-station road map on my bony
knees, I would look out the window for familiar landmarks. When in
doubt, you followed a railroad line or a main highway. Period joke: A dumb
pilot was told to follow the Super Chief no matter what; when the train
entered a tunnel, so did the pilot. End of joke.

At Bolling Field, I recognized the so-called Hammond flivver plane.
Gene had recently told the press that a plane had been developed so safe
that anyone could fly it and so practical that anyone who could afford a
flivver car could buy it—in mass production, that is. At present, there was

*A recent investigation of a certain newspaper of record shows that, contrary to family
tradition, I was *not* on the first flight. I made my first cross-country flight a few months
later, at the age of four. In any case, I am still a triumphant footnote: the first child ever
to cross the country by air-rail.

only the prototype. But it was my father's dream to put everyone in the air, just as Henry Ford had put everyone on the road. Since 1933, miles of newsprint and celluloid had been devoted to Gene Vidal's dream—or was it folly?

We had been up in the Hammond plane before, and I suppose it really was almost "foolproof," as my father claimed. I forget the plane's range and speed but the speed was probably less than a hundred miles an hour. (One pleasure of flying then: sliding the window open and sticking out your hand, and feeling the wind smash against it.) As a boy, the actual flying of a plane was a lot simpler for me than building one of those model planes that the other lads were so adept at making and I all thumbs in the presence of balsa wood, paper, and glue—the Dionysiac properties of glue were hardly known then. But those were Depression years, and we Americans a serious people. That is how we beat Hitler, Mussolini, and Tojo.

Next to the Hammond, there was a Pathé newsreel crew, presided over by the familiar figure of Floyd Gibbons, a dark patch covering the vacancy in his florid face where once there had been an eye that he had lost—it was rumored—as a correspondent in the war to make the world safe for democracy, and now for a flivver aircraft in every garage. Since my father appeared regularly in newsreels and *The March of Time,* a newsreel crew was no novelty. At age seven, when asked what my father did, I said, He's in the newsreels. But now, since I had been taken so mysteriously out of class, could it be . . . ? I felt a premonitory chill.

As we drove on to the runway (no nonsense in those days when the director came calling), Gene said, "Well, you want to be a movie actor. So here's your chance." He was, if nothing else, a superb salesman. Jaded when it came to flying, I was overwhelmed by the movies. Ever since Mickey Rooney played Puck in *A Midsummer Night's Dream,* I had wanted to be a star, too. What could Rooney do that I couldn't? Why was I at St. Albans, starting Latin, when I might be darting about the world, unconfined by either gravity or the director's Stinson? "I'll put a girdle round about the earth in forty minutes!" Rooney had croaked. Now I was about to do the same.

As we parked, Gene explained that I was to take off, circle the field once, and land. After I got out of the plane, I would have to do some acting. Floyd Gibbons would ask me what it was like to fly the flivver plane, and I was to say it was just like driving a flivver car. The fact that I had never even tried to drive a car seemed to my father and me irrelevant as we prepared for my screen debut. As it turned out, I didn't learn to drive until I was twenty-five years old.

My earlier footnotehood was clear-cut. I was indeed the first child to cross the country by air. But now I was a challenger. In 1927, one Jack Chapman, aged eleven, had soloed. Since there had been so much public complaint (suppose he had gone and killed a cow?), my father's predecessor had made it the law that no one under sixteen years of age could solo. Now here I was a few months younger than Chapman had been in 1927, ready to break the prepubescent record. But the law said that I could not fly unattended. Ordinarily, my father—true pioneer—would have ignored this sort of law. But the director of Air Commerce could not—at least in front of *Pathé News of the Week*—break a law that he was sworn to uphold.

As I stood by the door to the plane, staring glassy-eyed at the cobra-camera, a long discussion took place. How was I to solo (thus proving that the Hammond flivver was if not foolproof boyproof) and yet not break the 1927 law? Floyd Gibbons proposed that my father sit behind me. But Gene said, no. He was already so familiar a figure in the Trans-Luxes of the Republic that the audience would think that he had done the flying. Finally, Fred Geisse, an official of the bureau (and, like me, a nonpilot), got in first and crouched behind the pilot's seat. The cameras started to turn. With a slight but lovable Rooneyesque swagger, I climbed aboard.

===

Recently, I saw some footage from the newsreel. As I fasten my seat belt, I stare serenely off into space, not unlike Lindbergh-Earhart. I even looked a bit like the god and goddess of flight who, in turn, looked spookily like each other. I start up the engine. I am still serene. But as I watched the ancient footage, I recalled suddenly the terror that I was actually feeling. Terror not of flying but of the camera. This was my big chance to replace Mickey Rooney. But where was my script? My director? My talent? Thinking only of stardom, I took off. With Geisse behind me kindly suggesting that I keep into the wind (that is, opposite to the way that the lady's stocking on the flagpole was blowing), I circled the field not once but twice and landed with the sort of jolt that one of today's jet cowboys likes to bring to earth his DC-10.

The real terror began when I got out of the plane and stood, one hand on the door knob, staring into the camera. Gibbons asked me about the flight. I said, Oh, it wasn't much, and it wasn't, either. But I was now suffering from terminal stage fright. As my voice box began to shut down, the fingers on the door knob appeared to have a life of their own. I stammered incoherently. Finally, I gave what I thought was a puckish Rooneyesque grin which exploded on to the screen with all the sinister force of Peter Lorre's *M*. In that final ghastly frame, suddenly broken off as if edited by someone's teeth in the cutting room, my career as boy film star ended and my career as boy aviator was launched. I watched the newsreel twice in the Belasco Theater, built on the site of William Seward's Old Club House. Each time, I shuddered with horror at that demented leer which had cost me stardom. Yet, leer notwithstanding, I was summer famous; and my contemporaries knew loathing. The young Streckfus Persons (a.k.a. Truman Capote) knew of my exploit. "Among other things," Harper Lee writes of the boy she based on Capote, "he had been up in a mail plane seventeen times, he had been to Nova Scotia, he had seen an elephant, etc." In the sixties, when I introduced Norman Mailer to my father, I was amazed how much Mailer knew of Gene's pioneering.

I record this trivia not to try to regain my forever-lost feetnotehood but to try to recall the spirit of the early days of aviation, a spirit itself now footnote to the vast air and aerospace industries of today. In Anthony Sampson's *Empires of the Sky*, only a dozen pages are devoted to the first quarter-century of American aviation. There are also three times as many references to something called Freddie Laker as there are to Lindbergh. Well, *sic transit* was always the name of the game, even now when the focus is on space itself. Finally, I am put in mind of all this by a number of recent books on aviation, of which the most intriguing and original is *The Winged Gospel* by Joseph J. Corn, in which the author recalls the quasi-religious fervor that Americans experienced when men took to the air and how, for a time, there was "a gospel of flight," and Gene Vidal was its "high priest."* Flight would make men near-angels, it was believed; and a peaceful world one.

---

*Joseph J. Corn, *The Winged Gospel: America's Romance with Aviation, 1900–1950* (London: Oxford University Press, 1984).

2

Ever since the development of the balloon in eighteenth-century France, so-called "lighter-than-air craft" were a reality. Heavier-than-air craft were considered mad inventors' dreams until the brothers Orville and Wilbur Wright created the first heavier-than-air plane and flew it at Kitty Hawk, North Carolina, on December 17, 1903. Curiously enough, it took five years before the press could figure out exactly *what* it was that they had done. At that time the world was full of inventors like the Wright brothers; but the others were either inventing lighter-than-air craft such as the dirigible, or experimenting with gliders. Only a few certified nuts believed in the practicality of heavier-than-air craft. One of these "crackpots" was Henry Adams's friend at the Smithsonian Institution, Dr. S. P. Langley, and he was on much the same theoretical tack as the Wright brothers. But they left earth first.

It was not until Orville Wright flew a plane at Fort Myer outside Washington in the presence of five thousand people that the world realized that man had indeed kicked gravity and that the sky was only the beginning of no known limit. Like so many of the early airship makers, the Wright brothers were bicycle mechanics. But then the bicycle itself had been a revolutionary machine, adding an inch or two to the world's population by making it possible for boys to wheel over to faraway villages where taller (or shorter) girls might be found. At least in the days when eugenics was a science that was the story. Other bicycle manufacturers soon got into the act, notably Glenn H. Curtiss, who was to be a major manufacturer of aircraft.

Although the first generation of flyers believed that airplanes would eventually make war unthinkable, the 1914–18 war did develop a new glamorous sort of warfare, with Gary Cooper gallantly dueling Von Stroheim across the bright heavens. By 1918 the American government had an airmail service. In 1927 the twenty-five-year-old Lindbergh flew the Atlantic and became, overnight, the most famous man on earth, the air age beautifully incarnate. In 1928 Amelia Earhart flew the Atlantic and took her place in the heavens as yin to Lindbergh's yang.

———

It is hard to describe to later generations what it was like to live in a world dominated by two such shining youthful deities. Neither could appear in public without worshipers—no other word—storming them. Yet each was obliged to spend a lot of time not only publicizing and selling aircraft but encouraging air transport. Of the two, Lindbergh was the better paid. But, as a deity, the commercial aspect was nothing to him, he claimed, and the religion all. On the other hand, Earhart's husband, the publisher and publicist George Palmer Putnam (known as G.P.), worked her very hard indeed. The icons of the air age were big business.

*Time* magazine, September 28, 1931:

To Charles Townsend Ludington, socialite of Philadelphia, $8,000 might be the price of a small cabin cruiser such as he sails on Biscayne Bay. . . . But the $8,073.61 profit which showed on a balance sheet upon [his] desk last week was as exciting to him as a great fortune. It was the first year's net earning of the Ludington Line, plane-per-hour passenger service between New York, Philadelphia and Washington.

As practically sole financiers of the company [Nicholas and Charles Townsend] Ludington might well be proud. But they would be the first to insist that all credit go to two young men who sold them the plan and then made it work: brawny, handsome Gene Vidal, West Point halfback of 1916–20, one-time Army flyer; and squint-eyed, leathery Paul ("Dog") Collins, war pilot, old-time airmail pilot.

*Time*style still exerts its old magic, while *Time*checkers are, as always, a bit off—my father graduated from West Point in 1918. An all-American halfback, he also played quarterback. But he *was* one of the first army flyers and the first instructor in aeronautics at West Point. Bored with peacetime army life and excited by aviation, he quit the army in 1926. Already married to the "beauteous" (*Time* epithet) Nina Gore, daughter of "blind solon" (ditto) Senator T. P. Gore, he had a year-old son for whom *Time* had yet to mint any of those Lucite epithets that, in time (where "All things shall come to pass," Ecclesiastes), they would.

═══

New airlines were cropping up all over the country. After 1918, anyone who could nail down a contract from the postmaster general to fly the mail was in business. Since this was the good old United States, there was corruption. Unkind gossips thought that an army flyer whose father-in-law was a senator would be well placed to get such a contract. But during the last years of President Hoover, Senator Gore was a Democrat; and during the first term of President Roosevelt, he was an enemy of the New Deal. Gore was no help at all to Gene. But anyone who could fly was automatically in demand at one or another of the small airlines that carried (or did not carry) the mail.

In 1929, C. M. Keys combined a couple of airlines and started Transcontinental Air Transport, or TAT. For a quarter million dollars cash, Keys hired, as a sort of consultant, Charles Lindbergh; he also gave the Lone Eagle shrewd advice on how to avoid income tax. Thus, TAT was dubbed "The Lindbergh Line." Keys was perhaps the first true hustler or robber baron in American aviation: "He had been an editor of *The Wall Street Journal* and had worked with Walter Hines Page on the old *World's Work;* Keys was also an important aviation promoter. He got into the manufacturing end of the industry during the war and eventually won control of Curtiss Aeroplane & Motor Company. . . ."* In other words, a businessman who "got control" of companies; who bought and sold them. TAT also acquired ex–airmail flyer Paul Collins and Gene Vidal.

Like most of the early airlines, TAT was a combined air-rail service. Passenger planes did not fly at night or over the turbulent Alleghenys. On a TAT transcontinental flight, the passengers left New York by rail in the evening; then, in Columbus, Ohio, they boarded a Ford trimotor (eight passengers maximum) and flew to Waynoka, Oklahoma. Here they transferred to the Santa Fe railroad for an overnight haul to Clovis, New Mexico, where another plane flew them into Los Angeles—or Burbank, to be precise. It is a tribute to the faith of the air-gospellers that they truly believed that this grueling two-day journey would, in time, be preferable to the comforts of a Pullman car. Interestingly enough, many descendants of the original railroad barons were immediately attracted to aviation, and names like Harriman and Whitney and Vanderbilt crop up on the boards of directors. These young men were prescient. By the end of the Second War, the railroads that had dominated American life since the Civil War, buying not only politicians but whole states, would be almost entirely superseded by civil aviation and the Teamsters union. But the railroad lords suffered not at all; they simply became airlords.

The transition was hardly overnight. In TAT's eighteen months of service, the line lost $2,750,000. There were simply not enough customers at sixteen cents a mile; also, more important, there was no mail contract.

*Henry Ladd Smith, *Airways* (New York: Knopf, 1942), p. 141.

≡

TAT's headquarters were at St. Louis, and my only memory of the summer of 1929 (other than bleeding eardrums) was of city lights, as seen from a downtown hotel window. For anyone interested in period detail, there were almost no colored lights then. So, on a hot airless night in St. Louis, the city had a weird white arctic glow. Also, little did I suspect as I stared out over the tropical city with its icy blinking signs, that a stone's throw away, a youth of eighteen, as yet unknown to me and to the world, Thomas Lanier Williams, was typing, typing, typing into the night, while across the dark fields of the Republic . . .

Paul Collins describes the end of TAT *(Tales of an Old Air-Faring Man):* *

About Christmastime 1929 all the St. Louis executives were called to a meeting in New York including Joseph Magee, the general manager; Gene Vidal, his assistant; Luke Harris, Jack Herlihy, and me. We were introduced in Mr. Keyes's [*sic*] office to one Jack Maddux, President of Maddux Airlines, an operation that flew from Los Angeles to San Francisco. . . . Mr. Keyes [*sic*] stated that a merger had been effected between TAT and Maddux.

The ineffable Keys then waited until the assembled management of TAT had returned to St. Louis, where they were all fired.

Simultaneously, the Great Depression began. Small airlines either merged or died. Since a contract to fly the mail was the key to survival, the postmaster general, one Walter F. Brown, was, in effect, the most powerful single figure in aviation. He was also a political spoilsman of considerable energy. In principle, he wanted fewer airlines; and those beholden to him. As of 1930, United Air Lines carried all transcontinental mail. But Brown decided that, in this case, there should be two transcontinental carriers: one would have the central New York–Los Angeles route; the second the southern Atlanta–Dallas–Los Angeles route. As befitted a Herbert Hoover socialist, Brown did not believe in competitive bidding. The southern route would go to Brown-favored American Airlines and the central route to an airline yet to be created but already titled Transcontinental and Western Air, today's Trans World Airlines.

*Foundation Press, University of Wisconsin–Stevens Point.

Brown then forced a merger between TAT (willing) and Western Air Express (unwilling). But as neither flew the mail, Brown's promise of a federal contract for the combined operation did the trick. Since Brown was not above corporate troilism, a third airline, a shy mouse of a company called Pittsburgh Aviation Industries Corporation (PAIC), became a member of the wedding. How on earth did such a mouse get involved with two working airlines? Well, there were three Mellons on PAIC's board of directors, of whom the most active was Richard, nephew of Andrew, former secretary of the treasury. The nobles missed few tricks in the early days of aviation. As it turned out, the first real boss of TWA was a PAIC man, Richard W. Robbins. And so, on August 25, 1930, TWA was awarded the central airmail route even though its competitor, United, had made a lower bid. There was outcry, but nothing more. After all, the chief radio engineer for TWA was the president's twenty-eight-year-old son, Herbert Hoover, Jr. In those days, Hoover socialism was total; and it was not until his successor, Franklin D. Roosevelt, that old-fashioned capitalism was restored.

===

During all this, Gene Vidal had retreated to Senator Gore's house in Rock Creek Park, Washington, D.C. Certain that he had learned enough about the airline business to start one, he convinced the brothers Ludington that a regular New York–Philadelphia–Washington service was practical. He also came up with the revolutionary notion that the planes would fly "every hour on the hour": New York to Washington round trip was twenty-three dollars. When the Ludingtons insisted that costs be kept to a minimum, Gene, ever ingenious, said, "We'll operate at forty cents a mile, taking only a livable salary. Anything under forty cents, we'll agree to take in stock." The Ludingtons were charmed.

In September 1930, the Ludington Line began regular service. Tickets were sold in railway terminals. Gene personally built the first counter in Washington, using two crates with a board across. Everything was ad hoc. On one occasion, in Philadelphia, passengers from New York to Washington were stretching their legs while passengers from Washington to New York were doing the same. Then each group was shepherded into the wrong plane and the passengers to Washington went back to New York and those to New York back to Washington.

What to serve for lunch? My mother, always dieting, decided that consommé was bound to be popular. Fortunately, in those less litigious times, the first batch of badly scalded passengers gallantly did not sue. Later, hard-boiled eggs and saltine crackers made the sort of lunch that stayed down longest. As the passengers dined, and the plane lurched, and the smell of exhaust filled the cabin, cylindrical cardboard ice-cream containers were tactfully passed around. The fact that what was supposed to contain ice cream was used, instead, for vomit was my first metaphysical experience, an intimation of the skull beneath the skin. During the Second War, as first mate of an army ship in the Aleutians, I would grimly stuff our shaky passengers with crackers and hard-boiled eggs; and it is true: They do stay down longest.

At the end of the first year, the Ludington Line showed the profit duly noted by *Time*. As organizer and general manager, my father persuaded Amelia Earhart to become a vice president; he also hired Felix Du Pont to be the agent in Washington. He persuaded Herbert Hoover to light up the Washington monument at dusk because, sooner or later, a plane was bound to hit it. On the other hand, he ignored the mandatory fire drills at the Washington terminal on the sensible ground that "We have a real fire," as one of his mechanics put it, "most every day." Between New York and Washington, he put up twenty-four billboards. Slowpoke passengers on the Pennsylvania railroad could read, at regular intervals, "If you'd flown Ludington, you'd have been there." Were it not for Hoover socialism, so successful and busy a passenger airline would have got a mail contract. But Postmaster General Brown chose to give the franchise to Eastern Air Transport, who were eager to carry the mail at eighty-nine cents a mile versus Ludington's twenty-five cents. But that has always been the American way; who dares question it? The Ludingtons lost heart; and in February 1933 they sold out to Eastern—even though Hoover socialism had been rejected at the polls and there was now a new president, eager to restore prosperity with classic capitalistic measures.

Franklin Roosevelt was something of an aviation freak and, thanks in part to some backstage maneuvering on the part of Amelia Earhart and her friend Eleanor Roosevelt, Eugene L. Vidal became the director of the Bureau of Air Commerce at the age of thirty-eight. He was a popular figure not only in aviation circles but with the press. Henry Ladd Smith wrote: "Gene Vidal had fared so badly at the hands of Postmaster General Brown and the Republican administration that there was a certain poetic justice in his appointment. . . ."* But Smith felt that there was more honor than power in the job. The bureau was divided into three parts and Vidal "had all the responsibilities that go with the title, but few of the powers. Unhappy Mr. Vidal took all the blame for mistakes, but he had to share credit with his two colleagues. . . ." I don't think Gene felt all that powerless, although he certainly took a good deal of blame. Mainly he was concerned with, in Mr. Corn's words,

the dream of wings for all . . . in November 1933 [he] announced that the government would soon spend half a million dollars to produce a "poor man's airplane." The machine would sell for $700. . . . He planned to launch the project with a grant from Harold Ickes's Public Works Administration (PWA), one of the numerous government agencies established in the depression to battle unemployment.†

Although a lot of out-of-work engineers and craftsmen would be employed, Ickes saw nothing public in private planes, and Gene was obliged to use his power to buy planes for the bureau's inspectors. He ordered five experimental prototypes. The results were certainly unusual. There was one plane whose wings could be folded up; you could then drive it like an automobile. Although nothing came of this hybrid, its overhead rotor was the precursor of the helicopter, still worshiped as a god by the Vietnamese. Finally, there was the Hammond Y-1, which I was to fly.

Along with the glamor of flight, there was the grim fact that planes often crashed and that the bodies of the passengers tended to be unpretty, whether charred or simply in pieces strewn across the landscape. Knute Rockne, Grace Moore, Carole Lombard died; and at least half of the people I used to see in my childhood would, suddenly, one day, not be there. "Crashed" was the word; nothing more was said. As director, Gene was obliged to visit the scenes of every major accident, and he had gruesome tales to report. One survivor sued the bureau because the doctor at the scene of the accident refused to replace in his scrotal sac the testicles that lay nearby.

In 1934 the Democratic senator Hugo Black chaired a Senate commit-

*Smith, *Airways*, p. 283.
†Corn, *The Winged Gospel*.

tee to investigate the former Republican postmaster general Brown's deal-
ings with the airlines. Black's highly partisan committee painted Brown
even darker than he was. Yes, he had played favorites in awarding mail
contracts but no one could prove that he—or the Grand Old Party—had
in any specific way profited. Nevertheless, Jim Farley, the new postmaster
general, charged Brown with "conspiracy and collusion" while the president, himself a man of truly superhuman vindictiveness, decided to punish
Brown, the Republican party, and the colluded-with airlines.

What could be more punitive—and dramatic—than the cancellation of
all U.S. airmail contracts with private companies? Since the army had
flown the mail back in 1918, let them fly the mail now. The president
consulted the director of Air Commerce, who told him that army flyers
did not have the sort of skills needed to fly the mail. After all, he should
know; he was one. Undeterred, the president turned to General Benjamin
D. Foulois, the chief of the air corps, who lusted for appropriations as all
air corps chiefs do; and the general said, of course, the air corps could fly
the mail.

===

On February 9, 1934, by executive order, the president canceled all airmail
contracts; and the Army flew the mail. At the end of the first week, five
army pilots were dead, six critically injured, eight planes wrecked. One
evening in mid-March, my father was called to the White House. As Gene
pushed the president's wheelchair along the upstairs corridor, the president, his usual airy self, said, "Well, Brother Vidal, we seem to have a bit
of a mess on our hands." Gene always said, "I found that 'we' pretty
funny." But good soldiers covered up for their superiors. What, FDR
wondered, should they do? Although my father had a deep and lifelong
contempt for politicians in general ("They tell lies," he used to say with
wonder, "even when they don't have to") and for Roosevelt's cheerful
mendacities in particular, he did admire the president's resilience: "He was
always ready to try something new. He was like a good athlete. Never worry
about the last play. Only the next one." Unfortunately, before they could
extricate the administration from the mess, Charles Lindbergh attacked
the president; publicly, the Lone Eagle held FDR responsible for the dead
and injured army pilots.

Roosevelt never forgave Lindbergh. "After that," said Gene, "he would
always refer to Slim as 'this man Lindbergh,' in that condescending voice

of his. Or he'd say 'your friend Lindbergh,' which was worse." Although Roosevelt was convinced that Lindbergh's statement was entirely inspired by the airlines who wanted to get back their airmail contracts, he was too shrewd a politician to get in a shooting match with the world's most popular hero. Abruptly, on April 20, 1934, Postmaster General Farley let the airlines know that the Post Office was open to bids for mail contracts because, come May, the army would no longer fly the mail. It was, as one thoughtful observer put it, the same old crap game, with Farley not Brown as spoilsman.

In 1935, "lifelong bachelor" (as *Time* would say) Senator Bronson Cutting was killed in an air crash. He was a popular senator (survived to this day by his estimable niece, Iris Origo) and the Senate promptly investigated. My father was grilled at length.

The bureau was accused of wasting time and money in a futile effort to develop a "flivver plane" for the masses. . . . Vidal himself did not fare so badly. The committee rebuked him mildly and reported that he appeared "lacking in iron," but since Vidal was hardly in the position to enforce orders, perhaps even this accusation was unfair.*

My father's affection for politicians was not increased by the Senate hearings. But the real prince of darkness had now entered his life, Juan Trippe, and a lifelong struggle began. Even after I was grown, at the Maidstone Club in East Hampton, I used to observe the two men, who never exactly *not* spoke to each other and yet never did speak.

=

Juan Trippe was a smooth-looking man with very dark eyes. Grandson of a bank robber, as Gene liked to recall, Trippe had gone to Yale; got into the airline business in 1926, backed by two Yale friends, C. V. Whitney and William Rockefeller (what on earth do the rich *do* nowadays?). While Lindbergh was officially associated with my father and the Ludington Line, Slim was also being wooed by Trippe, who had acquired a small Florida–Cuba airline called Pan American. By 1931, Trippe had replaced Keys as the principal robber baron of the airways. Unlike Keys, he was wonderfully well connected socially and politically. For Pan American's

*Smith, *Airways*, p. 248.

original board, he managed to collect not only a Whitney but a Mellon son-in-law, David Bruce, and Robert Lehman. During Black's investigation of Brown, Trippe had been caught disguising his profits in what is now standard conglomerate procedure but in those sweet days was fraud; worse, Trippe was a Republican. But smoothness is all, and, in due course, Trippe charmed Farley and Gene; and, for a time, the sly president.

Trippe's ambitions for Pan American were worldwide. He already had South America; he now wanted the Pacific and China; the Atlantic and Europe. But he would need considerable help from the administration to get the routes nailed securely down. Smoothly, he invited the director of the Bureau of Air Commerce to tour South America. A good time was had by all and, en route, Gene collected a number of exotic decorations from various exotic presidents. Then, back in Washington, Trippe presented Gene with a long list of requests. The guileless director explained to his recent host that the law required *competitive* bidding and that the United States, unlike old Europe, did not have "chosen instruments." Naturally, if Pan American wanted to enter in competition with other airlines . . .

Trippe took his revenge. He went to his friend William Randolph Hearst—no longer a Roosevelt enthusiast—and together they orchestrated a press campaign against Gene Vidal, Jim Farley and FDR—in that order. It is my impression that Lindbergh may have sided with Trippe. There is a curious photograph in *The Chosen Instrument.** My father is at the center, speaking into a microphone. Trippe is smoothly obsequious to his right, while Igor Sikorsky and Lindbergh are also present. The caption: "Attending the delivery of the Sikorsky S-42 in May 1934," followed by the names of all those present except for the director, whose endorsement was the point to the photograph. Thanks in part to Trippe's inspired press campaign, Gene quit the government in 1937, and the bureau was broken up. The Civil Aeronautics Board was then created; on January 1, 1985 it, too, ended, a victim of Reaganism.

Although Trippe got most of the world, he never forgave Gene. Some years later, when my father was put up for membership in Philadelphia's Racquet Club, Trippe tried to blackball him because Gene's father's name was Felix. "A *Jewish* name," said Juan, smoothly. Those were racist days.

*Marylin Bender and Selig Altschul, *The Chosen Instrument* (New York: Simon and Schuster, 1982).

When my father pointed out that in our section of *Romano-Rhaetia,* Felix is a common Christian name, he inadvertently revealed the family's darkest secret. Upon arrival (1848) in the Great Protestant Republic, the Roman Catholic Vidals had promptly turned Protestant. Obviously, during the Republic's high noon, no mass was worth exclusion from the Racquet Club, against whose windows were pressed so many wistful Kennedy and Lee (born Levy) noses. Recently, a journalist told me that while interviewing Trippe, he noticed the old man was reading one of my books. When the journalist told him that the author was Gene Vidal's son, Trippe shook his head with wonder. "My, my," he said. "Hard to believe, isn't it?" Oh, there were real shits in those days.

3

I have no memory of Lindbergh. But Amelia Earhart was very much a part of my life. She wrote poetry and encouraged me to write, too. She had a beautiful speaking voice, which I am sure I would have recognized during the war if she had really been, as certain fabulists believe, Tokyo Rose, a captive of the Japanese. Since she usually dressed as a boy, it was assumed that she had what were then called Sapphic tendencies. I have no idea whether or not she did but I do know that she wore trousers because she thought her legs were ugly; and if she were truly Sapphic, I doubt that she would have been so much in love with my father. She had milk-white eyelashes.

In the fall of 1936, Amelia, Gene, and I went to the Army–Navy game at West Point. On the way back, as her fans peered excitedly into our train compartment, she described how she planned to fly around the world, following, more or less, the equator. I asked her what part of the flight worried her the most. "Africa," she said. "If you got forced down in those jungles, they'd never find you." I said that the Pacific looked pretty large and wet to me. "Oh, there are always islands," she said. Then she asked Gene: "Wouldn't it be wonderful to just go off and live on a desert island?" He rather doubted it. Then they discussed just *how* you could survive; and what would you do if there was no water? and if there was no water, you would have to make a sun-still and extract salt from sea water and how was that done? As we approached Grand Central Station, I suddenly decided that I wanted a souvenir of Amelia. Shortly before she left on her flight around the world, she sent me the blue-and-white checked leather belt that she often wore. She gave my father her old watch. She also made a new will, as she usually did before a dangerous flight. She left Gene her California house, on condition that if he didn't want it (he didn't), he would give it to her mother, something she did not trust G.P., her husband, to do.*

===

Although my father was as fond of conspiracy theories as any other good American, he rejected most of the notions that still circulate about Amelia's last flight. Of course, he was at a disadvantage: He knew something about it. When Amelia's plane vanished on July 2, 1937, somewhere between Lae, New Guinea, and Howland Island in the Pacific—where there are all those islands—the president sent the navy to look for her. He also asked Gene to help out and act as a sort of coordinator. If Amelia had been on a spy mission for the American government, as is still believed in many quarters,† the commander in chief hadn't been told about it. Years later, Eleanor Roosevelt used to talk a lot about Amelia. When I asked her if she had ever been able to find out anything, she said no. More to the point, since Mrs. Roosevelt had been devoted to Amelia, if there *had* been a secret mission, Mrs. Roosevelt would have certainly revealed it after the war and demanded all sorts of posthumous recognition for her friend. But Mrs. Roosevelt was certain that there had been no spy mission; on the other hand, she—like my father—thought there *was* something fishy about the whole business.

Shortly before Amelia left the States, she told my father that since she would have to take a navigator with her, she was going to hire Fred Noonan, formerly Pan American's chief navigator. Gene was alarmed: Noonan was a drunk. "Take anyone but Noonan," he said. "All right then," said Amelia, "why not you?" To Gene's surprise she wasn't joking. Although Gene had recently divorced my mother and G.P. was simply Amelia's manager, Gene's affection for Amelia was not equal to her love for him. "I'm not that good a navigator," he said. She then hired Noonan, who swore he was forever off the sauce. The flight began.

From India, Amelia rang G.P. and Gene together. She reported "per-

---

*G.P. managed to suppress Amelia's final will; my father didn't inherit the California property. I don't know what became of Amelia's mother.

†For a gorgeously off-the-wall "search" for Amelia, read *Amelia Earhart Lives*, by Joe Klaas (New York: McGraw-Hill, 1970). Apparently, in the sixties, she was alive and well and living in New Bedford; she who had so deeply hated Rye.

sonnel trouble": code for Noonan's drinking. Gene advised her to stop the flight. But she chose to keep on. Amelia rang again; this time from New Guinea. "Personnel trouble" had delayed her next hop—to Howland Island. This time both Gene and G.P. told her to abandon the flight. But she thought "personnel" might be improving. She was wrong. The night before they left Lae, Noonan was drunk; worse, he had had only forty-five minutes' sleep. When they took off, he was still drunk.

=

Gene's theory of what happened is this: Amelia was going through a disagreeable early menopause; she deeply disliked her husband; she hated the publicness of her life and she was, at some romantic level, quite serious about withdrawing to a desert island—symbolically if not literally. Years earlier, she had made a number of conditions when she allowed G.P. to marry her. The marriage was to be, as they called it then, "open." Also, "I may have to keep some place where I can go to be by myself now and then, for I cannot guarantee to endure at all times the confinements of even an attractive cage." Finally, Gene thought it unlikely that even a navy so sublimely incompetent that, four years later, it would allow most of its fleet to be sunk at Pearl Harbor, would ever have engaged such a nervy lady to spy on Japan, while *she* would have pointed out that a pioneer circumnavigation of the globe was quite enough for one outing.

According to Gene, there were only two mysteries. One of Amelia's last radio messages was, "742 from KHAQQ: We must be on you but we cannot see you. Gas is running low. Been unable to reach you by radio. Flying at one thousand feet. One half-hour's gas left." Gene said that this was not a true report. She had a good deal more than a half-hour's gas left. Why did she lie? The second mystery was that of the radio frequency. Amelia's last message was at 8:46 A.M.; after that, some fourteen minutes passed with her frequency still coming in strong at what is known as "maximum 5." "Then," said Gene, "the frequency didn't break off, the way it does when you crash. Someone switched it off." So what happened? It was Gene's hunch that she had indeed found an island—and landed. "But what about Fred Noonan?" I asked. "He sounds even worse than G.P." Gene's response was grim: "If Amelia wanted to get rid of him, she'd have got rid of him. Hit him over the head with one of his bottles. She was like that."

Over the years, there were many stories of a white woman sighted on this or that island. The only intriguing one, according to G.P., was from a Russian sailor whose ship had passed a small island on which a white woman signaled them; she was wearing nothing except a man's drawers. "The funny thing is," said G.P. to my father, "she always wore my shorts when she flew, but I wore boxer shorts, and the sailor said this woman was wearing those new jockey shorts." Gene never told G.P. that for some years Amelia had been wearing Gene's "new jockey shorts." In any event, the ship had not stopped; and no one ever followed up.

$$\equiv$$

Four years before Amelia's last flight, she and Gene started what became Northeast Airlines, with Paul Collins as president. Although Gene was never very active in the airline, he remained a director to the end of his life. According to Mr. Corn, Vidal never gave up his dream "of mass-produced personal planes, and in private life began experiments with molded plywood, a material he thought appropriate for the purpose." This is true enough, except that he also experimented, more successfully, with fiberglass. But by the time he died in 1969, the world was far too full of people even to dream of filling the skies with private planes in competition with military aircraft and the planes of those airlines, three of which he had had a hand in founding. I do know that he found modern civil aviation deeply boring; and though he shared the general ecstasy when a man got to the moon, the gospel of flight that he and Lindbergh and Earhart preached was by then a blurred footnote to the space age, where technology is all and, to the extent that there is a human aspect to space, it involves team players with the right stuff. Neil Armstrong first stepped on the moon but it was Werner von Braun and a cast of thousands who put him there. Mr. Armstrong did not fly to the moon; and for all his personal pluck and luck, he is already perceived as a footnote, a name for Trivial Pursuit.

It was different on December 17, 1934, when my father asked all the nation's pilots "to take off at 10.30 in the morning and to stay in the air for half an hour. They would thus be aloft at the precise time at which, thirty-one years earlier, Orville Wright had also been airborne. The response to Vidal's call was impressive . . . an estimated 8,000 aircraft participated in the ritual."[*]

Today it is marvelous indeed to watch on television the rings of Saturn

*Corn, *The Winged Gospel*, p. 64.

close and to speculate on what we may yet find at galaxy's edge. But in the process, we have lost the human element; not to mention the high hope of those quaint days when flight would create "one world." Instead of one world, we have "star wars," and a future in which dumb, dented human toys will drift mindlessly about the cosmos long after our small planet's dead.

THE NEW YORK REVIEW OF BOOKS
*January 17, 1985*

# Frederic Prokosch:
# The European
# Connection

1

In August 1939, I crossed the border from France into Italy. At thirteen I was already Henry James's passionate pilgrim; and the principal object of my pilgrimage was those remnants of the Roman empire which I had come to know so well from that glorious film *The Last Days of Pompeii,* not to mention its Plautine counterpart, the sympathetic Eddie Cantor's *Roman Scandals:* a thousand compelling celluloid images complemented by the texts of *Tales from Livy* and Suetonius's mind-boggling gossip.

At the train's first stop in Italy—Ventimiglia?—fascist guards gave the fascist salute just as they had done in all those newsreels where Hitler and Mussolini were perpetual Gog and Magog to our days, grotesque cinematic fictions soon to break out of the honey-odored darkness of the art-deco Trans-Lux theaters and become real-life monsters in spades.

Yet on my first trip down the Italian peninsula, in the company of a group of schoolboys and masters, I seldom looked out the train's windows. I was reading a paperback edition of *The Seven Who Fled* by Frederic Prokosch. For the next week I was in two places at once. I was in the Rome that I had so long imagined. I was also fleeing across an Asia that had been entirely imagined by Prokosch. One hot, airless August morning, as I walked up the Via Tritone and into the Piazza Barberini, I realized that I was, simultaneously, in the desert southwest of Urga and in prewar (yes, we knew it was prewar then) Rome, facing the Bristol Hotel, where lived, unknown to me, another writer that I was soon to read, George Santayana, whose *The Last Puritan* was to have much the same revelatory effect on me as the romantic eroticism of *The Seven Who Fled.*

From the ages of seventeen to twenty I was in the American army. Wherever I was stationed—at least in the United States—I would go to the post library and look up Prokosch. In the years since I first discovered him he had published three more novels. He was something of a cult in the army, and on the outside, too. During the summer of 1945 I was on leave at East Hampton, Long Island. I had finished my first novel. I had another six months to serve in the army.

═══

I cannot remember how I met Prokosch but one day there he was on the beach. Somehow it had never occurred to me that the two fascinating words that made up his name might actually belong to a living person, aged thirty-eight. It is true that I had looked carefully at the photographs on the dust jackets. But one might just as well have been looking at pictures of Byron. Certainly the dust-jacket biographies were brief and uninformative. He seemed to spend a lot of time in Europe; and that was it. Now there he was on the white beach, a dark-haired, black-eyed man, who looked more like a pirate than a writer.

In *Voices: A Memoir*, Prokosch writes of that summer: "I took a room in one of the cottages of the Sea Spray Inn. . . . Every evening I'd go wandering along the beach and watch the breakers. There were days when they kept pounding at the sand with their shining fists and there were days when they slid shoreward with a snakelike malevolence." In this one offhand description, Prokosch displays his characteristic investiture of nature with the human and the human with the natural—Ruskin's so-called "pathetic fallacy" which was to be denounced yet again by the French "new novelists" as the unforgivable (for an entire literary season) anthropomorphizing of nature's neutral otherness. Nevertheless, central to Prokosch's vision of the material world is a creation that can only be recorded by the human eye, itself both subject and object—the sole measurer of light and inevitable victim of darkness. For Prokosch, a landscape observed is an extension of the human, particularly if the landscape is one that he himself has invented, like the Asia of *The Asiatics* and *The Seven Who Fled.*

Personally, I found Prokosch amiable but distant. Now that I have read *Voices,* I can see that he was not used to being the found writer of a younger writer; rather, he himself was a dedicated finder of older artists and wise men, and the memoir that he has written is curiously selfless. The voice one hears is not so much his as the voices of those whom he has admired or at least listened closely to. By and large, he has chosen not to praise himself, the memoirist's usual task. Instead he has tried to distill the essence of each voice rather than what might have been exactly said. Since he and I often saw the same people at the same time (in the case of Santayana, we must have been alternating our visits to the Convent of the Blue Nuns, neither letting on to the other that he was making pilgrimages to the old man's cell), it is fascinating for me to hear what Santayana said to him as opposed to what he said to me. Particularly when . . .

≡

But, first, who is Frederic Prokosch? He was born in Wisconsin in 1908, the son of a Sudeten-Czech linguist and philologist. Prokosch's childhood was surprisingly Twainesque: Prairie du Sac, Wisconsin; Austin, Texas; and rural Pennsylvania, where his father taught at Bryn Mawr. As a youth, Prokosch's interests were about evenly divided between the arts—literature, painting—and tennis. Eventually, Professor Edouard Prokosch moved on to Yale, where Frederic got a doctorate in Middle English. In 1935 Prokosch was at King's College, Cambridge, when *The Asiatics* was published. Like Byron, he was suddenly famous.

*The Seven Who Fled* (1937) was equally successful. He also published poetry, which was praised by Yeats. During the war he worked for the Office of War Information in Lisbon and Stockholm. To date, he has written sixteen novels, four volumes of poetry, and he has translated into English Louise Labé and Friedrich Hölderlin. For thirty years he has been completely out of fashion in America (a place the late Philip Rahv used to call Amnesia), but the French continue to find his novels fascinating, and he has been praised in that country by critics as various as Gide and Camus and Queneau, while the first translation into French of *The Seven Who Fled* was made by Marguerite Yourcenar. He lives now in the south of France. He continues to write; he makes, by hand, miniature editions of poets whom he admires; he collects butterflies (I wish he had published more of his correspondence with Nabokov, another literary lepidopterist).

For those concerned with Significant Literary Trends in Modern Literature (so different from our own high culture's English Studies' English Studies), Prokosch is a precursor of the currently fashionable Latin American school of writing, which has managed to break more than a hundred years of beautifully resonant silence with the sort of precise rendering of imagined human landscapes that Prokosch had invented and perfected in the thirties. Since Prokosch's novels have always been available in French translations, his inventions have much influenced those Latin Americans who have always looked—and continue to look—to Paris for guidance. García Márquez would not write the way that he does if Prokosch had not written the way that he did. At a time when the American novel was either politically *engagé* or devoted to the homespun quotidian, Prokosch's first two novels were a half-century ahead of their time. This did him no good in the medium-long run.

———

After forty-four years, I have reread *The Seven Who Fled*. To my surprise, I actually remembered some of it. I also found that much of what had been magical for me still works. But then the picaresque novel has the unique advantage of *being* . . . Also, what is not dated cannot truly date; and if the writer has chosen to render imagined people in an imagined landscape with history firmly kept to the margin of *his* story, the work will always be what it is, in the present tense. On the other hand, the last two pages of the first edition which I have been reading are ominously dated.

First, there is a page with the words: "The Harper Prize Novel Contest *Its History and Terms.*" On the next page, the publisher tells us that the judges of the 1937 contest are Louis Bromfield, Sinclair Lewis, and Thornton Wilder. Recently, I read that Tennessee Williams (circa 1937) said that his favorite writer was Louis Bromfield while I remember writing (circa 1950) that Thornton Wilder was mine. The publisher now hits hard the Ozymandias note: "The first Harper Prize was awarded in 1922 to Margaret Wilson's *The Able McLaughlins,* which also received the Pulitzer Prize. The second winner was Anna Parrish's *The Perennial Bachelor.* The third was *The Grandmothers* by Glenway Wescott, the fourth Julian Green's *The Dark Journey,* the fifth Robert Raynold's *Brothers in the West,* and the sixth Paul Horgan's *The Fault of Angels.* The seventh award went to H. L. Davis's *Honey in the Horn,* which also won the Pulitzer Prize. To this distinguished list is now added *The Seven Who Fled* by Frederic Prokosch."

Happily, we have now got literature sorted out and we all know exactly who's who and why. The absolute permanence of the *oeuvre* (there is no other word, in French at least) of Joyce Carol Oates, say, is, very simply, a fact that no American English teacher—as opposed, perhaps, to an English American teacher—would for an instant challenge. But then the nice thing about being now is being right, and the bad thing about being then is being wrong, not to mention forgotten. Could any of these prize-winning books have been any good? It beats me. Of the lot, I read and somewhat admired *The Grandmothers.* I have read Julian Green but not *The Dark Journey.* The rest are simply dusty titles, swept up by time's winged wastebasket wherein alabaster cities as well as fruited plains are all as one forgot by Amnesia the Beautiful.

*The Seven Who Fled* is filled with energy and color. The somewhat unfocused romanticism of Prokosch's poetry works very well indeed when deployed as prose narrative. From Kashgar, at the center of Asia, seven Europeans flee the armies of the youthful General Ma, who ranges up and down Tashkent while Russia and China begin to press upon the borders of that disintegrating state. In the thirties, much was made of the fact that Prokosch had never set foot in the Asia that he had invented for *The Asiatics* and *The Seven Who Fled.* Since then, other writers have invented jungles in South America not to mention those brilliant invisible cities of Asia that Calvino's Marco Polo saw.

For each of the seven characters, there is at least one reverie of an earlier non-Asiatic time. For the Englishman Layeville there is a glimpse of the world in which Prokosch himself had been living:

And Cambridge. Those ingratiating days of hesitation and unreality! Those platonic hours upon the grass lit by the rays of sunlight slanting through the leaves, or among the scattered dusty books lit by rays that slanted through the high windows. Their very unreality indeed gave them a magical and melancholy innocence, not that of childhood, but that of pure seclusion. The elaborate pleas for a new order; the eloquent disputations of social justice; ardors and ambitions which made every moment seem important and profound.

Yes, Prokosch met Guy Burgess at Cambridge; no, Prokosch was not political. But his character Layeville is fulfilled in youth at school:

So that, little by little, he became familiar with the chilling pangs endured by those who have lost, somewhere amongst the ardors of childhood and youth, all power to love.

There is an astonishing sexual tension in Prokosch's early books that is as hard to define as it is impossible not to sense. The sexual takes unexpected forms. One of the seven kills another man, a gratuitous but altogether necessary act that is, in its dreamlike rendering, highly sexual, presaging Genet and Paul Bowles. As a writer, Prokosch is not so much a conscious mind as a temperament through which the human condition, as imagined by him, flows—and merges with the nonhuman. For Prokosch, each of the seven who flees is both generalized essence and specified ape, while the dark gravel-strewn Gobi beneath the sheltering sky that does not shelter is simply an extension of a shifting, living cosmos where man is in all things that man observes; and the only constant is change—hence, the romantic's agony. Or:

He could see that the snow was leading a life of its own, precisely like the earth or the sea: but sterile, secret, silvery, its love so to speak turned forever upon fragments of its own self and destined to fruitlessness and silence. A million crystals of infinite complexity, living for nothing else but the gradual destruction of their own perfect selves, growing slowly into each other, moving silkily downward during each moment of sunlight, motionless again at night, and then in the warm sun again becoming amorous and weak, like vast degenerate tribes drifting together, flowing away; demonstrating how close to one another were purity and decay, perfection and death.

Thus he makes the snow a metaphor for the human; and makes the snow snow; and makes sentences: "Sentences must stir in a book like leaves in a forest," wrote Flaubert, "each distinct from each, despite their resemblance."

2

The title of Prokosch's current memoir is significant: *Voices.* In a sense, it is an ironic commentary on the ancient complaint that he was always, as a novelist, too much concerned with place and not enough with people. Actually, it was his special genius to realize that place approached as if it were character *is* human since only a human mind can evoke a landscape never before seen on earth except in the author's mind. But now Prokosch has turned from those dreams of imaginary places (and recollections of the past, as in his reconstruction of Byron in *The Missolonghi Manuscript*) to the voices that he has heard in life and now recollects in memory.

Most young writers are eager, for a time at least, to meet the great figures of the day. At nineteen I was fascinated to meet Prokosch because his books had had a profound effect on my early adolescent self. He found this amusing: "How *sensitive* you must have been!" And the pirate's laugh would roar. Later he found it amusing that in the summer of 1948—when I was not enjoying the success of my third novel, *The City and the Pillar* —I should want to meet Gide and Santayana and Sartre. . . . He gave me the impression that this sort of busy-ness was somehow vulgar. I wish now that I had known then that he himself had been a resolute collector of all sorts of rare artist-butterflies and that he had continued to add to his collection until he withdrew himself entirely from the literary world, as most writers who write eventually do.

But, plainly, the voices he once heard persist in memory, and now he has put them down. From youth, he tells us, he had got into the habit of taking down conversations. He had begun with his father's friend Thomas Mann, who came to call on the family at Bryn Mawr. "I kept staring with fascination at the back of Thomas Mann. The stars were beginning to shine and a mist hung over the hockey field. His head rose from his shoulders like a moss-grown rock and the words he was uttering spread from his skull like antlers." Among those words: " 'The fatal thing,' he said, 'is that Tolstoy had no irony. It is a miracle that he managed to write as well as he did. Irony in a novel is like the salt in a pea soup. It gives the flavor, the nuance. Without the salt it is insipid.' " This is *echt* Mann, for whom food was always a metaphor, and the heavier the food the heavier the metaphor. "After he left I went to my bedroom and wrote it all down, and this was the first of the dialogues that I scribbled faithfully in my notebooks."

Prokosch glimpsed "an abyss at the core of greatness" in Mann. The abyss or vastation or, simply, *Weltschmerz* was to be a recurring theme in Prokosch's own travels among Heine's foreign cities: "It was a journey in search of the artist as a hero, as an enigma, as a martyr, as a revelation, and finally as a fragment of humanity."

While an undergraduate at Haverford, Prokosch and a culture-vulture classmate spent a summer in Paris, where they called on Gertrude Stein and Alice B. Toklas. The ladies were just back from Spain. Gertrude relates: "The Goyas were very nice and the El Grecos were more than adequate but I felt no rapport with the Murillos or the Zurbaráns. Alice said that she profoundly distrusted the Zurbaráns but we trusted Mallorca when we came to Mallorca." As for Paris, Gertrude confessed that in the early days, "there were moments when I was homesick but they gradually grew less frequent. I still had friends in America and I wrote them some letters and we ate cornbread with molasses and apple pie on Sundays and on certain occasions a bit of cheese with the pie. One has these native habits and it is foolish to defy them. . . . Even Alice who is a gypsy has her own deep Americanism."

Prokosch has always had a habit of asking the apparently simple—even simpleminded—question. He asks Gertrude Stein if she has a definite philosophy. This nets him some splendid Stein:

"A writer must always try to have a philosophy and he should also have a psychology and a philology and many other things. Without a philosophy and a psychology and all these various other things he is not really worthy of being called a writer. I agree with Kant and Schopenhauer and Plato and Spinoza and that is quite enough to be called a philosophy. But then of course a philosophy is not the same thing as a style . . ."

Later Prokosch and friend lie in wait for a style as incarnated by James Joyce at Sylvia Beach's bookshop. Incidentally, it is the friend who is ravished by Stein and Joyce. At this point, Prokosch is still as interested in tennis as in literature; but he has read *Ulysses* and Mrs. Woolf, and when the reluctant lion is trapped over tea in the shop's back room, he asks Joyce what he thinks of Virginia Woolf and is told that

she married her wolfish husband purely in order to change her name. Virginia Stephen is not a name for an exploratory authoress. I shall write a book some day about the appropriateness of names. Geoffrey Chaucer has a ribald ring, as is proper and correct, and Alexander Pope was inevitably Alexander Pope . . . and Shelley was very Percy and very Bysshe.

When confronted with the "stream of consciousness," Joyce's response is sour: "When I hear the word 'stream' uttered with such a revolting primness, what I think of is urine and not the contemporary novel. And besides, it isn't new, it is far from the *dernier cri*. Shakespeare used it continually, much too much in my opinion, and there's *Tristram Shandy*, not to mention the *Agamemnon* . . ."

Prokosch was a good tennis player; at squash, he was a champion. Suddenly, one hears the somewhat surprising voice of Bill Tilden, who had written, *"Never* change a winning game, and *always* change a losing one," a maxim that must be reversed when applied to art. "One day I finally cornered Bill Tilden . . ." Prokosch got the master to autograph one of his books on tennis. Tilden had also written two novels, which Prokosch had read. Tilden dismisses them as "perfect trash. I always yearned to become a novelist. But I didn't have it in me. Just rubbish, that's all they are." But for Tilden—and the young Prokosch—tennis was an art form, too. Unhappily, the Tilden that Prokosch met was at the end of his career: "My legs are giving way. Will the last act be tragic?"

For Prokosch there were two golden ages, divided by the war: Cambridge at the end of the thirties and Rome at the end of the forties. He seems to have enjoyed his literary success without ever having taken on the persona of the great author. Also, surprisingly, Dr. Prokosch has never taught school; never sought prizes or foundation grants; never played at literary politics. He seems to have been more interested in the works or voices of others than in himself as a person (as opposed to himself as a writer), a characteristic that tends to put him outside contemporary American literature; and contemporary American literature, sensing this indifference to the games careerists play, extruded him entirely from the canon.

He was like no one else, anyway. He had always been a kind of expatriate at a time when the drums of America First had begun to beat their somewhat ragged martial tattoo. Finally, he was dedicated to literature in a way hard for his contemporaries to grasp as they pretended to be boxers or bullfighters—not to mention bullshitters, Zelda Fitzgerald's nice phrase for the huge hollow Hemingway who had set the tone for a generation that only now is beginning to get truly lost. Hail, Amnesia!

Prokosch went his own way; and listened to his voices. At Cambridge he invites an ancient don to tea. The old man tells him, "You are rather naïve to have written a masterpiece. I agree with the critics. *The Asiatics is* a little masterpiece. But is your air of simplicity just a part of your cunning, or is your cunning just an aspect of your inner simplicity?" Although this is the sort of self-serving conversation that memoirists are prone to include to show how much the famous admired them, I quote the exchange because Prokosch seldom gets this personal about himself; he keeps tributes to his genius at a delicate minimum. Prokosch has no response other than "Both, maybe." To which Housman (yes, it was he; later to become famous as the TV spokesperson for a Los Angeles bank) replied, "In every American there is an air of incorrigible innocence, which seems to conceal a diabolical cunning." Prokosch broods on Housman; on Eliot; on beauty . . . and on Auden.

Beauty, first. The absolutely relative or relatively absolute nature of beauty was not as firmly established in those prewar days as it is now. It was generally agreed then that beauty was good; and that the good is hard to achieve. "Of this wisdom," wrote Walter Pater, "the poetic passion, the desire of beauty, the love of art for art's sake has most; for it comes to you professing frankly to give nothing but the highest quality to your moments as they pass, simply for those moments' sake." In a way, this is incontrovertible; but the way that Pater put what Prokosch echoes is not our present way. Today all abstract nouns are questioned save those abstractions that are used to measure the ones that have gone out of fashion. We signal and we sign; we structure and we deconstruct; and for a long time a good deal of the century's philosophy has been a division of logic. Although Prokosch's idea of beauty in art is very old-fashioned indeed, the way in which he himself deploys his own art is a formidable reminder that beauty, no matter by what sign or name acknowledged, can be a fact whose refutation is a highly risky business even for the most confident literary bureaucrat.

≡

The voice of Auden is the most significant in Prokosch's memoirs. Auden was his almost exact contemporary. By the time that Prokosch had published his first volume of poems (after the two celebrated novels), Auden was already the most famous young poet in English. From the beginning Prokosch acknowledged not only Auden's mastery but his own indebtedness to him. This is a rare thing for a contemporary to do: When it comes to envy and malice, our century's poets make even the dizziest of American novelists appear serene and charitable.

Prokosch had fallen under Auden's spell long before they finally met in New York City at the Yale Club. Auden had just arrived from England. "He wore a pin-striped suit, a wrinkled shirt, and a checkered tie. I had the impression that he had tried to look tidy for the Yale Club. His thick unruly hair was parted far on the right. There was a wart on his right cheek and he cocked his head to the right, so that his body as well as his mind seemed to tilt into the asymmetrical." Auden asks Prokosch to propose him for American citizenship. Prokosch says he would be delighted. They talk of Delmore Schwartz's new book, *In Dreams Begin Responsibilities.* "Auden listened inquisitively and nodded his head politely. He seemed, by some secret antennalike instinct, to be appraising all the strengths and all the weaknesses in Delmore Schwartz." But at the mention of Dylan Thomas "he looked irritable and queasy" while a reference to Prokosch's recent book of poems, *The Carnival,* and its debt to *early* Auden, appeared to trouble Auden with "the ambivalence of my admiration and his politeness was fringed with little tentacles of hostility."

And I suddenly realized that there were four of us at the table: two speakers and two listeners who were hiding behind the speakers, each with his own hidden attitudes and doubts and suspicions. And abruptly, as we glanced across the table uneasily, we were engulfed in a silence of mutual shyness and distrust.

I said, "Tell me, Wystan. Why did you decide to escape to America?"

*"Escape!* What in the world makes you think it was an escape? It was not an escape. And what's more, it was not a *decision.* It was an instinct, a desire. Please don't try to intellectualize. One has impulses and instincts. There was no yearning to escape. And there was nothing that remotely resembled a decision!"

Although Prokosch tells us nothing of his own private life, he does describe a Turkish bath in Forty-second Street where "I was repelled by the cockroaches and the smell of secretions but intrigued by the atmosphere of silence and cunning.

"As I sat in the steam room I caught sight of Wystan Auden. He looked like a naked sea beast as he prowled through the steam, and his skin looked phosphorescent under the damp electric bulb." Auden's voice is now from a nightmare. "He rambled on wildly, as though secretly distraught." He compares the steam room to Kafka; talks of Dostoevsky: "All is focused on obsession. All this vice all around us, there's a touch of lunacy, isn't there? It's so mad and ridiculous in its Dostoevskyan fashion. 'To extreme sickness,' said Pascal, 'one must apply extreme remedies.' " Very clever, of course, but what did he mean by *extreme remedies*?

He clutched at the marble slab, as though seized with a fit of dizziness, then faded into the steam like a fog-bound vessel.

Years later Prokosch sees Auden, alone at a café in Venice. Prokosch begins:

"I've been to see the de Chiricos."

"Ah, you've been to see the de Chiricos," said Auden remotely.

"They were very disappointing," I said, blowing a smoke ring.

"Oh, I see. They were *disappointing,*" said Auden sarcastically.

"Almost sinisterly so," I muttered, half-imploringly.

"Indeed. Were they really? Almost *sinisterly* so!" He perked up a bit. His teeth protruded slightly.

I had an unerring knack for always saying the wrong thing to Auden. Whatever I wanted to say, however simple or sincere, the moment I opened my mouth it sounded gauche, vapid, insolent.

He seemed somehow to revel in this air of mutual embarrassment. He seemed to swell up into a sleek, didactic majesty.

I said, "Venice has changed."

"Venice," he snorted, "is constantly changing. With all that sky and water, how can it keep from changing incessantly?"

"I used to think of Tiepolo whenever I thought of Venice."

"Of Tiepolo. How interesting. So it reminded you of Tiepolo?"

"But I now think of Tintoretto. It has a beard, like Tintoretto."

"A beard. Yes. I see. Like Tintoretto. How very amusing."

Perhaps he was drunk. Impossible to be sure. He had already started on his desolate journey downward. The wrinkles were deepening, the pouches were thickening. The eyelids looked scaly and shifty, reptilian. Even the eyes were no longer the old Auden eyes, which used to be quick and alert as hummingbirds. They had turned into eyes that seemed to gloat over a malady, to brood over some accumulating inner calamity.

"Tintoretto," he said, with an accusatory precision. He seemed to ponder over the word, to linger over its contours. He cocked his head a little, as though looking for a new perspective. His hair was very tousled and his fingernails were purple. He stared across the piazza with an air of agitation.

And for an instant I caught that old familiar whiff of a festering unhappiness. . . . There was something almost regal in this massive, drunken misery. I felt almost reconciled to this grim, penultimate Auden. I yearned to cry out, "Come, let's drop all this pretense! Let's be friends after all! Let's forgive and forget!"

But I couldn't bring myself to say it. He slumped back in his chair. He seemed to catch on the wing this momentary impulse in me and all of a sudden he seemed to be listening to a voice in the distance and the folds of his face took on a ruinous splendour. This quick, molten beauty was the last glimpse I had of him. It was like a quick shaft of lightning on a war-shattered landscape.

I said, "Well, goodbye. It was nice to see you, Wystan."

"Yes. Of course. Tintoretto. It's odd about Tintoretto . . ."

I must say it takes guts to record such a scene at one's expense.

The Santayana voice that Prokosch records is not at all the voice that I heard. The old man says to Prokosch, "One must always, without necessarily being a pessimist, be prepared for the worst. For the end of what we call our Western civilization—I include the Athenian—and all that grandeur of Christian romanticism."

His head sagged a little. His eyes began to water. His voice rose imperceptibly, as though for a final effort. "We are sailing ever deeper into the dark, uncharted waters. The lights in the lighthouses are beginning to go out. Is there anything to guide us? Is there anyone worth listening to? I wake up in the middle of the night and I'm cold with terror. . . ."

I fear that my Santayana was a stoic like me, and I could not imagine him cold with terror at the thought of civilization's end. Even at eighty-five, the clear black eyes did not water but shone as bright and as hard as obsidian. When I said to him, with youthful despair, that the world had never been in so terrible a state, Santayana could not have been more brisk, or chilling. "My own lifetime has been spent in a longer period of peace and security than that of almost anyone I could conceive of in the European past." When I spoke with horror and revulsion of the possibility that Italy . . . *bella Italia* . . . might go communist in the next month's election, Santayana looked positively gleeful. "Oh, let them! Let them try it! They've tried everything else, so why not communism? After all, who knows what new loyalties will emerge as they become part of a—of a wolf pack." I was sickened and revolted by his sangfroid, by his cynicism, by his, yes, blancmange. I was also much amused by his response to my sad comment on the speed with which literary reputations were lost in Amnesia. "It would be insufferable," he said swiftly, "if they were not." Could *he* have heard time's winged wastebasket hovering near?

=

Among Prokosch's voices there are some marvelously comical ones, including Lady Cunard and Hemingway in deadly combat for the mucho-macho drawing-room championship award. An exchange between Edith Sitwell and Edmund Wilson is also splendid. It is 1948 or 1949. The Sitwells are being lionized by *tout* New York.

The butler slid past with a tray of boiled shrimps. Edmund Wilson approached the sofa with a glass in his hand. He plucked a shrimp from the tray and dipped it in the mayonnaise. He held it in the air as he sipped his whisky. I watched with frozen horror as the shrimp slid from its toothpick and gracefully landed on Miss Sitwell's coiffure. But Miss Sitwell ignored it and continued with serenity.

"It is always the incantatory element which basically appeals to me . . ."

" 'The Hollow Men' is pure incantation," said Edmund Wilson. He kept peering at the shrimp with a scrupulous curiosity. "I heard Eliot read it aloud once. It was a marvel of rhythmicality."

"Even in Dryden," said Miss Sitwell, "there is a sense of abracadabra . . ."

I kept staring at the shrimp with a feverish fascination. It lay poised on Miss Sitwell like an amulet of ivory. I visualized it in terms of the Victorian, the Elizabethan, the Gothic. I suddenly began rather to like Edith Sitwell.

I suddenly began rather to admire Frederic Prokosch twenty years ago when he visited me on the Hudson River where I lived. I took him to a party attended by a number of hicks and hacks and hoods from a nearby outpost of Academe. Naturally, they regarded Prokosch with contempt.

They knew that he had once been famous in Amnesia but they had forgotten why. Anyway, Auden had won. And Auden had said that there can only be one poet per epoch.

A great deal was said about poetry; and some of it was said by poets —teacher-poets, true, but poets nevertheless; winners of prizes ("They got more prizes now than they got poets": Philip Rahv, circa 1960, Amnesia). Prokosch was entirely ignored. But he listened politely as the uses of poetry in general and of the classics in particular were brought into question. Extreme positions were taken. Finally, one poet-teacher pulled the chain, as it were, on all of Western civilization: The classics, as such, were totally irrelevant. For a moment, there was a blessed silence. Then Prokosch began to recite in Latin a passage from Virgil; and the room grew very cold and still. "It's Dante," a full professor whispered to a full wife.

When Prokosch had finished, he said mildly, "Those lines are carved in marble in the gardens of the Villa Borghese at Rome. I used to look at them every day and I'd think, that is what poetry is, something that can be carved in marble, something that can still be beautiful to read after so many centuries."

Now in his seventy-fifth year, Prokosch ends his memoir with: "I live in a valley below Grasse in a cottage enclosed by cypresses. Behind me loom the hills where the walls are perched in the sunlight. Below me flows the cold green canal of the Siagne. Every morning I look at the dew which clings to the olive trees and I wonder what strange new excitement the day will hold for me. . . . My voyage is at its end. I think how glorious to grow old!" But "then I sit by the window and drink a cup of coffee and labor once again in my ceaseless struggle to produce a masterpiece."

So he is still at work, writing, as he ends. "I am no longer afraid of loneliness or suffering or death. I see the marvelous faces of the past gathering around me and I hear once again the murmuring of voices in the night." One must have created for oneself a very good day indeed to have so beautiful a prospect of the night.

THE NEW YORK REVIEW OF BOOKS

*May 12, 1983*

# CHAPTER 4

# TENNESSEE WILLIAMS: SOMEONE TO LAUGH AT THE SQUARES WITH

1

Although poetry is no longer much read by anyone in freedom's land, biographies of those American poets who took terrible risks not only with their talents but with their lives, are often quite popular; and testimonies, chockablock with pity, terror and awe, provide the unread poet, if not his poetry, with a degree of posthumous fame. Ever since Hart ("Man overboard!") Crane dove into the Caribbean and all our hearts, the most ambitious of our poets have often gone the suicide route:

There was an unnatural stillness in the kitchen which made her heart skip a beat; then she saw Marvin, huddled in front of the oven; then she screamed: the head of the "finest sestina-operator of the Seventies" [*Hudson Review,* Spring 1971] had been burned to a crisp.

If nothing else, suicide really *validates,* to use lit-crit's ultimate verb, the life if not the poetry; and so sly Marvin was able to die secure in the knowledge that his emblematic life would be written about and that readers who would not have been caught dead, as it were, with the work of the finest sestina-operator of the seventies will now fall, like so many hyenas, on the bio-bared bones of that long agony his life: high school valetudinarian. Columbia. The master's degree, written with heart's blood (on Rimbaud in *transition*). The awakening at Bread Loaf, and the stormy marriage to Linda. Precocious—and prescient—meteoric success of "On First Looking Into Delmore Schwartz's Medicine Cabinet" (*Prairie Schooner,* 1961). The drinking. The children. The pills. Pulitzer lost; Pulitzer regained. Seminal meeting with Roethke at the University of Iowa in an all-night diner. What conversation! Oh, they were titans then. But —born with one skin too few. All nerves; jangled sensibility. Lithium's failure is Lethe's opportunity. Genius-magma too radioactive for leaden human brain to hold. Oh! mounting horror as, one by one, the finest minds of a generation snuff themselves out in ovens, plastic bags, the odd river. Death and then—triumphant transfiguration as A Cautionary Tale.

By and large, American novelists and playwrights have not had to kill themselves in order to be noticed: There are still voluntary readers and restless playgoers out there. But since so many American writers gradually drink themselves to death (as do realtors, jockeys, and former officers of the Junior League), these sodden buffaloes are now attracting the sort of Cautionary Tale-spinner that usually keens over suicide-poets. Although the writer as actor in his time is nothing new, and the writer as performing self has been examined by Richard Poirier as a phenomenon ancillary to writer's writing, for the first time the self now threatens to become the sole artifact—to be written about by others who tend to erase, in the process, whatever writing the writer may have written.

=

Scott Fitzgerald, that most self-conscious of writers, made others conscious of himself and his crack-up through the pages known as *The Crack-Up.* Ever since then, American journalists and academics have used him as our paradigmatic Cautionary Tale on the ground that if you are young, handsome, talented, successful, and married to a beautiful woman, you will be destroyed because your life will be absolutely unbearable to those who teach and are taught. If, by some accident of fate, you are *not* destroyed, you will have a highly distressing old age like Somerset Maugham's, which we will describe in all its gamy incontinent horror. There is no winning, obviously. But then the Greeks knew that. And the rest is—Bruccoli. Today the writer need not write his life. Others will do it for him. But he must provide them with material; and a gaudy descent into drink, drugs, sex, and terminal name dropping.

As Tennessee Williams's powers failed (drink/drugs/age), he turned himself into a circus. If people would not go to his new plays, he would see to it that they would be able to look at him on television and read about him in the press. He lived a most glamorous crack-up; and now that he is dead, a thousand Cautionary Tales are humming along the electrical circuits of a thousand word processors en route to the electrical circuits of thousands upon thousands of brains already overloaded with tales of celebrity-suffering, the ultimate consolation—and justification— to those who didn't make it or, worse, didn't even try.

In 1976, I reviewed Tennessee Williams's *Memoirs*. We had been friends from the late forties to the early sixties; after that, we saw very little of each other (drink/drugs), but I never ceased to be fond of what I called the Glorious Bird. Readers of my review, who have waited, I hope patiently, to find out Tennessee's reaction should know that when next we met, he narrowed his cloudy blue eyes and said, in tones that one of these biographers would call "clipped," "When your review appeared my book was number five on the nonfiction best-seller list of *The New York Times*. Within two weeks of your review, *it was not listed at all.*"

I last saw him three or four years ago. We were together on a televised Chicago talk show. He was in good form, despite a papilla on the bridge of his nose, the first sign, ever, of that sturdy rubbery body's resentment of alcohol. There were two or three other guests around a table, and the host. Abruptly, the Bird settled back in his chair and shut his eyes. The host's habitual unease became panic. After some disjointed general chat, he said, tentatively, "Tennessee, are you asleep?" And the Bird replied, eyes still shut, "No, I am not asleep but sometimes I shut my eyes when I am bored."

===

Two testimonials to the passion and the agony of the life of Tennessee Williams have just been published. One is a straightforward biography of the sort known as journeyman; it is called *The Kindness of Strangers* (what else?) by Donald Spoto. The other is *Tennessee: Cry of the Heart* (whose heart?) by a male sob sister who works for *Parade* magazine.

The first book means to shock and titillate in a *responsible* way (drink, drugs, "wildly promiscuous sex"); that is, the author tries, not always successfully, to get the facts if not the life straight. The second is a self-serving memoir with a Capotean approach to reality. In fact, I suspect that Crier of the Heart may indeed be the avatar of the late Caravaggio of gossip. If so, he has now taken up the fallen leper's bell, and we need not ask ever for whom it tolls.

Crier tells us that he lived with Williams, from time to time, in the seventies. He tells us that Williams got him on the needle for two years, but that he bears him no grudge. In turn, he "radicalized" Williams during the Vietnam years. Each, we are told, really and truly hated the rich. Yet, confusingly, Crier is celebrated principally for his friendships with not one (1) but two (2) presidential sisters, Pat Kennedy Lawford and the late Ruth Carter Stapleton. He is also very much at home in counterrevolutionary circles: "A year before Tennessee died, I visited Mrs. Reagan at the White House and we had a long conversation alone in the Green Room after lunch. She asked about Tennessee, and Truman Capote, among others . . ." Oh, to have been a fly on that Green wall! But then when it comes to the rich and famous, Crier's style alternates between frantic to tell us the very worst and vatic as he cries up what to him is plainly the only game on earth or in heaven, Celebrity, as performed by consenting adults in Manhattan.

═══

Since most of Crier's references to me are wrong, I can only assume that most of the references to others are equally untrue. But then words like *true* and *false* are irrelevant to this sort of venture. It is the awful plangency of the Cry that matters, and this one's a real hoot, as they used to say on the Bird Circuit.

On the other hand, responsible Mr. Spoto begins at the beginning, and I found interesting the school days, endlessly protracted, of Thomas Lanier Williams (he did not use the name Tennessee until he was twenty-eight). The first twenty years of Williams's life provided him with the characters that he would write about. There is his sister, Rose, two years older than he, who moved from eccentricity to madness. There is the mother. Edwina, who gave the order for Rose's lobotomy, on the best medical advice, or so she says; for Rose may or may not have accused the hard-drinking father, Cornelius, at war with sissy son, Tom, and relentlessly genteel wife, of making sexual advances to her, which he may or may not have made. In any case, Tom never ceased to love Rose, despite the blotting out of her personality. Finally, there was the maternal grandfather, the Reverend Dakin; and the grandmother, another beloved Rose, known as Grand.

In 1928, the Reverend Dakin took the seventeen-year-old Williams to Europe. Grandson was grateful to grandfather to the end, which did not come until 1955. Many years earlier, the reverend gave his life savings to unkind strangers for reasons never made clear. The Bird told me that he thought that his grandfather had been blackmailed because of an encounter with a boy. Later, the reverend burned all his sermons on the lawn. In time, Tennessee's sympathies shifted from his enervating mother to his now entirely absent father. These are the cards that life dealt Williams; and he played them for the rest of his life. He took on no new characters, as opposed to male lovers, who tend either to appear in his work as phantoms or as youthful versions of the crude father, impersonated, much too excitingly, by Marlon Brando.

A great deal has been made of Williams's homosexual adventures; not least, alas, by himself. Since those who write about him are usually more confused about human sexuality than he was, which is saying a lot, some instruction is now in order.

===

Williams was born, 1911, in the heart of the Bible belt (Columbus, Mississippi); he was brought up in St. Louis, Missouri, a town more southern than not. In 1919, God-fearing Protestants imposed Prohibition on the entire United States. Needless to say, in this world of fierce Christian peasant values anything pleasurable was automatically sin and to be condemned. Williams may not have believed in God but he certainly believed in sin; he came to sex nervously and relatively late—in his twenties; his first experiences were heterosexual; then he shifted to homosexual relations with numerous people over many years. Although he never doubted that what he liked to do was entirely natural, he was obliged to tote the usual amount of guilt of a man of his time and place and class (lower-middle-class WASP, southern-airs-and-graces division). In the end, he suffered from a sense of otherness, not unuseful for a writer.

But the guilt took a not-so-useful turn: He became a lifelong hypochondriac, wasting a great deal of psychic energy on imaginary illnesses. He was always about to die of some dread inoperable tumor. When I first met him (1948), he was just out of a Paris hospital, and he spoke with somber joy of the pancreatic cancer that would soon cause him to fall from the perch. Years later I discovered that the pancreatic cancer for which he had been hospitalized was nothing more than a half-mile or so of homely tapeworm. When he died (not of "an unwashed grape" but of suffocation caused by the inhaling of a nasal-spray top), an autopsy was performed and the famous heart ("I have suffered a series of cardiac seizures and arrests since my twelfth year") was found to be in fine condition, and the liver that of a hero.

Just as Williams never really added to his basic repertory company of actors (Cornelius and Edwina, Reverend Dakin and Rose, himself and Rose), he never picked up much information about the world during his half-century as an adult. He also never tried, consciously at least, to make sense of the society into which he was born. If he had, he might have figured out that there is no such thing as a homosexual or a heterosexual person. There are only homo- or heterosexual acts. Most people are a mixture of impulses if not practices, and what anyone does with a willing partner is of no social or cosmic significance.

So why all the fuss? In order for a ruling class to rule, there must be arbitrary prohibitions. Of all prohibitions, sexual taboo is the most useful because sex involves everyone. To be able to lock up someone or deprive him of employment because of his sex life is a very great power indeed, and one seldom used in civilized societies. But although the United States is the best and most perfect of earth's societies and our huddled masses earth's envy, we have yet to create a civilization, as opposed to a way of life. That is why we have allowed our governors to divide the population into two teams. One team is good, godly, straight; the other is evil, sick, vicious. Like the good team's sectarian press, Williams believed, until the end of his life, in this wacky division. He even went to an analyst who ordered him to give up both writing and sex so that he could be transformed into a good-team player. Happily, the analyst did not do in the Bird's beak, as Freud's buddy Fliess ruined the nose of a young lady, on the ground that only through breaking the nose could onanism be stopped in its vile track. Also, happily, the Bird's anarchy triumphed over the analyst. After a troubling session on the couch, he would appear on television and tell Mike Wallace all about the problems of his analysis with one

Dr. Kubie, who not long after took down his shingle and retired from shrinkage.

===

Both *The Glass Menagerie* and *A Streetcar Named Desire* opened during that brief golden age (1945–1950) when the United States was everywhere not only regnant but at peace, something we have not been for the last thirty-five years. At the beginning, Williams was acclaimed by pretty much everyone; only *Time* magazine was consistently hostile, suspecting that Williams might be "basically negative" and "sterile," code words of the day for fag. More to the point, *Time*'s founder, Henry Luce, had been born in China, son of a Christian missionary. "The greatest task of the United States in the twentieth century," he once told me, "will be the Christianization of China." With so mad a proprietor, it is no wonder that Time-Life should have led the press crusade against fags in general and Williams in particular.

Although Williams was able to survive as a playwright because he was supported by the drama reviewers of *The New York Times* and *Herald Tribune*, the only two newspapers that mattered for a play's success, he was to take a lot of flak over the years. After so much good-team propaganda, it is now widely believed that since Tennessee Williams liked to have sex with men (true), he hated women (untrue); as a result, his women characters are thought to be malicious caricatures, designed to subvert and destroy godly straightness.

But there is no actress on earth who will not testify that Williams created the best women characters in the modern theater. After all, he never ceased to love Rose and Rose, and his women characters tended to be either one or the other. Faced with contrary evidence, the anti-fag brigade promptly switch to their fallback position. All right, so he didn't hate women (as real guys do—the ball-breakers!) but, worse, far worse, *he thought he was a woman.* Needless to say, a biblical hatred of women intertwines with the good team's hatred of fags. But Williams never thought of himself as anything but a man who could, as an artist, inhabit any gender; on the other hand, his sympathies were always with those defeated by "the squares"; or by time, once the sweet bird of youth is flown. Or by death, "which has never been much in the way of completion."

Finally, in sexual matters (the principal interest of the two Cautionary

Tales at hand), there seems to be a double standard at work. Although the heterosexual promiscuity of Pepys, Boswell, Byron, Henry Miller, and President Kennedy has never *deeply* upset any of their fans, William's ("feverish") promiscuity quite horrifies Mr. Spoto, and even Crier from the Heart tends to sniffle at all those interchangeable pieces of trade. But Williams had a great deal of creative and sexual energy; and he used both. Why not? And so what?

=

Heart's Crier describes how I took Williams to meet another sexual athlete (good-team, natch), Senator John F. Kennedy. Crier quotes the Bird, who is speaking to Mrs. Pat Lawford, Kennedy's sister and Crier's current friend: "Gore said he was invited to a lunch by Mr. Kennedy and would I like to come along? Of course I did, since I greatly admired your brother. He brought such vitality to our country's life, such hope and great style. He made thinking fashionable again." Actually, the Bird had never heard of Kennedy that day in 1958 when we drove from Miami to Palm Beach for lunch with the golden couple, who had told me that they lusted to meet the Bird. He, in turn, was charmed by them. "Now tell me again," he would ask Jack, repeatedly, "what you are. A governor or a senator?" Each time, Jack, dutifully, gave name, rank, and party. Then the Bird would sternly quiz him on America's China policy, and Jack would look a bit glum. Finally, he proposed that we shoot at a target in the patio.

While Jackie flitted about, taking Polaroid shots of us, the Bird banged away at the target; and proved to be a better shot than our host. At one point, while Jack was shooting, the Bird muttered in my ear, "Get that ass!" I said, "Bird, you can't cruise our next president." The Bird chuckled ominously: "They'll never elect those two. They are much too attractive for the American people." Later, I told Jack that the Bird had commented favorably on his ass. He beamed. "Now, that's *very* exciting," he said. But, fun and games to one side, it is, of course, tragic that both men were, essentially, immature sexually and so incapable of truly warm *mature* human relations. One could weep for what might have been.

Crier from the Heart has lots and lots of scores to settle in the course of his lament and he brings us bad news about all sorts of famous people who may have offended him. Certainly, he wears if not his heart his spleen on his sleeve. Mary Hemingway confessed to him that she and her husband Ernest were "never lovers. Mr. Hemingway was beyond that by then." Bet you didn't know that! As for the rich whom he and Tennessee so radically hate, they are finally incarnated not by the Rockefellers or by the Mellons but by a couple of hard-working overachievers called de la Renta, whose joint fortune must be a small fraction of the Bird's. To be fair, Crier has his compassionate side. A piece of trade had no money, and Tennessee was passed out. So Crier took the Bird's checkbook and "wrote out a check for six hundred dollars made out to cash, and took it downstairs to the hotel desk and had it cashed. I went back upstairs, handed Chris the money, and kissed him goodbye.

"It was the only time I ever forged Tennessee's name to a check, and I do not regret it." For such heroic continence, *canaille oblige.*


2

Thirty-seven years ago, in March 1948, Tennessee Williams and I celebrated his thirty-seventh birthday in Rome, except that he said that it was his thirty-*fourth* birthday. Years later, when confronted with the fact that he had been born in 1911 not 1914, he said, serenely, "I do not choose to count as part of my life the three years that I spent working for a shoe company." Actually, he spent ten months, not three years, in the shoe company, and the reason that he had changed his birth date was to qualify for a play contest open to those twenty-five or under. No matter. I thought him very old in 1948. But I was twenty-two in the spring of *annus mirabilis* when my novel *The City and the Pillar* was a best seller (Mr. Spoto thinks the book was published later) and his play, *A Streetcar Named Desire,* was taking the world by storm, as it still does.

I must say I was somewhat awed by Tennessee's success. Of course, he went on and on about the years of poverty but, starting with *The Glass Menagerie* (1944), he had an astonishingly productive and successful fifteen years: *Summer and Smoke* (1947), *The Rose Tattoo* (1951), *Cat on a Hot Tin Roof* (1955), *Suddenly Last Summer* (1958), *Sweet Bird of Youth* (1959). But even at that high moment in Rome, the Bird's eye was coldly realistic. "Baby, the playwright's working career is a short one. There's always somebody new to take your place." I said that I didn't believe it would happen in his case, and I still don't. The best of his plays are as permanent as anything can be in the age of Kleenex.

All his life, Tennessee wrote short stories. I have just finished reading the lot of them, some forty-six stories. The first was written when Tom was seventeen—a sister avenges her brother in lush prose in even lusher Pharaonic Egypt ("The Vengeance of Nitocris")—and published in *Weird Tales*. The last is unpublished. "The Negative" was written when Tennessee was seventy-one; he deals, as he so often came to do, with a poet, losing his mind, art; at the end, "as he ran toward this hugely tolerant receiver, he scattered from his gentleman's clothes, from their pockets, the illegibly scribbled poetry of his life."

To my mind, the short stories, and not *Memoirs*, are the true memoir of Tennessee Williams. Whatever happened to him, real or imagined, he turned into prose. Except for occasional excursions into fantasy, he sticks pretty close to life as he experienced or imagined it. No, he is not a great short-story writer like Chekhov but he has something rather more rare than mere genius. He has a narrative tone of voice that is wholly convincing. In this, he resembles Mark Twain, a very different sort of writer (to overdo understatement); yet Hannibal, Missouri, is not all that far from St. Louis, Missouri. Each is best at comedy and each was always uneasy when not so innocently abroad. Tennessee loved to sprinkle foreign phrases throughout his work, and they are *always* wrong.

=

Tennessee worked every morning on whatever was at hand. If there was no play to be finished or new dialogue to be sent round to the theater, he would open a drawer and take out the draft of a story already written and begin to rewrite it. I once found him revising a short story that had just been published. "Why," I asked, "rewrite what's already in print?" He looked at me, vaguely; then he said, "Well, obviously it's not finished." And went back to his typing.

In Paris, he gave me the story "Rubio y Morena" to read. I didn't like it. So fix it, he said. He knew, of course, that there is no fixing someone else's story (or life) but he was curious to see what I would do. So I reversed backward-running sentences, removed repetitions, eliminated half those adjectives and adverbs that he always insisted do their work in pairs. I was proud of the result. He was deeply irritated. "What you have done is remove my *style*, which is all that I have."

Tennessee could not possess his own life until he had written about it. This is common. To start with, there would be, let us say, a sexual desire for someone. Consummated or not, the desire ("something that is made to occupy a larger space than that which is afforded by the individual being") would produce reveries. In turn, the reveries would be written down as a story. But should the desire still remain unfulfilled, he would make a play of the story and then—and this is why he was so compulsive a working playwright—he would have the play produced so that he could, at relative leisure, like God, rearrange his original experience into something that was no longer God's and unpossessable but *his*. The Bird's frantic lifelong pursuit of—and involvement in—play productions was not just ambition or a need to be busy; it was the only way that he ever had of being entirely alive. The sandy encounters with his first real love, a dancer, on the beach at Provincetown and the dancer's later death ("an awful flower grew in his brain") instead of being forever lost were forever his once they had been translated to the stage where living men and women could act out his text and with their immediate flesh close at last the circle of desire. "For love I make characters in plays," he wrote; and did.

═══

I had long since forgotten why I called him the Glorious Bird until I reread the stories. The image of the bird is everywhere in his work. The bird is flight, poetry, life. The bird is time, death: "Have you ever seen the skeleton of a bird? If you have you will know how completely they are still flying." In "The Negative" he wrote of a poet who can no longer assemble a poem. "Am I a wingless bird?" he writes; and soars no longer.

Although the Bird accepted our "culture's" two-team theory, he never seriously wanted to play on the good team, as poor Dr. Kubie discovered on prime-time television. He went right on having sex; he also went right on hating the "squares" or, as he put it, in the story "Two on a Party" (1954), where Billy (in life the poet Oliver Evans) and Cora (Marion Black Vaccaro) cruise sailors together:

It was a rare sort of moral anarchy, doubtless, that held them together, a really fearful shared hatred of everything that was restrictive and which they felt to be false in the society they lived in and against the grain of which they continually operated. They did not dislike what they called "squares." They loathed and despised them, and for the best of reasons. Their existence was a never-ending contest with the squares of the world, the squares who have such a virulent rage at everything not in their book.

The squares had indeed victimized the Bird but by 1965, when he came to write *The Knightly Quest*, he had begun to see that the poor squares' "virulent rage" is deliberately whipped up by the rulers in order to distract them from such real problems as, in the sixties, the Vietnam War and Watergate and Operation Armageddon then—and now—under way. In this story, Tennessee moves Lyndon Johnson's America into a near future where the world is about to vanish in a shining cloud; and he realizes, at last, that the squares have been every bit as damaged and manipulated as he; and so he now writes an elegy to the true American, Don Quixote, an exile in his own country: "His castles are immaterial and his ways are endless and you do not have to look into many American eyes to suddenly meet somewhere the beautiful grave lunacy of his gaze." Also, Tennessee seems to be trying to bring into focus the outlandish craziness of a society which had so wounded him. Was it possible that he was not the evil creature portrayed by the press? Was it possible that they are wrong about *everything*? A light bulb switches on: "All of which makes me suspect that back of the sun and way deep under our feet, at the earth's center, are not a couple of noble mysteries but a couple of joke books." Right on, Bird! It was a nice coincidence that just as Tennessee was going around the bend (drink, drugs, and a trip to the bin in 1969) the United States was doing the same. Suddenly, the Bird and Uncle Sam met face to face in *The Knightly Quest*. Better too late than never. Anyway, he was, finally, beginning to put the puzzle together.

=

"I cannot write any sort of story," said Tennessee to me, "unless there is at least one character in it for whom I have physical desire."

In story after story there are handsome young men, some uncouth like Stanley Kowalski; some couth like the violinist in "The Resemblance Between a Violin Case and a Coffin." Then, when Tennessee produced *A Streetcar Named Desire*, he inadvertently smashed one of our society's most powerful taboos (no wonder Henry Luce loathed him): He showed the male not only as sexually attractive in the flesh but as an object for something never before entirely acknowledged by the good team, the lust of women. In the age of Calvin Klein's steaming hunks, it must be hard for those under forty to realize that there was ever a time when a man was nothing but a suit of clothes, a shirt and tie, shined leather shoes, and a gray, felt hat. If he was thought attractive, it was because he had a nice smile and a twinkle in his eye. In 1947, when Marlon Brando appeared on stage in a torn sweaty T-shirt, there was an earthquake; and the male as sex object is still at our culture's center stage and will so remain until the likes of Boy George redress, as it were, the balance. Yet, ironically, Tennessee's auctorial sympathies were not with Stanley but with his "victim" Blanche.

=====

I have never known anyone to complain as much as the Bird. If he was not dying of some new mysterious illness, he was in mourning for a dead lover, usually discarded long before the cancerous death, or he was suffering from the combination of various cabals, real and imagined, that were out to get him. Toward the end, he had personified the ringleaders. They were a Mr. and Mrs. Gelb, who worked for *The New York Times.* Because they had written a book about Eugene O'Neill, the Bird was convinced that the Gelbs were using the *Times* in order to destroy him so that they could sell more copies of their book about O'Neill, who would then be America's *numero uno* dramatist. Among Crier's numerous errors and inventions is the Eugene O'Neill letter, "the only one he ever wrote to Tennessee," who "read it to me, first explaining that he had received it after the opening of *The Glass Menagerie. . . .* It was a very moving and a very sad letter, and I don't know what became of it." The letter was written not after *Menagerie* but *Streetcar,* and Tennessee never read it to Crier or to anyone else because neither Tennessee nor I, in Rome 1948, could make head or tail of it. O'Neill was suffering from Parkinson's disease; the handwriting was illegible. The Bird and I had a running gag over the years that would begin, "As Eugene O'Neill wrote you . . ." Except for O'Neill, the Bird's sharp eye saw no dangerous competition. Once, at a function, where the guests were asked to line up alphabetically, Thornton Wilder approached the Bird and said, "I believe Wilder comes before Williams." To which the Bird responded, *"Only* in the alphabet."

I did not see much of him in the last years. I don't recall when he got into the habit of taking barbiturates (later, speed; and worse). He certainly did his mind and body no good; but he was tough as they come, mind and body. The current chroniclers naturally emphasize the horrors of the last years because the genre requires that they produce A Cautionary Tale. Also, since the last years are the closest to us, they give us no sense at all of what he was like for most of his long life. Obviously, he wasn't drunk or drugged all that much because he lived to write; and he wrote, like no one else.

I remember him best one noon in Key West during the early fifties (exact date can be determined because on every jukebox "Tennessee Waltz" was being mournfully sung by Patti Page). Each of us had finished work for the day. We met on South Beach, a real beach then. We made our way through sailors on the sand to a terraced restaurant where the Bird sat back in a chair, put his bare feet up on a railing, looked out at the bright blue sea, and, as he drank his first and only martini of the midday, said, with a great smile, "I like my life."

THE NEW YORK REVIEW OF BOOKS
*June 13, 1985*

# CHAPTER 5

# RICHARD NIXON: NOT *THE BEST MAN'S* BEST MAN

O f all my literary inventions, Richard Nixon is the most nearly autonomous. Like all great literary creations—Beowulf, Gargantua, Little Nell—one does not know what on earth he might do next. When I first invented him as a character called Joe Cantwell in the play and later the movie *The Best Man,* I thought to myself, There! I have done it. For at least a generation I have fixed on the page—or, in this case, on the stage and upon some strips of celluloid—a splendid twentieth-century archetype. But little did I suspect that my invention would suddenly take on a life of its own and that I would be forced to return again and again to this astonishing protean creature whose genius it is to be always the same.

My last major effort was in 1972, when *An Evening with Richard Nixon* was produced on Broadway. But this time my invention did an end run around me, as he would put it in his jock jargon. When the play opened, most of the press had decided to support Nixon's Committee to Re-Elect the President (the acronym was CREEP—remember?), and my revelations about shoe boxes filled with money and break-ins and illegal spying and other high capers were not only premature but they were the one thing that no American journalist can abide—bad taste. In fact, so bad was my taste that an apostle of good taste at *The New York Times* (a paper that is good taste incarnate—and utter refinement, too) said that I had said "mean and nasty things about our President." The apostle was English and did not know that although the sovereign of his native islands is called Our Queen, the emperor of the West is known to us aficionados as The Goddamned President.

Needless to say, I cannot stop following the adventures of my invention . . . *my* invention! He is ours in a way that the queen is not England's, because she was invented by history, while Nixon made himself up, with a lot of help from all of us. As individuals, the presidents are accidental; but as types, they are inevitable and represent, God help us, us. We are Nixon; he is us.

Although hypocrisy has been the name of the American game for most of this century, Nixon's occasional odd bursts of candor are often stunning. Of General Eisenhower, whose despised (by Ike) vice president he was, Nixon wrote in *Six Crises:* "Eisenhower was a far more complex and devious man than most people realized"—a truth not generally known even now. Then comes the inimitable Nixon gloss: Eisenhower was complex and devious "in the best sense of those words."

The Machiavelli of Whittier, California, often says what he means when he means to say something quite different, and that is why one cannot stop listening to him. In Nixon we are able to observe our faults larger than life. But we can also, if we try, see in this huge, dusty mirror our virtues as well. So the time has now come for us to regard the thirty-seventh president in the light, if not of eternity, of the twentieth century, now drawing to its unmourned close.

Currently, in a series of books signed with Nixon's name, he himself is trying to rearrange his place in that long cavalcade of mediocrity—and worse—that has characterized the American presidency since the death of Franklin Roosevelt.

Nixon's chroniclers have their work cut out for them, because he is simply too gorgeous and outsize an American figure for any contemporary to put into a clear perspective. To understand Nixon's career you would have to understand the United States in the twentieth century, and that is something that our educational, political, and media establishments are not about to help us do. After all: no myth, no nation. They have a vested interest in maintaining our ignorance, and that is why we are currently stuck with the peculiar notion that Nixon just happened to be the one bad apple in a splendid barrel. The fact that there has not been a good or serious president since Franklin Roosevelt is ignored, while the fact that Nixon was corrupt some of the time, and complex and devious all of the time, is constantly emphasized in order to make him appear uniquely sleazy—and the rest of us just grand. Yet Nixon is hardly atypical. Certainly his predecessor, Lyndon Johnson, far surpassed Nixon when it came to mendacity and corruption. But the national myth requires, periodically, a scapegoat; hence Nixon's turn in the barrel.

Actually, corruption has been more the rule than the exception in our political life. When Lincoln was obliged to appoint a known crook as secretary of war, he asked a congressman from the appointee's state if he thought that the new cabinet minister would actually steal in office. "Well," said the congressman thoughtfully, "I don't think he'd steal a red-hot stove."

Neither personally nor auctorially did I feel sorry for Nixon during the days of Watergate and his resignation. After all, he was simply acting out his Big Loser nature, and, in the process, he turned being a Big Loser into a perfect triumph by managing to lose the presidency in a way bigger and more original than anyone else had ever lost it before. That takes gumption. No, I only began to feel sorry for him when the late, much-dreaded Fawn M. Brodie, a certifiable fool (of the dead only the truth), wrote one of her pseudo-psychobiographies of him and plowed him under as if he were a mere Thomas Jefferson (a previous victim of her somber art) in pursuit of mulatto nymphets. Enough is enough, I said to myself; do not inflict this Freudian horseshit on Nixon—*my* Nixon.

So let us now praise an infamous man who has done great deeds for his country. The clatter you just heard is that of knives falling on the floor of the American pantheon, where now, with slow and mechanical and ever-so-slightly-out-of-sync tread, the only great president of the last half of the twentieth century moves toward his rightful niche. Future historians—and with some thanks to Nixon, there may even be future historians—will look to Nixon as the first president who acted upon the not-exactly-arcane notion that the United States is just one country among many countries and that communism is an economic and political system without much to recommend it at the moment and with few voluntary adherents.

Simultaneously Nixon realized that coexistence with the Soviet Union is the only game that we can safely play. Nixon also saw the value of exploiting the rift between Russia and China.

In a book called *Leaders,* Nixon praises de Gaulle, from whom he learned two lessons. First, power accrues to the ruler whose actions are unpredictable. Although this tactic might work at a local level for the leader of a minor country, such a system of unexpectedness on the part of the emperor of the West could send what is known euphemistically as the Wrong Signal to the emperor of the East, in which case there would never be enough shovels to protect us from the subsequent nuclear rain. The second—more practical—lesson was in de Gaulle's view that nations are nations, and while political systems come and go, national interests continue for millennia. Like every good and bad American, Nixon knows almost no history of any kind. But he was quick to pick up on the fact that the Russians and the Chinese each have a world view that has nothing at all to do with communism, or whatever happens to be the current official name for Heaven's Mandate.

Nixon proceeded to do the unexpected. He buried the hatchet with the Son of Heaven, Mao, by going to see him—as is proper for the Barbarian from beyond the Four Seas if he wishes to enjoy the patronage of the Lord of the Middle Kingdom. Then, from this position of strength, Nixon paid a call on the Czar of all the Russias, whose mouth, to say the least, was somewhat ajar at what Nixon had done in China. With one stroke, Nixon brought the world's three great powers (all nuclear) into the same plane of communication. There was no precedent for what he had done. Kennedy worshipers point to Kennedy's celebrated we-are-all-in-this-together speech at American University; but Kennedy was a genuine war lover in a way that Nixon was not, despite his locker-room-macho imitation of what he took to be Kennedy's genuine locker-room macho. Actually, neither one ever qualified for the team; they were just a standard pair of weaklings.

Although Nixon is the one who will be remembered for ending, four years too late, the Vietnam War, he is currently obliged to share some of the glory with a curious little man called Henry Kissinger. In the war of the books now going on between Nixon and Kissinger, Kissinger is trying hard to close the fame gap. The Kissinger books give the impression that while Nixon was holed up in the Executive Office Building, swilling martinis and listening to the emetic strains of Richard Rodgers's score for *Victory at Sea*, the American Metternich was leading the free world out of the Valley of the Shadow. But, ultimately, a Kissinger is just a Kissinger, something the burglar uses to jimmy a lock. While Nixon allowed the Vietnam War to drag on for four years, hoping that something would turn up, Kissinger did as he was told.

Even so, if the Kissinger books are to be believed, he was a lot tougher than Nixon when it came to dealing with Hanoi. After the election of '72, Kissinger tells us, "basically, [Nixon] now wanted the war over on almost any terms. . . . He had a horror of appearing on television to announce that he was beginning his new mandate by once again expanding the war." But Kissinger was made of sterner stuff. Although he praised (to Nixon's face) the Christmas bombing of North Vietnam, he was taking a tougher line than Nixon in negotiations despite "Nixon's brooding disquietude with my new-found celebrity. . . ." Also, Kissinger, being Kissinger, did not want the press to think that he had concurred in the brutal bombing. "I did not indicate to any journalist that I had opposed the decision to use B-52s," he tells us firmly, then adds, "but I also did little to dampen the speculation, partly in reaction to the harassment of the previous weeks, partly out of a not very heroic desire to deflect the assault from my person."

Meanwhile, Nixon quotes from his diary at the time the decision to bomb was made: "Henry talked rather emotionally about the fact that this was a very courageous decision. . . ." Later, when the war ran out of gas, the diarist reports: ". . . I told [Kissinger] that the country was indebted to him for what he had done. It is not really a comfortable thing for me to praise people so openly. . . . On the other hand, Henry expects it. . . . He, in turn, responded that without my having the, as he puts it, courage to make the difficult decision of December 18th, we would not be where we are today."

The unsatisfactory end to the most unsatisfactory and pointless war in American history will be, like Kissinger himself, a footnote to a presidency that will be remembered for the bold initiative to China combined with a degree of détente with the Soviet Union.

Today we are all of us in Nixon's debt for seizing an opportunity *(ignore his motives: the world is governed by deeds, not motives)* in order to make sense of close to one third of a century of dangerous nonsense.

Finally, I am happy to say that the ever-restless householder of Saddle River, New Jersey, continues to surprise. In the spring of last year he addressed a fund-raising event at the Disneyland Hotel, in Orange County, California. For the right-wingers present, he was obliged to do a bit of the Russians-are-coming; then he made absolute sense.

"The Soviet Union needs a deal," Nixon said. "And we should give them one. But for a price." Noting that the West has a five-to-one edge in economic power over the Soviets, Nixon said that this advantage should be used as an "economic lever." Because "simply to have a program that would lead to a balance of nuclear terror is not enough. We must try to add to that a new dimension of the use of America's and the free world's economic power as both a carrot and a stick." Predictably, the press did not pick up on any of this, but history will; and since we are all of us Nixon and he is us, the fact that he went to Peking and Moscow in order to demonstrate to all the world the absolute necessity of coexistence proves that there is not only good in him but in us as well—hope, too.

ESQUIRE
*December 1983*

# CHAPTER 6

# HOLLYWOOD!

One morning last spring (June 1982), I cast a vote for myself in the Hollywood hills; then I descended to the flats of Beverly Hills for a haircut at the barber shop in the Beverly Wilshire Hotel, where I found the Wise Hack, now half as old as time; his remaining white hairs had just been trimmed; he was being manicured, the large yellow diamond still sparkles on that finger which he refers to as a "pinkie." The Wise Hack's eyes have lost a bit of their sparkle but then eyes that have looked with deep suspicion into those of F. Scott Fitzgerald *and* of Y. Frank Freeman have earned their mica glaze.

When I greeted him, he said, accusingly, "Why do you want to be governor of this schmatteh state?" When I said that I didn't want to be *governor* (I was a candidate for the U.S. Senate) he nodded slyly. "That's what *I* told people," he said, cryptic as always. Then: "It's over there. In my briefcase. This Xerox copy. You can borrow it. Everybody's in it. Not that I know a lot of these young hotshots they got nowadays with their beads and long hair. Remember when there was only the one head of the studio and he was there forever? But a lot of old-timers are in it, too. Ray's in it. Real hatchet job like that one that—you know, what's her name, did to Dore . . ." I supplied the name of Lillian Ross. He nodded, "I warned Dore at the time . . ."

In due course, I read the Xerox of a book—or tome as the Wise Hack would say—called *Indecent Exposure* by a journalist named David McClintick, who has examined at great length the David Begelman scandal of five years ago. As I read the book, the Wise Hack supplied me with a running commentary. Although the Wise Hack's memory for names is going fast, he has perfect recall of what goes on—or went on—behind Hollywood's closed doors. "You see, the book is told from the point of view of this one young hotshot who, when Columbia Pictures was on its ass, was made president in New York by Ray Stark and Herbert Allen, Jr., then this hotshot Alan Hirschfield . . . You know him?" A sharp look, suddenly. I said as far as I know I have never met Mr. Hirschfield. But then like the Wise Hack I can't keep straight all the young executives who come and go, talking of Coca-Cola—Columbia's new owner.

I did know the unfortunate Begelman, who had been my agent, and I had once made a film with Ray Stark twenty years ago while . . . But as the Wise Hack always says, "First you identify your characters. Then you show us your problem. Then you bring on your hero. Then you kick him in the balls. Then you show how he takes that kick. Does he feel sorry for himself? Never. Because," and I would recite along with the Wise Hack movieland's inexorable law: "Self-pity is not box office."

=

In 1973 Columbia Pictures was close to bankruptcy. The studio's principal supplier of films, Ray Stark, went to his old friend Charles Allen of the investment firm Allen and Company and persuaded him to buy into the studio. Stark proceeded to interest Allen's thirty-three-year-old nephew, Herbert Allen, Jr., in Columbia's management. Together they selected an employee of Allen and Company, one Alan Hirschfield, to be the president of Columbia Pictures, headquartered in New York. Thus has Hollywood always been governed. The power and the money are in New York; the studio and the glamor are in Hollywood. According to the Wise Hack, the day after Pearl Harbor was attacked, there was not a dry eye in the commissary at MGM when L. B. Mayer exhorted each of the assembled artists and artisans "to say to himself a silent prayer—at this time of national emergency—for our great president—Nicholas M. Schenck in New York."

David Begelman was made chief of production of Columbia Pictures in Hollywood. Begelman had been a highly successful agent and packager of films. He turned, as they say, Columbia Pictures around. After four years of Begelman's management the studio was a great success. Begelman got most of the praise, which somewhat irritated Hirschfield. Even so, everything was going very nicely for everyone until . . .

In 1976 Begelman forged the actor Cliff Robertson's name to a check for ten thousand dollars made out to Robertson by Columbia. Robertson would never have known of the check if he had not got an IRS form in the mail. It is of some psychological interest that although Robertson had once been a client of Begelman, a *froideur*, as they say in Bel Air, developed between the two men when Begelman took the side of Cinerama against his client in a dispute over money. Begelman's attempts to cover up the Robertson forgery failed, and Columbia's board of directors suspended Begelman as president of the company, notified the SEC, and ordered an audit of Begelman's affairs. The press reported that there had been "financial irregularities"; the word *forgery* was not mentioned.

A second forged check surfaced, made out to the director Marty Ritt, as well as a payment to an imaginary Frenchman whose name Begelman had appropriated from one of Hollywood's leading maîtres d'hotel—Begelman's subconscious had its witty side. After a thorough investigation, the auditors reported to the board of Columbia that Begelman had embezzled $61,008; he had also taken, in unauthorized expenses, $23,000. The board was stunned by these amounts.

"Why so little?" asked the Wise Hack, not at all rhetorically. "A real thief in that job can steal millions. This was the petty cash. Let's face it, David's a sick man. That's all." Since the Wise Hack's estimate was pretty much that of the board of directors, Begelman was reinstated on condition that he pay back what he had taken and agree to go to the village medicine man—at this time and in that place, a shrink. Plainly, they were all nuts. Now begins the agony and the ecstasy of Mr. McClintick's tale.

≡

In an author's note, Mr. McClintick tells us that "everything in this book is real [as opposed to true?], every episode, scene, weather reference, conversation, and name (except for that of a single confidential informant)." Since Columbia's board meetings are reported with such a wealth of "real" dialogue, it would appear that the author's Deep Throat is Mr. Hirschfield himself. Certainly, he must have an astonishing memory. If not, how else could he have supplied the author with so many detailed conversations? After all, in Mr. McClintick's own words, "The minutes are summaries and contain no actual dialogue." Perhaps Mr. Hirschfield taped himself and his fellow board members.

But this is only idle supposition—one must proceed carefully with Mr. McClintick because on the page entitled "Acknowledgments" he gives "thanks also to Robert D. Sack, the finest libel lawyer in America and, not insignificantly, an astute editorial critic." Plainly, what we are in for is hardball. Curiously enough, neither author nor libel lawyer cum editorial critic is exactly straightforward on the problem of attribution. On the next page there are two epigraphs. One is an aria by John Huston on how Hollywood is a jungle. The other is a remark by David Chasman: "The New Hollywood is very much like the Old Hollywood." To the innocent reader it looks as if both Huston and Chasman had made these statements to the author. The Huston aria is dated 1950; the Chasman 1981. I had no idea of the provenance of the Chasman quotation but surely Mr. McClintick should have given prompt credit to Lillian Ross, from whose remarkable book *Picture* he lifted Huston's speech. Instead, under "Notes," on page 524, he identifies his source.

Despite the author's note, *Indecent Exposure* belongs to a relatively new genre of writing in which real people are treated as if they are characters in a fiction. Villains "smirk"; heroes "stride"; Begelman "sidled over." Although Mr. McClintick has proudly billed his book as "A True Story of Hollywood and Wall Street," he does not hesitate to enter the minds of real people. "Caressed by Muzak, Begelman sat at his elaborate *faux marbre* desk and thought about the check and about Cliff Robertson. . . . Using Robertson's name to steal the money in the first place had been a big mistake, even though it had seemed perfectly logical at the time." Incidentally, "the finest libel lawyer in America" and "astute editorial critic" does not have much of an eye or ear for English—or even the *faux anglais* of Bel Air. Dangling participles adorn Mr. McClintick's pages like hangman's nooses. Or, later, "Sitting at home on a Sunday three months later, facing an imminent investigation, Begelman decided to proceed with his plan for concealing the Pierre Groleau embezzlement." How does our author know that Begelman was sitting rather than standing? or whether or not Muzak caressed or annoyed Begelman? And wouldn't it be more dramatic to have him on the toilet instead of at his desk when he thinks about the check? Since all of this is plainly unknowable, all of this becomes untrue.

═══

It is Mr. McClintick's thesis that good-guy Alan Hirschfield wanted to get rid of Begelman because he was a crook but he couldn't because the real power brokers at Columbia, Herbert Allen and Ray Stark, did not share his high moral standards. Mr. McClintick's Hirschfield is a highly moral man—if somewhat indecisive, because he fears not only for his job but he suspects "blackmail" might be used against him because his wife Berte was employed by the research firm E. J. Wolf & Associates, who did work for Columbia.

Thus, Mr. McClintick sets up his hero: "Reporters, especially women, enjoyed interviewing him. He was an attractive man—a six-footer of medium build with an athletic bearing, hair that was expertly coiffed even though thinning and graying, and a countenance that revealed his droll, playful personality through twinkling eyes and the trace of a smile. Relaxed and informal, he laughed easily and often, and his speaking voice was the kind of soft, gentle adult voice that children find comforting." I looked in the back of the book for affidavits from children; there were none.

Hirschfield is also from Oklahoma, which gives him a "somewhat home-town naïveté that was a deeply ingrained part of Alan's character—the Oklahoma in him—as Berte saw it. . . ." Mr. McClintick is no doubt an eastern city bumpkin, unaware that Oklahoma's rich and marvelous corruption makes Hollywood's wheeling and dealing seem positively innocent. In the text, Hirschfield usually "strides"; occasionally he "ambles." Sometimes he is "discombobulated"; even "a man in agony"; once—only once—he "whined." He is a good family man, as all good men are, and "the company of his children—Laura, thirteen; Marc, eleven; and Scott, eight—always invigorated Alan, no matter what problems might be plaguing him."

Now let us look at the villains of the book. "Although [Herbert Allen] was trim and fit, he had slightly sunken eyes which gave him a somewhat gaunt, tired look and projected coolness, cynicism, nonchalance, and even indifference, much more often than joy or sadness." This does not sound at all like a well-coiffed person to me. The author keeps fretting about those eyes. "While Herbert's slightly sunken eyes appeared to reveal fatigue and worry . . . they were an inherited characteristic," and his Uncle Charles has them, too. Even so . . . Although Mr. Hirschfield's sexual life is not discussed (marital strain is alluded to only toward the end), Herbert Allen's girlfriends are noted by name and his suite on the Carlyle Hotel's thirty-first floor is made to sound jumping: ". . . he was a bit compulsive about the physical standards he set for his women. He would mull over fine points of physique with cronies, etc.," but then Allen was "divorced in 1971—after nine years of marriage and four children." What any of this has to do with the Begelman case is a question best asked of the ghost of Jacqueline Susann, which hovers over these often steamy pages.

═══

On the other hand, the relationship between Allen and Hirschfield is interesting. The latter was an employee of Allen and Company, a powerful investment firm run by Herbert's uncle, Charles Allen. "Hirschfield considered himself superior in intellect and business acumen to Herbert Allen, Jr., the firm's scion . . . who was four and half years younger than Hirschfield and, unlike Hirschfield, born to great wealth." This has the ring of truth. "He, not Herbert, had saved Columbia. He, not Herbert, was one of the brightest young show-business executives in the nation." Worse, the little that Herbert knew about movies he had learned from old-fashioned oldsters like Ray Stark. Fortunately, "none of Hirschfield's feelings was stated or even hinted in Herbert's presence, however. While never best friends, Alan and Herbert always had had a close, comfortable relationship which continued in the summer of 1977." Summertime for Iago.

It is odd how widely Mr. McClintick misses the point of the relationship between Allen and Hirschfield. He writes as if they were equals. They are not. Allen is, as the author puts it, a "scion"; Hirschfield is a hired hand. From Mr. McClintick's account it would appear that in the course of the drama Hirschfield may have had occasional delusions of equality—if he did, he destroyed himself because, as every scion knows from the moment he first teethes on that silver spoon, the one with the money wins because that is the American way. Since workers in the Hollywoods often make hundreds of thousands of dollars a year, there is a tendency to think of them as rich. They are not or, as John O'Hara once said of the best-selling writer, "He has the income of a millionaire without the million dollars." David Begelman was also a hired hand. But he had developed an expertise: He could put together successful films. That is a gift so rare—and often so temporary, fashions change rapidly in movieland—that the board of Columbia forgave him his trespasses by invoking mental illness and let him go on as before. With perfect hindsight, this was a stupid thing to do; but it was done and Hirschfeld made no demur.

≡

Mr. McClintick describes Ray Stark at considerable length. "As long as anyone in Hollywood could remember, Ray Stark had been known to friend and foe alike as 'The Rabbit.' " The Wise Hack shook his head and wheezed, "News to me. And I go back to the first rewrite on that Hong Kong thing—*The World of Herman Orient*"—he meant *The World of Susie Wong;* the Wise Hack tends to mix up movie titles but he is precise when it comes to movie deals. "Although many people assumed that the tag originated as a sexual reference," Mr. McClintick delicately sows a seed, "it was a physical description coined by Fanny Brice, who was to become Stark's mother-in-law in the 1940s. . . . Although he was far from being what Herbert Allen called him—'the most important producer in Hollywood post-1948' (he had produced little of artistic distinction, and his films had won very few Academy Awards, none as best picture)—Ray Stark had accomplished something that the entertainment industry admires more than anything else because it is so elusive—commercial consistency." He means Stark's pictures made money.

In thirty years Stark had gone from hired hand (he was a writer's agent and then a movie producer) to movie mogul. When Columbia started to come apart in 1973, Stark could deal as an equal with the Allen family. Together Stark and the scion hired both Hirschfeld and Begelman. Stark himself continued to make his own pictures; sometimes at Columbia and soemtimes not. Mr. McClintick discusses at length the relationship between the sixty-two-year-old Stark and the thirty-three-year-old Herbert Allen: Never at a loss for a Freudian cliché, he speculates that Stark is in need of a surrogate son, following "the death, apparently by suicide, of Ray's son, Peter."

"Cheap shot," muttered the Wise Hack. "Anyway, Ray knew Herbert before the kid died." We were seated in the study of the Wise Hack's house. "I got the letters, too," he added, with a McClintickesque tight smile. "What letters?" The Wise Hack's style is often Delphic. "Here," he handed me two badly Xeroxed letters. "These have been going around the town. Just like the book." One of the letters was from our author Mr. David McClintick to Ray Stark. The other was Stark's answer.

=

On September 5, 1980, Mr. McClintick wrote Stark a magisterial letter. He was, he said, disappointed that he had not been able to "break through the stiffness, awkwardness and discomfort that have always characterized our relationship if it can be called a relationship."

"When Herbert and I first discussed my book nearly two years ago, he said that he would give me full cooperation and that he would do everything he could to encourage you and David Begelman to cooperate as well." Apparently, Herbert Allen and David Begelman each gave fifteen hours of time to the author—"these sessions were painful," McClintick concedes; doubtless the principals must find the resulting use of their time even more painful. "By contrast," Mr. McClintick chides, "you have granted me precisely one hour in connection with my book. (A previous hour in your office in December 1977 concerned an article for *The Wall Street Journal*.) Not only was the time far too short, but the atmosphere was hardly conducive to a relaxed and candid conversation. Furthermore, you saw fit to bring a witness—a gesture to which frightened people sometimes resort, but which I found odd in these circumstances, and even a little rude."

Unlike Allen and Begelman and the novel's hero, Hirschfield, Stark was not about to help Mr. McClintick turn him into a fictional character. But Stark had no choice; Mr. McClintick is an auteur, a creator of true fictions or fictive truths in the great line of those *ci-devant* novelists Capote and Mailer. He can invent Ray Stark as both Mailer and Capote, separately, invented Marilyn Monroe.

Mr. McClintick mounts his high horse. "Ray, I'm sure that you feel that the one hour you gave me fulfills your commitment." The word *commitment* is the giveaway—the auteur knows that he—and he alone—is the creator of this particular universe and none of his characters is going to be autonomous. "You have told me repeatedly how you rarely give any time to journalists, implying that I should be deeply honored to receive even one hour. All I can say is that I am not just another Hollywood gossip monger. I am one of the top investigative reporters in this country (Pulitzer Prize nominee) and am writing a serious book about events in which you played a major role . . . the book will include the deepest and most detailed portrait of you that has ever been written or ever will be written until someone does your biography or you do your autobiography . . ." At this moment any semi-autonomous character in a true fiction would have taken to his heels.

Stark's response is benign: "I respect you as a Pulitzer Prize nominee and, therefore, I must respect your power of observation and presume by this time you should know that I am a very private person. I doubt whether you can find a dozen quotes or two interviews given by me in the last ten years. . . . You and I have talked congenially, I believe, several times. Once at a premiere in New York and at length, I thought, in my office in California. It may have only been for an hour according to your time, but since my interest span is short, it seemed like several hours to me." Stark notes that one of his associates joined them for lunch not "as a witness because long ago I found it very difficult to refute what a writer may interpret or write regardless of there being a witness. She was along to refresh my memory.

"That misinterpretation on your part only strengthens my reluctance to break what has been my lifelong policy against interviews and personal publicity. . . . The fact that you want to give 'the deepest and most detailed portrait of me that has ever been written' certainly motivates me *not* to talk to you." Thus one of Pirandello's characters tries to leave the stage. Stark notes that "it is difficult for me to express to you that I have nothing to hide. It is merely that I have no desire to have my privacy invaded." He ends, cheerfully, "I wish that all of your efforts are fruitful for you. At least now you are in possession of one of the longest and most revealing letters that I have ever written to a member of the press."

=

Mr. McClintick's revenge is outright. He accuses Stark of various crimes and then says that these accusations are either untrue or unverifiable. He quotes one of Hirschfield's tirades: "Ray is in no position to threaten or blackmail. I assure every one of you that with two phone calls—to the SEC and IRS—Ray will be busy for the rest of his life. I will not hesitate to make those calls." If that is not an accusation of corporate and personal crookedness, it is hard to know what is. But our auteur has put an asterisk beside this "quotation." At the bottom of the page, there is a footnote in the smallest type that my eye can read: "This was a threat, made in the passion of a heated meeting, which turned out to be empty. Hirschfield had no evidence of any wrongdoing by Stark that would have been of interest to the SEC or IRS." This is good to know but why quote a libel that one knows to be untrue?

Later, our auteur goes even further. Somehow, Mr. McClintick obtained a copy of a letter that the columnist Liz Smith wrote to Ray Stark. "I was trying," she writes, "to explain why I had to come down harder on the Begelman affair than you might want me to, considering your friendship. All these items on my desk saying he owes you $600,000 and you had a deal with him to take all your worthless as well as good projects for Columbia, and on and on. All that has been kept out of my column. I consider that friendship, Ray . . ."

Now for the pussy-footnote: "Of course the 'items' about a $600,000 debt and Begelman's buying Stark's 'worthless' projects for Columbia were omitted from Smith's column not because of friendship but because she could not verify them as anything more than unfounded rumors." So our auteur prints slanders based on "unfounded rumors" that Liz Smith did not see fit to print, in order to make us think that Stark and Begelman were defrauding Columbia. There is no experience quite like being caught in an American journalist's true fiction where the laws of libel—not to mention grammar—often seem not to obtain.

===

The Begelman *affaire* is of more interest as a study in contemporary journalistic practices than it is of skulduggery in the movie business. After Begelman's reinstatement, the press found out what happened. As the storm of publicity broke over Columbia (Mr. McClintick's style is contagious) Stark and Allen remained Begelman's allies. Hirschfield waffled. Since every bad novel must have a good-guy hero, Mr. McClintick would have us believe that, from the beginning of the scandal, Hirschfield had been morally outraged and sickened by Begelman's crimes. If he had been, then he was very much out of character—or at least out of that character which our auteur has invented for him. Apparently after Hirschfield became president of Columbia, he hired a man who had been fired "from CBS Records for misappropriation of funds and was under federal indictment for income tax evasion. . . .

" 'What if Clive goes to jail?' Herbert Allen asked Hirschfield.

" 'Then he'll run it from Danbury [a federal prison in Connecticut],' Hirschfield replied, only half in jest." Later, at another studio, Hirschfield kept in office a man caught with his hand in the till. As our amateur gorgeously puts it: "Hollywood is a town that takes delight in spitting in the face of irony."

The press did a good bit of spitting, too, and Hollywood was subjected to creative as well as investigative reporting. Characteristically, *The New York Times* took the low road. They assigned that excellent young novelist and West Point graduate Lucian K. Truscott IV to thread the Hollywood maze. He did his best—but West Point and the army are not much use when it comes to reading audits. Truscott heard all the old rumors, including the perennial one that organized crime and the movie business have often had carnal, as it were, knowledge of one another. Although there is probably a good deal of truth in this, one must first discover an authentic smoking gun. Truscott's piece, according to Mr. McClintick, "was strewn with falsehoods, large and small." Old Charles Allen was labeled "The Godfather of the New Hollywood"; a photograph of crime lord Meyer Lansky was published—and, of course, there was Begelman.

"Word on the article was beginning to circulate, the price of Columbia's stock was plummeting, and at noon Friday, the New York Stock Exchange stopped trading the stock because an influx of sell orders had made orderly trading impossible." When it comes to mischief, never underestimate the power of *The New York Times*. But, for once, the *Times* had met its match. "That afternoon, Allen & Company announced publicly that it would sue *The New York Times* for $150 million for publishing false and defamatory statements. . . . Three months later, after elaborate negotiations between lawyers for the two sides, *The New York Times* found it necessary to publish perhaps the most elaborate retraction, correction, and apology in the history of major American newspapers up to that time." There is an obscure footnote to the effect that a Mr. Abe Rosenthal, identified as the executive editor of the paper, was away at the time that the price was published. Social notes from all over.

≡

In due course, Begelman left Columbia. Then Hirschfield departed after he was caught trying secretly to get Sir James Goldsmith to buy Columbia away from the Allens—the sort of behavior that is bound to make irritable your average sunken-eyed employer. Although Hirschfield had always denied that he wanted to leave New York for Hollywood, he indeed went to Hollywood in a big way; currently, he is head of production at Twentieth Century–Fox. Meanwhile, Columbia, Stark, Allen and Company continue to prosper; and so it goes . . . Hollywood is what it is.

Traditionally, bad writers like to take fierce Moral Stands. They depict their characters in the blackest of black and the whitest of white. Ostensibly, Mr. McClintick is cleaning out the Augean stables of the Republic. He will give us the lowdown about Hollywood (all that money, all those movie stars!), a glittering cancer that is munching away at the very heart of what is, after all—in the immortal phrase of a writer very much like Mr. McClintick, Spiro Agnew—the greatest nation in the country. But, surely, the author knows that Hollywood is no more corrupt than Detroit or Washington. This is a nation of hustlers and although it is always salutary to blow the whistle on the crooks, it is hard to see, in this particular case, just what all the fuss is about. Begelman's forgeries are psychologically interesting—but hardly worth a book when we still know so little about the man. The loyalty of the board of directors to Begelman *could* be interpreted as just that; hence, something rather rare in Hollywood. In any case, it was the board that notified the SEC; called in the auditors; and let Begelman, finally and messily, go. Hirschfield's problems with Herbert Allen, Jr., belong to the realm not of mortality but of the higher hustlerdom and we know, at a glance, what makes him run.

The implicit moral of *Indecent Exposure* (thus, irony spits back) is not the story that the book tells but the book itself as artifact, the work of a writer who believes that he can take real people and events and remake them, as it were, in his own image. Worse, he is so filled with an odd animus toward most of his characters that he repeats accusations that he knows to be untrue so that he can then recant them, slyly, in footnotes to the text. If the "finest libel lawyer in America" told the writer that he could get away with this sort of hit-and-run tactic, I can only defer to what is, after all, a superior knowledge of our republic's greasy laws; but as "an astute editorial critic" he should have advised the creator to forget all about instructing us in what Mr. McClintick refers to "as the lessons of power and arrogance" (which he is in no position either to learn or to apply), and simply tell the truth as far as the truth can ever be determined. This is what used to be known as journalism, an honorable trade, as demonstrated thirty years ago by Lillian Ross in her book *Picture,* where she recorded, in deadly detail, only what she herself had seen and heard at MGM during the making of *The Red Badge of Courage.* The result was definitive; and the really "real" thing.

THE NEW YORK REVIEW OF BOOKS
*September 23, 1982*

# CHAPTER 7

# RONNIE AND NANCY:
# A LIFE IN PICTURES

1

I first saw Ronnie and Nancy Reagan at the Republican convention of 1964 in San Francisco's Cow Palace. Ronnie and Nancy (they are called by these names throughout Laurence Leamer's book *Make-Believe: The Story of Nancy and Ronald Reagan*) were seated in a box to one side of the central area where the cows—the delegates, that is—were whooping it up. Barry Goldwater was about to be nominated for president. Nelson Rockefeller was being booed not only for his communism but for his indecently uncloseted heterosexuality. Who present that famous day can ever forget those women with blue-rinsed hair and leathery faces and large costume jewelry and pastel-tinted dresses with tasteful matching accessories as they screamed "Lover!" at Nelson? It was like a TV rerun of *The Bacchae,* with Nelson as Pentheus.

I felt sorry for Nelson. I felt sorry for David Brinkley when a number of seriously overweight Sunbelt Goldwaterites chased him through the kitchens of the Mark Hopkins Hotel. I felt sorry for myself when I, too, had to ward off their righteous wrath: I was there as a television commentator for Westinghouse. I felt sorry for the entire media that day as fists were actually shaken at the anchorpersons high up in the eaves of the hall. I felt particularly sorry for the media when a former president named Eisenhower, reading a speech with his usual sense of discovery, attacked the press, and the convention hall went mad. At last Ike was giving it to those commie-weirdo-Jew-fags who did not believe in the real America of humming electric chairs, well-packed prisons, and kitchens filled with every electrical device that a small brown person of extranational provenance might successfully operate at a fraction of the legal minimum wage.

═══

As luck would have it, I stood leaning on the metal railing that enclosed the boxed-in open place where, side by side, Ronnie and Nancy were seated watching Ike. Suddenly, I was fascinated by them. First, there was her furious glare when someone created a diversion during Ike's aria. She turned, lip curled with Bacchantish rage, huge unblinking eyes afire with a passion to kill the enemy so palpably at hand—or so it looked to me. For all I know she might have been trying out new contact lenses. In any case, I had barely heard of Nancy then. Even so, I said to myself: There is a lot of rage in this little lady. I turned then to Ronnie. I had seen him in the flesh for a decade or so as each of us earned his mite in the Hollyjungle. Ronnie was already notorious for his speeches for General Electric, excoriating communists who were, apparently, everywhere. I had never actually spoken to him at a party because I knew—as who did not?—that although he was the soul of amiability when not excoriating the international monolithic menace of atheistic godless communism, he was, far and away, Hollywood's most grinding bore—Chester Chatterbox, in fact. Ronnie never stopped talking, even though he never had anything to say except what he had just read in the *Reader's Digest,* which he studied the way that Jefferson did Montesquieu. He also told show-biz stories of the sort that overexcites civilians in awe of old movie stars, but causes other toilers in the industry to stampede.

I had heard that Reagan might be involved in the coming campaign. So I studied him with some care. He was slumped in a folding chair, one hand holding up his chins; he was totally concentrated on Eisenhower. I remember thinking that I had made the right choice in 1959 when we were casting *The Best Man,* a play that I had written about a presidential convention. An agent had suggested Ronald Reagan for the lead. We all had a good laugh. He is by no means a bad actor, but he would hardly be convincing, I said with that eerie prescience which has earned me the title the American Nostradamus, as a presidential candidate. So I cast Melvyn Douglas, who could have made a splendid president in real life had his career not been rejuvenated by the play's success, while the actor whom I had rejected had no choice but to get himself elected president. I do remember being struck by the intensity with which Reagan studied Eisenhower. I had seen that sort of concentration a thousand times in half-darkened theatres during rehearsals or Saturday matinees: The understudy examines the star's performance and tries to figure how it is done. An actor prepares, I said to myself: Mr. Reagan is planning to go into politics. With his crude charm, I was reasonably certain that he could be elected mayor of Beverly Hills.

In time all things converge. The campaign biography and the movie star's biography are now interchangeable. The carefully packaged persona of the old-time movie star resembles nothing so much as the carefully packaged persona of today's politician. Was it not inevitable that the two would at last coincide in one person? That that person should have been Ronald Reagan is a curiosity of more than minor interest. George Murphy had broken the ice, as it were, by getting elected to the Senate from California. Years earlier Orson Welles had been approached about a race for the Senate. Welles is highly political; he is also uncommonly intelligent. "I was tempted, but then I was talked out of it," he said over lunch —cups of hot butter with marrow cubes at Pat's Fish House in Hollywood. "Everyone agreed I could never win because I was an actor and divorced." He boomed his delight.

=

Since Mr. Leamer is as little interested in politics and history as his two subjects, he is in some ways an ideal chronicler. He loves the kind of gossip that ordinary folks—his subjects and their friends—love. He takes an O'Haran delight in brand names while the "proper" names that are most often seen in syndicated columns ravish him. On the other hand, he is not very interested in the actual way politics, even as practiced by Ronnie, works. Although Reagan's eight years as governor of California are of some interest, Leamer gets through the-time-in-Sacramento as quickly as possible, with only one reference to Bob Moretti, the Democratic speaker of the assembly who, in effect, ran the state while Ronnie made his speeches around state, country, world on the dangers of communism. When in town, Ronnie played with his electric trains (something omitted by Mr. Leamer). On the other hand, there are twenty-four references to "wardrobe" in the index. So, perhaps, Mr. Leamer has got his priorities right after all. In any case, he never promised us a Rosebud.

Leamer begins with the inaugural of the fortieth president. First sentence: "On a gilded California day, Ronald and Nancy Reagan left their home for the last time." That is *echt Photoplay* and there is much, much more to come. Such lines as: "She had begun dating him when he thought he would never love again." You know, I think I will have some of those Hydrox cookies after all. "Unlike many of his backers, Ronnie was no snob. He believed that everybody should have his shot at this great golden honeypot of American free enterprise." The Golden Horde now arrives in Washington for the inaugural. "Ostentatious," growled that old meanie Barry Goldwater, nose out of joint because the man who got started in politics by giving The Speech for him in 1964 kept on giving The Speech for himself, and so, sixteen years and four wonderful presidents later, got elected Numero Uno.

Leamer tells us about their wardrobes for the great day. Also, "as a teenager and a young woman, [Nancy] had had her weight problems, but now at fifty-nine [Leamer finks on Nancy: Long ago she sliced two years off her age] she was a perfect size six. Her high cheekbones, huge eyes, delicate features and extraordinary attention to appearance made her lovelier than she had ever been." According to the testimony of the numerous ill-reproduced photographs in the book, this is quite true. The adventures simply of Nancy's nose down the years is an odyssey that we *Photoplay* fans would like to know a lot more about. At first there is a bulb on the tip; then the bulb vanishes but there is a certain thickness around the bridge; then, suddenly, retroussé triumph!

The inaugural turns out to be a long and beautiful commercial to Adolfo, Blass, Saint Laurent, Galanos, de la Renta, and Halston. At one point, Ronnie reads a poem his mother had written; there were "tears in his eyes." During the ceremonies, Ronnie said later, "It was so hard not to cry during the whole thing." But then Ronnie had been discovered, groomed, and coiffed, by the brothers Warner, who knew how to produce tears on cue with Max Steiner's ineffable musical scores. So overwhelming was Maestro Steiner that at one point, halfway up the stairs to die nobly in *Dark Victory*, Bette Davis suddenly stopped and looked down at the weeping director and crew and said, "Tell me now. Just who is going up these goddamned stairs to die? Me or Max Steiner?" She thought the teary music a bit hard on her thespian talents. No, I don't like the Oreos as much as the Hydrox but if that's all there is . . .

"As her husband spoke . . . her eyes gleamed with tears," while "the Mormon Tabernacle choir brought tears to his eyes." Tears, size sixes, Edwards-Lowell furs, Jimmy and Gloria Stewart, Roy Rogers and Dale Evans, new noses and old ideas, with charity toward none . . . then a final phone call to one of Nancy's oldest friends who says: "Oh, Nancy, you aren't a movie star now, not the biggest movie star. You're the star of the whole world. The biggest star of all." To which Nancy answers, "Yes, I know, and it scares me to death." To which, halfway around the world, at Windsor Castle, an erect small woman of a certain age somewhat less than that of Nancy is heard to mutter, "What is all this shit?"

≡

Mr. Leamer's book is nicely organized. After "A Gilded Dawn," he flashes back to tell us Nancy's story up until she meets Ronnie (who thought he would never love again); then Mr. Leamer flashes back and tells us Ronnie's story up until that momentous meeting. Then it is side by side into history. Curiously enough Nancy's story is more interesting than Ronnie's because she is more explicable and Mr. Leamer can get a grip on her. Ronnie is as mysterious a figure as ever appeared on the American political stage.

Nancy's mother was Edith Luckett, an actress from Washington, D.C. She worked in films and on the stage: "Edith's just been divorced from a rich playboy who's not worth the powder to blow him up." There is a lot of fine period dialogue in *Make-Believe*. Edith's father was a Virginian who worked for the old Adams Express Company where, thirty-one years earlier, John Surratt had worked; as you will recall, Surratt was one of the conspirators in the Abraham Lincoln murder case. Mr. Leamer tactfully omits this ominous detail.

Edith's marriage to Ken Robbins, "a handsome stage-door johnny . . . from a far better family than Edith's," is skimpily, even mysteriously, described by Mr. Leamer. Where did they meet? When and where were they married? Where did they live? All we are told is that "when Ken entered the service in 1917, he and Edith were newlyweds. But he had his duties and she had her career. . . . Ken had been released from the army in January 1919. Edith had tried to keep the marriage going with her twenty-three-year-old husband [with her career? his duties?], but all she had to show for it was a baby, born on July 6, 1921, in New York City. Ken hadn't even been there." After two years of dragging Nancy around with her ("using trunks as cradles," what else?) Edith parked baby with her older sister, Virginia, in Maryland, while Ken went to live with his mother in New Jersey. So when were Edith and Ken divorced? It does not help that Mr. Leamer constantly refers to Ken as Nancy's "natural father."

Nancy was well looked after by her aunt; she was sent to Sidwell Friends School in Washington, some four years before I went there. Mr. Sidwell was an ancient Quaker whose elephantine ears were filled with hair while numerous liver spots made piebald his kindly bald head. I used to talk to him occasionally: *Never once did he mention Nancy Robbins.*

Meanwhile, Edith had found Mr. Right, Loyal Davis, M.D., F.A.C.S., a brain surgeon of pronounced reactionary politics and a loathing of the lesser breeds, particularly those of a dusky hue. The marriage of Edith and Loyal (I feel I know them, thanks to Mr. Leamer) seems to have been happy and, at fourteen, Nancy got herself adopted by Mr. Davis and took his name. Nancy Davis now "traveled at the top of Chicago's social world." She was a school leader. Yearbook: "Nancy's social perfection is a constant source of amazement. She is invariably becomingly and suitably dressed. She can talk, and even better listen intelligently . . ." Thus was child begetter of the woman and First Lady-to-be. Destiny was to unite her with a man who has not stopped talking, according to his associates and relatives, for threescore years at least.

Nancy went to Smith and to deb parties. She herself had a tea-dance debut in Chicago. She had beaux. She was a bit overweight, while her nose was still a Platonic essence waiting to happen. A friend of her mother's ZaSu Pitts, gave Nancy a small part in a play that she was bringing to Broadway. From an early age, Nancy had greasepaint in her eyes. The play opened on Broadway unsuccessfully but Nancy stayed on. She modeled, looked for work (found it in *Lute Song*), dated famous family friends, among them Clark Gable, who after a few drinks would loosen his false teeth, which were on some sort of peg and then shake his head until they rattled like dice. I wonder if he ever did that for Nancy. Can we ever really and truly know *anyone*? The Oreos are stale.

Hollywood came Nancy's way in the form of Benny Thau, a vice president of MGM. Nancy had a "blind date" with him. In 1949 Thau was a great power at the greatest studio. He got Nancy a screen test, and a contract. By now Nancy was, as Mr. Leamer puts it,

dating Benny Thau. Barbara, the pretty teen-age receptionist, saw Nancy frequently. Many years later she remembered that she had orders that on Sunday morning Nancy was to be sent directly into Benny Thau's suite. Barbara nodded to Miss Davis as she walked into the vice-president's office; nodded again when she left later.

No wonder Nancy thinks the ERA is just plain silly.

=

Now Mr. Leamer cuts to the career of Ronnie ("Dutch") Reagan. This story has been told so much that it now makes no sense at all. Dixon, Illinois. Father drank (Irish Catholic). Mother stern (Protestant Scots-Irish); also, a fundamentalist Christian, a Disciple of Christ. Brother Neil is Catholic. Ronnie is Protestant. Sunday School teacher. Lifeguard. Eureka College. Drama department. Debating society. Lousy grades. Lousy football player but eager to be a successful jock (like Nixon and Ike *et al.* . . . What would happen if someone who could really play football got elected president?). Imitates radio sportscasters. Incessantly. Told to stop. Gets on everyone's nerves. Has the last laugh. Got a job as . . . sportscaster. At twenty-two. Midst of depression. Gets better job. Goes west. Meets agent. Gets hired by Warner Brothers as an actor. Becomes, in his own words, "the Errol Flynn of the B's."

Mr. Leamer bats out this stuff rather the way the studio press departments used to do. He seems to have done no firsthand research. Dutch is a dreamer, quiet (except that he talks all the time, from puberty on), unread and incurious about the world beyond the road ahead, which was in his case a thrilling one for a boy at that time: sportscaster at twenty-two and then film actor and movie star.

Mr. Leamer might have done well to talk to some of the California journalists who covered Reagan as governor. I was chatting with one last year, backstage in an Orange County auditorium. When I said something to the effect how odd it was that a klutz like Reagan should ever have been elected president, the journalist then proceeded to give an analysis of Reagan that was far more interesting than Mr. Leamer's mosaic of *Photoplay* tidbits. "He's not stupid at all. He's ignorant, which is another thing. He's also lazy, so what he doesn't know by now, which is a lot, he'll never know. That's the way he is. But he's a perfect politician. He knows exactly how to make the thing work for him."

I made some objections, pointed to errors along the way, not to mention the storms now gathering over the republic. "You can't look at it like that. You see, he's not interested in politics as such. He's only interested in himself. Consider this. Here is a fairly handsome ordinary young man with a pleasant speaking voice who first gets to be what he wants to be and everybody else then wanted to be, a radio announcer [equivalent to an anchorperson nowadays]. Then he gets to be a movie star in the Golden Age of the movies. Then he gets credit for being in the Second World War while never leaving L.A. Then he gets in at the start of television as an actor and host. Then he picks up a lot of rich friends who underwrite him politically and personally and get him elected governor twice of the biggest state in the union and then they get him elected president, and if he survives he'll be reelected. The point is that here is the only man I've ever heard of who got everything that he ever wanted. That's no accident."

I must say that as I stepped out on to the stage to make my speech, I could not help but think that though there may not be a God there is quite possibly a devil, and we are now trapped in the era of the Dixon, Illinois, Faust.

$$\equiv$$

One thing that Mr. Leamer quickly picks up on is Ronnie's freedom with facts. Apparently this began quite early. "Dutch had been brought up to tell the truth; but to him, facts had become flat little balloons that had to be blown up if they were to be seen and sufficiently appreciated." In Hollywood he began a lifelong habit of exaggerating not only his own past but those stories that he read in the *Reader's Digest* and other right-wing publications. No wonder his aides worry every time he opens his mouth without a script on the TelePrompTer to be read through those contact lenses that he used, idly, to take out at dinner parties and suck on.

By 1938 Ronnie was a featured player in *Brother Rat*. He was and still is an excellent film actor. The notion that he was just another Jon Hall is nonsense. For a time he was, in popularity with the fans, one of the top five actors in the country. If his range is limited that is because what he was called on to do was limited. You were a type in those days, and you didn't change your type if you wanted to be a star. But he did marry an actress who was an exception to the rule. Jane Wyman did graduate from brash blonde wisecracker to "dramatic" actress (as Mr. Leamer would say). After the war, she was the bigger star. The marriage fell apart. Natural daughter Maureen and adopted son Michael could not hold them together. Plainly, Jane could not follow Ronnie's sage advice. "We'll lead an ideal life if you'll just avoid doing one thing: Don't think." Never has there been such a perfect prescription for success in late-twentieth-century American political life.

But war clouds were now gathering over the Hollywood Hills. Five months after Pearl Harbor was attacked, Ronnie, though extremely near-sighted, was available for "limited service." To much weeping and gorge-rising, Ronnie went not overseas but over to Culver City where he made training films for the rest of the war. *Modern Screen* headline: BUT WHEN RONNIE WENT RIDING OFF TO BATTLE, HE LEFT HIS HEART BEHIND HIM! *Photoplay:* I WON'T BE DOING THESE PICTURES. UNCLE SAM HAS CALLED ME . . . AND I'M OFF TO THE WAR.

Ronnie was now known for two important roles, one as the doomed "Gipper" in *Knute Rockne, All American* and the other as the playboy whose legs are sawed off ("Where's the rest of me?") in *King's Row.* As Ronnie's films moved once again B-ward, he moved toward politics. Originally, he had been a New Deal liberal, or something. Actually his real political activity was with the Screen Actors Guild where, by and large, in those days at least, first-rate working actors were seldom to be found giving much time to meetings, much less to becoming its president, as Reagan did.

When the McCarthy era broke upon America, Ronnie took a stern anticommie line within his own union. In 1951 in *Fortnight,* he wrote that "several members of Congress are known Communists" and as one whose reviews had not been so good lately, he went on to add that though good American newspapers were attacking "dirty Reds" their publishers didn't know that they were employing "drama and book critics who . . . were praising the creative efforts of their little 'Red Brothers' while panning the work of all non-Communists."

Ronnie then went to work vetting (or, as it was called then, "clearing") people in the movies who might be tainted with communism. This was done through the Motion Picture Industry Council. The witch hunt was on, and many careers were duly ruined. Ronnie believed that no commie should be allowed to work in the movies and that anyone who did not cooperate with his council or the House Committee on Un-American Activities (in other words, refused to allow the committee to ask impertinent questions about political beliefs) should walk the plank. To this day, he takes the line that there was never a blacklist in Hollywood except for the one that commies within the industry drew up in order to exclude good Americans from jobs. Ronnie has always been a very sincere sort of liar.

≡

As luck would have it, Nancy Davis cropped up on one of the nonexistent blacklists. Apparently there were other possibly pinker actresses named Nancy Davis in lotusland. She asked a producer what to do; he said that Reagan could clear her. Thus, they met . . . not so cute, as the Wise Hack would say. It was the end of 1949. They "dated" for two years. Plainly, she loved this bona fide movie star who never stopped talking just as she could never stop appearing to listen (what her stepfather Dr. Davis must have been like at the breakfast table can only be imagined). But the woman who had launched the marriage of Ronnie and Janie, Louella Parsons, the Saint Simon of San Simeon as well as of all movieland, could not understand why that idyllic couple had split up. She described in her column how "one of the lovely girls Ronnie seemed interested in for a while told me he recently said to her, 'Sure, I like you. I like you fine. But I think I've forgotten how to fall in love.' I wonder—do those embers of the once perfect love they shared still burn deep with haunting memories that won't let them forget?" If the popcorn isn't too old, we can pop it. But no salt and use oleomargarine.

Apparently, the embers had turned to ash. After two years, thirty-year-old Nancy married the forty-one-year-old Ronnie in the company of glamorous Mr. and Mrs. William Holden who posed, beaming, beside their new best friends at a time when they were their own new worst friends for, according to Mr. Leamer, as they posed side by side with the Reagans, "The Holdens weren't even talking to one another."

Nancy's career is now one of wifedom and motherhood and, of course, listening. Also, in due course, social climbing. She was born with a silver ladder in her hand, just like the rest of us who went to Sidwell Friends School. Naturally, there were problems with Ronnie's first set of children. Ronnie seems not to have been a particularly attentive father, while Nancy was an overattentive mother to her own two children. But she took a dim view of Ronnie's first litter. The Reagans settled on Pacific Palisades. Ronnie's movie career was grinding to an end; he was obliged to go to Las Vegas to be a gambling casino "emcee." As there were no commies working for the trade papers by then, the reviews were good.

2

The year 1952 is crucial in Reagan's life. The Hollywood unions had always taken the position that no talent agency could go into production on a regular basis since the resulting conflict of interest would screw agency clients. Eventually, federal law forbade this anomaly. But thirty years ago there was a tacit agreement between agencies and unions that, on a case-by-case basis, an occasional movie might be produced by an agency. The Music Corporation of America represented actor Ronald Reagan. Within that vast agency, one Taft Schreiber looked after Ronald Reagan's declining career. At the end of Reagan's term as president of the Screen Actors Guild, he did something unprecedented.

On July 3, 1952, after a series of meetings, Ronnie sent a letter to MCA granting the agency the blanket right to produce films.

Within a few years, MCA was a dominant force in show business. In television, the forty or so shows that Revue Productions produced each week far surpassed the output of other programming suppliers.

Now for the payoff:

Later that year [1954], Taft Schreiber . . . told Ronnie about a possible role introducing a new weekly television anthology series, "The GE Theater" . . . Schreiber owed his position as head of MCA's new Revue Productions to a SAG decision in which Ronnie played an instrumental role,

and so on.

≡

For eight years, Ronnie was GE's host and occasional actor; he also became the corporate voice for General Electric's conservative viewpoint. During Reagan's tours of the country, he gave The Speech in the name of General Electric in particular and free enterprise in general. Gradually, Reagan became more and more right wing. But then if his principal reading matter told him that the Russians were not only coming but that their little Red brothers were entrenched in Congress and the school libraries and the reservoirs (fluoride at the ready), he must speak out. Finally, all this nonsense began to alarm even GE. When he started to attack socialism's masterpiece, the TVA (a GE client worth 50 million a year to the firm), he was told to start cooling it, which he did. Then, "In 1962, pleading bad ratings, GE canceled the program."

During this period, Reagan was not only getting deeper and deeper into the politics of the far right, but he and Nancy were getting to know some of the new-rich Hollywood folk outside show biz. Car dealers such as Holmes Tuttle and other wheeler-dealers became friends. The wives were into conspicuous consumption while the husbands were into money and, marginally, conservative politics which would enable them to make more money, pay less tax, and punish the poor. Thanks to Ronnie's brother Neil, then with an advertising agency that peddled Borax, the future leader of Righteous Christendom became host to Borax's television series, "Death Valley Days." That same year Ronnie attended the Cow Palace investiture of Barry Goldwater.

"In late October, Goldwater was unable to speak at the big $1,000-a-plate fund raiser at the Ambassador Hotel in Los Angeles. . . . Holmes Tuttle asked Ronnie to pinch-hit." Tuttle sat next to wealthy Henry Salvatori, Goldwater's finance chairman. Tuttle suggested that they run Ronnie for governor of California in 1966. Salvatori didn't think you could run an actor against an old political pro like the Democratic incumbent Pat Brown. But when Ronnie went national with The Speech on television, Ronnie was in business as a politician, and his friends decided to finance a Reagan race. To these new-rich Sunbelters, "Politicians and candidates, even Ronnie, were an inferior breed. 'Reagan doesn't have great depth,' Salvatori admits, 'but I don't know any politician who does. He's not the most intelligent man who ever was, but I've never met a politician with great depth. I don't know of any politician who would be smart enough to run my business, but Reagan just might.' " There it all is in one nut's shell.

=

The rest is beginning now to be history. "In the spring of 1965, forty-one rich businessmen formed 'The Friends of Ronald Reagan.' " For fifty thousand dollars a year, they hired a public-relations firm that specialized in political campaigns to groom Ronnie. California politics were carefully explained to him and he was given a crash course in the state's geography, which he may have flunked. He often had no idea where he was, or, as a supporter remarked to Leamer, "once, he didn't know a goddamn canal and where it went. Another time, he was standing in the Eagle River and didn't know where the hell he was," etc. But he had his dream of the city on the hill and he had The Speech and he had such insights as: the graduated income tax was "spawned by Marx as the prime essential of the socialistic state."

Alas, Mr. Leamer is not interested in Reagan's two terms as governor. He is more interested in Nancy's good grooming and circle of "best dressed" friends; also, in the way her past was falsified: "Nancy Davis Reagan was born in Chicago, the only daughter of Dr. and Mrs. Loyal Davis," said a campaign biography. Although Nancy had denied seeing her "natural" father after her adoption, she had indeed kept in touch for a time; but when he was dying in 1972 and her natural cousin tried to get through to her, there was no response. Mr. Leamer goes on rather too much about Nancy's wealthy girlfriends and their clothes as well as her wealthy *cavaliere servente* Jerome Zipkin who has known everyone from my mother to W. Somerset Maugham. "Maugham's biographer, Ted Morgan, thinks the British author may have patterned Elliot Templeton, a snobbish character in *The Razor's Edge*, on his American friend." Since *The Razor's Edge* was published in 1944, when Mr. Zipkin was still under thirty, it is most unlikely that that exquisite Anglophile American snob (and anti-Semite) could have been based on the charming Mr. Zipkin. Actually, for those interested in such trivia, the character was based on Henry de Courcey May, a monocled figure of my youth, much visible at Bailey's Beach in Newport, Rhode Island; although this exquisite was adored by our mothers, we little lads were under orders never to be alone with nice Mr. May—or not-so-nice Mr. Maugham for that matter. But once, on the train from Providence, Mr. May . . . But that is for Mr. Leamer's next book.

In a bored way, Mr. Leamer rushes through the governorship, using familiar Reagan boiler plate: the highest taxes in the state's history, and so on. He skirts around the most interesting caper of all, the ranch that Reagan was able to acquire through the good offices of MCA. When some details of this transaction were reported in the press, I was at a health spa near San Diego where Jules Stein and his wife (lifelong friends, as Mr. Leamer would say) were also taking the waters. When I asked Jules about the ranch caper, he got very nervous indeed. "What exactly did they print?" he asked. I told him. "Well," he said, "I didn't know anything about that. It was Schreiber who looked after Ronnie." By then Schreiber was dead.

Mr. Leamer tells us more than we want to know about the Reagan children. There seems to be a good deal of bitterness in a family that is closer to that of the Louds than to Judge Hardy's. But this is par for the course in the families of celebrities in general, and of politicians in particular. A ballet-dancer son with his mother's nose did not go down well. A daughter who decided to run for the Senate (and support the ERA) did not go down well either. So in 1982 Ronnie and his brother, Neil, helped to defeat Maureen, which was a pity since she would have been a more honorable public servant than her father. Apparently he has now had second thoughts or something; he has appointed her consultant "to improve his image among women." The family seems a lot creepier than it probably is simply because Reagan, a divorced man, has always put himself forward as the champion of prayer in the schools, and monogamy, and God, and a foe of abortion and smut and pot and the poor.

Mr. Leamer races through the political life: Ronnie sets out to replace Ford as president but instead is defeated in the primaries of 1976. Mr. Leamer finds Ronnie a pretty cold fish despite the professional appearance of warmth. When one of Ronnie's aides, Mike Deaver, lost out in a power struggle within the Reagan campaign, he was banished; and Ronnie never even telephoned him to say, "How are tricks?"

As he did in his own family, Ronnie stood above the squabble. Indeed four years before, when Ronnie had been choking on a peanut, Deaver had saved his life.

For God's sake, Leamer, dramatize! as Henry James always told us to do. When and how did that peanut get into his windpipe? Where were they? Was it the Heimlich maneuver Deaver used?

In 1980 Reagan took the nomination from Bush, whom he genuinely dislikes, if Mr. Leamer is correct. Reagan then wins the presidency though it might be more accurate to say that Carter lost it. Nancy woos Washington's old guard, the Bright Old Things as they are dubbed, who were at first mildly charmed and then more and more bemused by this curious couple who have no interest at all in talking about what Washington's BOT have always talked about: power and politics and history and even, shades of Henry Adams and John Hay, literature and art. Henry James was not entirely ironic when he called Washington "the city of conversation." Ronnie simply bends their ears with stories about Jack Warner while Nancy discusses pretty things.

Mr. Leamer gets quickly through the politics to the drama: the shooting of Ronnie, who was more gravely injured than anyone admitted at the time. By now, Mr. Leamer is racing along: "Unknown to [Nancy's] staff . . . she was accepting dresses and gowns from major designers as well as jewels from Bulgari and Harry Winston." Seven pages later: "Unknown to Nancy's staff, much of this jewelry didn't belong to her; it had been 'borrowed' for an unspecified period from the exclusive jeweler to be part of a White House collection." Nancy wriggled out of all this as best she could, proposing to give her dresses to a museum while suggesting a permanent White House collection of crown jewels for future first ladies. Conspicuous consumption at the White House has not been so visible since Mrs. Lincoln's day. But at least old Abe paid out of his own pocket for his wife's "flub dubs."

—————

The most disturbing aspect of *Make-Believe* is that Ronnie not only is still the president but could probably be reelected. Almost as an afterthought, Mr. Leamer suddenly reveals, in the last pages of his book, the true Reagan problem, which is now a world problem:

What was so extraordinary was Ronnie's apparent psychic distance from the burden of the presidency. He sat in cabinet meetings doodling. Unless held to a rigid agenda, he would start telling Hollywood stories or talk about football in Dixon. Often in one-on-one conversations Ronnie seemed distracted or withdrawn. "He has a habit now," his brother, Neil, said. "You might be talking to him, and it's like he's picking his fingernails, but he's not. And you know then he's talking to himself."

"If people knew about him living in his own reality, they wouldn't believe it," said one White House aide. "There are only ten to fifteen people who know the extent, and until they leave and begin talking, no one will believe it."

Of all our presidents, Reagan most resembles Warren Harding. He is handsome, amiable, ignorant; he has an ambitious wife (Mrs. Harding was known as the Duchess). But in the year 1983 who keeps what brooch from Bulgari is supremely unimportant. What is important is that in a dangerous world, the United States, thanks to a worn-out political system, has not a president but an indolent cue-card reader, whose writers seem eager for us to be, as soon as possible, at war. To the extent that Reagan is aware of what is happening, he probably concurs. But then what actor, no matter how old, could resist playing the part of a wartime president? even though war is now the last worst hope of earth; and hardly make-believe.

Mr. Leamer's *Make-Believe* will be criticized because it is largely a compendium of trivia about personalities. Unfortunately, there is no other book for him to write—unless it be an updated version of *Who Owns America?*

THE NEW YORK REVIEW OF BOOKS
*September 29, 1983*

# CHAPTER 8

# ARMAGEDDON?

1

As the curtain falls on the ancient Acting President and his "Administration," it is time to analyze just what this bizarre episode in American history was all about. When Ronald Reagan's career in show business came to an end, he was hired to impersonate, first, a California governor and then an American president who would reduce taxes for his employers, the southern and western New Rich, much of whose money came from the defense industries. There is nothing unusual in this arrangement. All recent presidents have had their price tags, and the shelf life of each was short. What *was* unusual was his employers' cynical recognition that in an age of television one must steer clear of politicians who may not know how to act president and go instead for the best actor available for the job, the one who can read with warm plausibility the commercials that they have written for him.

Now it is quite possible to find an actor who does understand politics. Orson Welles and Gregory Peck come to mind; but would they have been sufficiently malleable? The producers were not about to experiment. They selected an actor who has never shown the slightest interest in actual politics as opposed to the mechanics of political elections in the age of television. That is why Reagan's economic and foreign policies have never made the slightest sense to anyone who knows anything about either. On the other hand, there is evidence that, unlike his wealthy sponsors, he has a sense of mission that, like Jesus', is not of this world.

The Great Obfuscator has come among us to dispense not only good news for the usual purposes of election but Good News. Reagan is nothing so mundane as an American president. Rather, he is here to prepare us for the coming war between the Christ and the Antichrist. A war, to be specific, between the United States and Russia, to take place in Israel. Hence, the mysterious and irrelevant, to most of us, exhortations about prayer in the schools, abortion, drugs, evil empires, and, mostly lately, the encroaching "sea of darkness." Hence, the military buildup that can never, ever cease until we have done battle for the Lord. Hence, the evangelical tone which makes the priestly eloquence of the late Woodrow Wilson sound like the current mayor of New York City. Hence, the perfect indifference to the disintegration of the American economy, educational system, industrial infrastructure; and, finally, really finally, the all-out one-time-only investment in a nuclear war to end all wars and Evil itself. This world is simply a used-up Kleenex, as Reagan's secretary of the interior, James Watt, acknowledged when he scorned the environmentalists with the first hint of what was in the works: "I do not know," he said to Congress in 1981, "how many future generations we can count on before the Lord returns." So why conserve anything, if Judgment Day is at hand?

For those, and I am one, who have been totally mystified by this president's weird indifference to the general welfare at home and the preservation of peace abroad, the most plausible answer has now been given in a carefully documented and deeply alarming book called *Prophecy and Politics: Militant Evangelists on the Road to Nuclear War.** The

*Westport, Connecticut: Lawrence Hill and Co., 1986.

Texas-born author, Grace Halsell, comes from a fundamentalist Christian family. She has been for many years a working journalist, the author of seven books, a speechwriter for the dread Lyndon Johnson, and a longtime student of the twice-born Christians and their current president.

According to Halsell's interpretation and synthesis of facts available to all, the old actor has been rehearsing for some time the part of the Great Anarch who lets the curtain fall on the late great planet earth, as prophesied in the Good Book and in that even Better Book, *The Late Great Planet Earth* by an ex–riverboat captain, Hal Lindsey, whose account of the ultimate showdown between Christ and Antichrist was much admired by Ronald Reagan as well as by the eighteen million other Christian fundamentalists who bought the book in the 1970s and who believe that we are living in the penultimate Dispensation. The what? Let me explain.

Let us begin not with the Old Testament sky-god but with one Clyde Ingerson Scofield, who was born in Michigan in 1843. Scofield had an innate end-of-the-world bent which was reinforced by an Anglo-Irish divine named John Nelson Darby, who "taught that God had two plans and two groups of people with whom to work. Israel was God's kingdom here on earth and the Church (Christianity) was God's heavenly kingdom." According to Scofield/Darby, the sky-god has divided history into seven seven-year plans, or "Dispensations." During each Dispensation, God relates to man in a different way. Obviously, this particular sky-god is highly bureaucratic, even Leninist in his approach. Although Scofield was easily able to identify seven Dispensations in scripture, others could not. Eager to shed light, Mr. Scofield then sat down and rewrote the Bible so that we could all share in the Bad News. In 1909, he published the first *Scofield Reference Bible.* Since then many millions of copies have been (and are being) sold of his mock Bible.

Essentially, the Scofield exegesis is both Manichean (material world evil, spirit good; therefore, man cannot live at peace, is flawed, doomed) and Zoroastrian (Ahura Mazda, the wise Lord, defeats the evil Ahriman at the end of "the time of long dominion"). During the last but one Dispensation, Christ will defeat the Antichrist at Armageddon, fifty-five miles north of Tel Aviv. Just before the battle, the Church will be wafted to Heaven and all the good folks will experience "Rapture," as Scofield calls it. The wicked will suffer horribly. Then after seven years of "burying the dead" (presumably there will be survivors), God returns, bringing Peace and Joy and the Raptured Ones.

The gospel according to Scofield is preached daily by such American television divines as Jerry Falwell, Pat Robertson, Jimmy Swaggart, Jim Bakker, *et al.;* and according to a Yankelovich poll (1984), 39 percent of the American people believe in the death of earth by nuclear fire; and Rapture. Among the 39 percent is Ronald Reagan, as we shall see.

In 1985, Grace Halsell went on a Falwell Old Time Gospel Hour Tour of the Holy Land. If any of the good Christians on this tour expected to gaze upon Bethelehem and Nazareth where their God's son was born and lived, they were doomed to disappointment. These trips have only one purpose: to raise money for Falwell and Israel, under the guise of preparing the pilgrims for the approaching Armageddon. At Halsell's request, her group finally met one nervous taciturn local Christian. Moslems were ignored. On the other hand, there were constant briefings by Israelis on their military might.

The Falwell indoctrination is, relentlessly, the imminent end of the world, the ambiguity of the role of the Jews (*why* won't they convert?), and the importance of the state of Israel whose invention in 1948 and victories in 1967 were all foretold, most excitingly, by Scofield: exciting because Dispensationalists can never be sure *which* Dispensation they happen to be living in. Is this the one that will end in Armageddon? If so, when will the seven years be up and the fireworks start? In 1982, poor Pat Robertson got out on a limb when he thought that Israel's invasion of Lebanon was the beginning of the longed-for end; rapturously, Pat declared on television: "The whole thing is in place now, it can happen at any time. . . . But by fall, undoubtedly something like this will happen which will fulfill Ezekiel." Happily for us, unhappily for Pat, 1982 wasn't the year. But I reckon if we all pray hard enough the end's bound to come real fast.

As Halsell and group gaze upon Armageddon, an innocent rural country-side, one of her companions fills her in on *the meaning of it all.* Reverently, he quotes St. John: "And he gathered them together into a place called in the Hebrew tongue Armageddon." When she inquires what this neutral sentence has to do with a final battle between Christ and Antichrist, she gets a barrage of bronze-age quotes: "The cities of the nation fell . . . and every island fled away and the mountains were not found." Apparently, the Euphrates then dries up and the Antichrist himself (you guessed it, Gorbachev) crosses into Israel to do battle with the Lord, who comes down from Heaven, with "a great shout" (played by Charlton Heston—once again

Ronald Reagan is, in Jack Warner's phrase, the star's "best friend"). The Lord and the Americans win hands down, thanks to SDI and the B-I bomber and the Fourteenth Regiment cavalry from Des Moines, Iowa, and a number of Republican elephants who happen to have strayed on to the field, trumpeting free enterprise, as the Lord requires.

Dispensationalists delight in the horror of this crucial (pun intended) battle, as predicted so gloatingly by Ezekiel: "Torrential rains and hailstone, fire and brimstone . . . a great shaking in the land . . . every kind of terror." But it is sly prescient old Zechariah, eye glued to that bronze-age crystal ball, who foretells atomic weapons: "Their flesh shall consume away while they stand upon their feet [Hiroshima, *mon assassin*], and their eyes shall consume away in their holes, and their tongue shall consume away in their mouth."

What about the Jews? asked Halsell. Since they won't be with Gorbachev (a.k.a. Gog and Magog), what happens to them? The answer is stern: "Two-thirds of all the Jews living here will be killed . . . " She asks, why, if the Jews are *His* chosen people, as the Dispensationalists believe? The answer glows with charity: "He's doing it mainly for his ancient people, the Jews. . . . He devised a seven-year Tribulation period mainly to purge the Jews, to get them to see the light and recognize Christ as their Savior. . . . Don't you see? God wants them to bow down before His only son, who is our Lord Jesus Christ." Anyway, forget the Jews because many, many other people will also be exterminated so that Christ may come again, *in peace.* Just why Jesus' Dad should have chosen nuclear war as the means of universal peace is as rare and impenetrable a mystery as the Trinity itself.

Although the three religions (Judaism, Christianity, and Islam) of the Book, as Moslems call the Old Testament, are alike in a common worship of a highly primitive sky-god (rejected by the more civilized Hindus, Buddhists, and Confucians) and variously adapted to different times, peoples, and climates, only Fundamentalist Christianity in our century has got so seriously into the end-of-the-world game, or Rapture, as it is described by the Dispensationalists who believe . . .

But why am *I* telling you this? Let Jerry Falwell, the millionaire divine of Lynchburg, Virginia, explain it to you as he did to the journalist Bob Scheer in the *Los Angeles Times* (March 4, 1981): "We believe that Russia, because of her need of oil—and she's running out now [no, she's not, Jerry]—is going to move in the Middle East, and particularly Israel because of their hatred of the Jew [so where's the oil there, Jerry?] and that it is at that time when all hell will break out. And it is at that time when I believe there will be some nuclear holocaust on this earth. . . ." Falwell then does the obligatory mishmash from Apocrypha—and the wild "real" thing, too: Russia "will be ultimately totally destroyed," he tells us. When Scheer says that if that happens the whole world will be destroyed, Falwell spells out the Dispensationalist doctrine: "No, not the whole world, because then our Lord is coming back to the earth. First, he comes to take the Church out [plainly, Falwell was never in the army—for us "to take out" means destroy; he means lift up, save]. Seven years later, after Armageddon, this terrible holocaust, He's coming back to this very earth so it won't be destroyed, and the Church is coming with him [up, down; out, in—the vertiginous Church], to rule and reign with Christ on the earth for a thousand years. . . ." A joyous millennium of no abortion, no sodomy, no crack, no Pure Drug and Food Act, no civil rights, but of schools where only prayers are said, and earth proved daily flat.

"We believe," says Falwell, "we're living in those days just prior to the Lord's coming." When Scheer asks for an expected time of arrival, Falwell assures him that although the Lord has warned them not to give dates, he himself has a hunch: "I do not think we have fifty years left. I don't think my children will live their full lives out. . . ." So we are now in the penultimate seven-year Dispensation, which will end with Armageddon.

Scheer suggests that after the nuclear weapons we drop on Russia and the ones they drop on us, the great planet earth will be very late indeed. But Falwell *knows* that there will be survivors, in addition to the taken-out Church. Personally, he has no fear of the nuclear holocaust because, as he said to Halsell's group, with a grin, "You know why I'm not worried? I ain't gonna be here."

2

Halsell notes: "A Nielsen survey released in October 1985 shows that 61 million Americans (40 percent of all regular viewers) listen to preachers who tell them that we can do nothing to prevent a nuclear war in our lifetime." But do the 61 million actually believe what they hear? I suspect that they probably do on the ground that so little other information gets to them. They are not book readers (the United States has dropped to twenty-fourth place among book-reading nations); the public educational system has been allowed to deteriorate as public money goes mostly to defense; while television news is simply entertainment and the principal entertainer (until the latest Iran scandal) is a professional actor who knows very little about anything other than his necessary craft, which is to sell emotions—and Armageddon. But, again, does the salesman believe in the product that he sells? Halsell thinks that he does.

On September 20, 1970, an evangelical Christian, George Otis, and several like-minded folk visited Reagan when he was governor of California. They spoke rapturously of Rapture. Then, according to Otis, they all joined hands in prayer and Otis prophesied Reagan's coming election to the presidency. According to Otis *(Visit with a King)* Reagan's arms "shook and pulsated" during this prophecy. The next summer (June 29, 1971) Reagan asked Billy Graham to address the California legislature; afterward, at lunch, Reagan asked Graham, "Well, do you believe that Jesus Christ is coming soon, and what are the signs of his coming if that is the case?" Graham did not beat about this burning bush. "The indication," he said, "is that Jesus Christ is at the very door."

Later in 1971 Governor Reagan attended a dinner where he sat next to James Mills, the president of the California state senate. Mills was so impressed by the dinner conversation that he wrote it all down immediately afterward, but published it much later *(San Diego Magazine,* August 1985), *pro bono publico,* if a bit late.

After the main course, the lights dimmed and flaming bowls of cherries jubilee were served. No doubt inspired by the darkness and the flames, Reagan suddenly asked, out of right field, if Mills had read "the fierce Old Testament prophet Ezekiel." Mills allowed that he had (after all, you don't get elected to the California State Senate if you say no); as it turned out, he did know Ezekiel. Then, "with firelit intensity," Reagan began to talk about how Libya had now gone communist, just as Ezekiel had foretold, and "that's a sign that the day of Armageddon isn't far off." When Mills reminded him that Ethiopia was also due to go over to Satan and he couldn't, somehow, see the Emperor Haile Selassie turning pinko or allowing the Reds to take over his country in order to make war "on God's Chosen People," Reagan agreed "that everything hasn't fallen into place yet. But there is only that one thing left that has to happen. The Reds have to take over Ethiopia." Mills thought this unlikely. Reagan thought it inevitable: "It's necessary to fulfill the prophecy that Ethiopia will be one of the ungodly nations that go against Israel." As it turned out, Reagan was right on target. Three years later Ethiopia went communist, or something very like it.

Mills was particularly impressed by Reagan's manner, which is usually amiable to the point of goofiness: Now he was "like a preacher [talking] to a skeptical college student." Reagan then told Mills: "All of the other prophecies that had to be fulfilled before Armageddon have come to pass. In the thirty-eighth chapter of Ezekiel it says God will take the children of Israel from among the heathen when they'd been scattered and will gather them again in the promised land. That has finally come about after 2,000 years. For the first time ever, everything is in place for the battle of Armageddon and the Second Coming of Christ."

When Mills said that the Bible clearly states that men will never have the fun of knowing just *when* this awesome event will take place, Reagan replied, "Everything is falling into place. It can't be too long now. Ezekiel says that fire and brimstone will be rained upon the enemies of God's people. That must mean that they will be destroyed by nuclear weapons . . . Ezekiel tells us that Gog, the nation that will lead all of the other powers of darkness ['sea of darkness,' he moaned just after he plunged into Irangate] against Israel, will come out of the north. What other powerful nation is to the north of Israel? None. But it didn't seem to make much sense before the Russian revolution, when Russia was a Christian country. Now it does, now that Russia has become communistic and atheistic, now that Russia has set itself against God. Now it fits the description perfectly." So you thought there would be an arms deal with the Soviet Union? A cutback of nuclear weapons? Not on, literally, our lives. To stop the arms race would be to give the victory to Gog.

Mills's conversation took place fifteen years ago. Nine years later, the nemesis of Gog was elected president. If he survives, Constitutionally or constitutionally, he now has two more years to see us on our way to, if not actually *into*, glory. Until recently, one could not imagine any American president with a sense of history openly expressing religious views that are so opposed to the spirit of the founders of the United States. Jefferson had a low opinion of religious—as opposed to ethical—Christianity, and no friendly view of the pre-Scofield Old Testament, while the non-Christian Lincoln's appeals to the Almighty were as vague as Confucius's ritual hymns to Heaven. The American republic was created by men of Enlightenment, who had little or no use for sky-god systems; certainly they would have regarded the Scofield-Falwell-Reagan sky-god as a totem more suitable for men who walk with their knuckles grazing the greensward than for the upright citizens of the last best hope of earth.

But Reagan knows nothing about Jefferson, and history is not his bag. On the other hand, " 'I was fortunate,' " he told TV evangelist Jim Bakker. " 'I had a mother who planted a great faith in me. . . .' " Garry Wills, in his recent book *Reagan's America*, tells us a great deal about Nelle Reagan who "was baptized in Tampico (Illinois), as a Disciple of Christ, by total immersion . . . on Easter Sunday, 1910." She was a great influence on her son, who taught Sunday School and then attended Drake University, a Disciples' college. With mounting horror, one realizes that he may not be what all of us had hoped (even prayed), a hypocrite. Until Reagan's recent misfortunes, he had not the United States but Armageddon on his mind.

During the presidential race of 1980, Reagan told Jim Bakker of the PTL network: "We may be the generation that sees Armageddon," while a writer for *The New York Times* reported that Reagan (1980) told a Jewish group that "Israel is the only stable democracy we can rely on as a spot where Armageddon could come." Apparently, the god of Ezekiel has a thing about the necessity of stable democratic elections *prior* to sorting out the Elect just before the Bang.

Although most American right-wingers are anti-Semites, the Armageddonists need a strong Israel in order to fulfil prophecy. So TV-evangelicals, Pentagon ("Those are the *real* anti-Semites," former Austrian Chancellor Bruno Kreisky muttered in my ear last October at Frankfurt), and rightwing politicians like Richard Nixon are all dedicated supporters of Israel. Sensibly and cynically, the Israelis exploit this religious madness.

Halsell reports that in October 1983, President Reagan told an Israeli lobby leader, Tom Dine, "You know, I turn back to your ancient prophets [Dine runs a home for retired ancient prophets where you can be denounced by the prophet of your choice] in the Old Testament, and I find myself wondering if we're the generation that's going to see that come about. I don't know if you noticed any of those prophecies lately, but believe me, they certainly describe the times we're going through." This was the year that Reagan decided to alert the nation to Gog. On March 8, 1983 he declared, "They [the Soviet Union] are the focus of evil in the modern world." Later, "I believe that communism is another sad, bizarre chapter in human history *whose last pages even now are being written* [my italics]." The old Acting President seems not to mind our approaching fiery fate. But then, of course, he's been saved, as he told George Otis. So, like Falwell, he ain't gonna be here either at the end.

3

The fifteenth of February, 1987, proved to be a bright sunny day in Hell, where I had come with nine hundred worthies from several dozen countries, to listen to Satan himself, Gorbachev, who spoke thoughtfully of the absolute necessity of abolishing all nuclear weapons on the ground that the fact of their existence endangers the human race. Plainly, the Lord of the Flies has not read the Good Book. If he had, he would know that this planet is just a staging area for that glorious place in the sky where, free of abortion and contraception and communism, the chosen will swirl about in the cosmic dust, praising the Lord for all eternity. In fact, not only did Gorbachev not seem to know the Truth that Reagan adheres to (so unlike mere irksome truth telling), he even suggested to us that this planet may be the only one that could support a human race. It would be, he said, a pity to lose everything through war or, more likely, accident. Then, to everyone's amazement, Gorbachev mentioned Chernobyl by name, breaking the first law of the TV politician—never acknowledge failure. Since Hitler's invasion, nothing has alarmed the Russians more than Chernobyl's fallout, which is everywhere, including the village where I live in southern Italy: There is cesium 137 at the bottom of my garden. Gorbachev owned up to the whole mess, something our Acting President would never do . . . indeed has not, specifically, done.

On April 10, 1986, in order to preserve freedom for all men everywhere, the Acting President ordered a resumption of underground nuclear testing. The test's code name was Mighty Oak; the place, Nevada. Several weeks before Chernobyl, Mighty Oak came a cropper. Some sort of unanticipated explosion went wrong. When nongovernment analysts duly noted increased radiation in the spring zephyrs, they were told by the Department of Energy that all was well. Then, on May 7, the department admitted that the level of the radioactive inert gas xenon 133 had been detected fifty miles from the site, at 550 picocuries per cubic meter. Of course things were, as always, worse in Russia. Now we learn that of our last six nuclear underground tests, three have made the atmosphere more than ever poisonous through mishap. In August 1986, Gorbachev announced a moratorium on such tests. But Reagan chooses to ignore the moratorium and stands tall.

As I stared at the stocky round-faced little man addressing us, I tried to imagine any American politician making as straightforward and intelligent an address to the likes of Trudeau and Galbraith, Milos Forman and Berio (needless to say the American press ignored the substance of the speech and zeroed in on the charismatic presence of one Yoko Ono). The only direct reference that Lucifer made to the Archangel from Warner Brothers concerned something that Reagan had said to him in Geneva: If the earth were ever to be invaded by Martians, the United States and the Soviet Union would, of course, be joint allies in a common cause. Gorbachev sighed: "I told the president that it was, perhaps, premature to prepare for such an invasion but as we had a common enemy right now, nuclear weapons, why couldn't we unite to get rid of them?" But the planter of Mighty Oaks was not to be seduced. How could he be? Nearly every major politician in the United States is paid for by what is known as "the defense industry." That is why close to 90 percent of the government's income is wasted on "defense."

Ordinarily, American conservatives (known, amusingly, as liberals) would have stopped this destruction of the economy and endangerment of life itself by the radical right (known, yet another thigh slapper, as conservatives). But things began to go awry with the invention of Israel. Many American conservatives decided that, for them, Israel comes first and so they chose to make common cause with the anti-Semitic but pro-Israel Jesus Christers, who lust for rapture.

Two years ago, Irving Kristol justified this shift in a house organ of the American Jewish Committee. Kristol noted that when the Jews were new to the American scene they "found liberal opinion and liberal politicism more congenial in their attitudes, more sensitive to Jewish concerns." So they voted for the liberal paladin, Franklin D. Roosevelt and his heirs. But now, Kristol writes, "is there any point in Jews hanging on, dogmatically and hypocritically, to their opinions of yesteryear when it is a new era we are confronting?" Because of Israel, "we are constrained to take our allies where and how we find them." Finally, "If one had informed American Jews fifteen years ago that there was to be a powerful revival of Protestant fundamentalism as a political as well as religious force, they would surely have been alarmed, since they would have assumed that any such revival might tend to be anti-Semitic and anti-Israel. But the Moral Majority is neither." But, of course, the Moral Majority is deeply anti-Semitic and will always remain so because the Jews killed our Lord (proving that no good deed ever goes unpunished: Were not those first-century Jews simply fulfilling The Divine Plan?), and the Jesus Christers are pro-Israel for reasons that have nothing to do with the Jews who are—except for exactly 144,000—going to get it along with the commies, at Armageddon.

Currently, there is little open debate in the United States on any of these matters. The Soviet Union must be permanently demonized in order to keep the money flowing to the Pentagon for "defense," while Arabs are characterized as subhuman terrorists. Israel may not be criticized at all (ironically, the press in Israel is far more open and self-critical than ours). We do have one token Palestinian who is allowed an occasional word in the press, Professor Edward Said, who wrote (*Guardian*, December 21, 1986): since the "1982 Israeli invasion of Lebanon . . . it was felt by the Zionist lobby that the spectacle of ruthless Israeli power on the TV screen would have to be effaced from memory by the strategy of incriminating the media as anti-Semitic for showing these scenes at all." A wide range of Americans were then exuberantly defamed, including myself (see page 115, "A Cheerful Response").

I wondered, as I listened to Gorbachev, if he had any notion of the forces arrayed against him in the United States. Obviously, he is aware of the Israeli lobby, but that is something that he can come to terms with: Neither the Israelis nor the Russians are interested in suicide. But the Dispensationalists are quite another matter. By accident, the producers of that one-time hit-show the United States of America picked for the part of president a star with primitive religious longings. We cannot blame them. How could they have known? They thought that he was giving all that money to defense simply to reward them for giving him the lead, which he was doing, in part; but he was also responding to Ezekiel, and the glory of the coming end.

On the other hand, Gorbachev said that because he believes in life, the nuclear arms race will end because this is the only world that we have. We applauded. He paused. Then, with perfect timing, he said, "I had expected warmer applause on that line." We gave it to him. He laughed. The speech was soon over.

I said to Norman Mailer, "I think there should be a constitutional amendment making it impossible for anyone to be president who believes in an afterlife." Mailer said, "Well, that rules me out." I was astonished and said so. "If there isn't an afterlife," he said, "then what's the point to all this?" Before I could answer, he said, "All right, all right. I know what you're going to say. There is no point." A pride of exotic bishops separated us.

Yes, that is what I would have said, and because there is no cosmic point to the life that each of us perceives on this distant bit of dust at galaxy's edge, all the more reason for us to maintain in proper balance what we have here. Because there is nothing else. No thing. This is it. And quite enough, all in all.

THE OBSERVER (LONDON)
*November 15, 1987*
*(But written as of March 1987)*

# CHAPTER 9

# THE DAY
# THE AMERICAN EMPIRE
# RAN OUT OF GAS*

On September 16, 1985, when* the Commerce Department announced that the United States had become a debtor nation, the
American Empire died. The empire was seventy-one years old and
had been in ill health since 1968. Like most modern empires, ours rested
not so much on military prowess as on economic primacy.†

After the French Revolution, the world money power shifted from

---

*This was, first, a speech given for the benefit of PEN, then printed in *The Nation*
(November 1985).

†In *The Guardian* (November 20, 1987) Frank Kermode wrote: "I happened to hear
Vidal expound this thesis in a New York theater, to a highly ribald and incredulous, though
doubtless very ignorant audience. . . ." Since then, my thesis has been repeated by others
so many times that it is now conventional wisdom.

Paris to London. For three generations, the British maintained an old-fashioned colonial empire, as well as a modern empire based on London's primacy in the money markets. Then, in 1914, New York replaced London as the world's financial capital. Before 1914, the United States had been a developing country, dependent on outside investment. But with the shift of the money power from Old World to New, what had been a debtor nation became a creditor nation and central motor to the world's economy. All in all, the English were well pleased to have us take their place. They were too few in number for so big a task. As early as the turn of the century, they were eager for us not only to help them out financially but to continue, in their behalf, the destiny of the Anglo-Saxon race: to bear with courage the white man's burden, as Rudyard Kipling not so tactfully put it. Were we not—English and Americans—all Anglo-Saxons, united by common blood, laws, language? Well, no, we were not. But our differences were not so apparent then. In any case, we took on the job. We would supervise and civilize the lesser breeds. We would make money.

By the end of the Second World War, we were the most powerful and least damaged of the great nations. We also had most of the money. America's hegemony lasted exactly five years. Then the cold and hot wars began. Our masters would have us believe that all our problems are the fault of the Evil Empire of the East, with its satanic and atheistic religion, ever ready to destroy us in the night. This nonsense began at a time when we had atomic weapons and the Russians did not. They had lost twenty million of their people in the war, and eight million of them before the war, thanks to their neoconservative Mongolian political system. Most important, there was never any chance, then or now, of the money power shifting from New York to Moscow. What was—and is—the reason for the big scare? Well, the Second War made prosperous the United States, which had been undergoing a depression for a dozen years, and made very rich those magnates and their managers who govern the republic, with many a wink, in the people's name. In order to maintain a general prosperity (and enormous wealth for the few) they decided that we would become the world's policeman, perennial shield against the Mongol hordes. We shall have an arms race, said one of the high priests, John Foster Dulles, and we shall win it because the Russians will go broke first. We were then

put on a permanent wartime economy, which is why close to two thirds*
of the government's revenues are constantly being siphoned off to pay for
what is euphemistically called defense.

As early as 1950, Albert Einstein understood the nature of the rip-off.
He said, "The men who possess real power in this country have no intention of ending the cold war." Thirty-five years later, they are still at it,
making money while the nation itself declines to eleventh place in world
per capita income, to forty-sixth in literacy and so on, until last summer
(not suddenly, I fear) we found ourselves close to two trillion dollars in
debt. Then, in the fall, the money power shifted from New York to Tokyo,
and that was the end of our empire. Now the long-feared Asiatic colossus
takes its turn as world leader, and we—the white race—have become the
yellow man's burden. Let us hope that he will treat us more kindly than
we treated him.† In any case, if the foreseeable future is not nuclear, it
will be Asiatic, some combination of Japan's advanced technology with
China's resourceful landmass. Europe and the United States will then be,
simply, irrelevant to the world that matters, and so we come full circle:
Europe began as the relatively empty uncivilized Wild West of Asia; then
the Western Hemisphere became the Wild West of Europe. Now the sun
has set in our West and risen once more in the East.

The British used to say that their empire was obtained in a fit of
absentmindedness. They exaggerate, of course. On the other hand, our
modern empire was carefully thought out by four men. In 1890 a U.S.
Navy captain, Alfred Thayer Mahan, wrote the blueprint for the American
imperium, *The Influence of Sea Power Upon History, 1660–1783*. Then
Mahan's friend, the historian-geopolitician Brooks Adams, younger
brother of Henry, came up with the following formula: "All civilization
is centralization. All centralization is economy." He applied the formula
in the following syllogism: "Under economical centralization, Asia is
cheaper than Europe. The world tends to economic centralization. Therefore, Asia tends to survive and Europe to perish." Ultimately, *that* is why
we were in Vietnam. The amateur historian and professional politician
Theodore Roosevelt was much under the influence of Adams and Mahan;

---

*Once Social Security is factored out of the budget, defense and defense-related expendi-
tures (e.g., interest on the debt) account for close to 90 percent of the money wasted.

†Believe it or not, this plain observation was interpreted as a racist invocation of "the
Yellow Peril"!

he was also their political instrument, most active not so much during his presidency as during the crucial war with Spain, where he can take a good deal of credit for our seizure of the Philippines, which made us a world empire. Finally, Senator Henry Cabot Lodge, Roosevelt's closest friend, kept in line a Congress that had a tendency to forget our holy mission— our manifest destiny—and ask, rather wistfully, for internal improvements.

From the beginning of our republic we have had imperial longings. We took care—as we continue to take care—of the indigenous population. We maintained slavery a bit too long even by a cynical world's tolerant standards. Then, in 1846, we produced our first conquistador, President James K. Polk. After acquiring Texas, Polk deliberately started a war with Mexico because, as he later told the historian George Bancroft, we had to acquire California. Thanks to Polk, we did. And that is why to this day the Mexicans refer to our southwestern states as "the occupied lands," which Hispanics are now, quite sensibly, filling up.

The case against empire began as early as 1847. Representative Abraham Lincoln did not think much of Polk's war, while Lieutenant Ulysses S. Grant, who fought at Veracruz, said in his memoirs, "The war was an instance of a republic following the bad example of European monarchies, in not considering justice in their desire to acquire additional territory." He went on to make a causal link, something not usual in our politics then and completely unknown now: "The Southern rebellion was largely the outgrowth of the Mexican War. Nations, like individuals, are punished for their transgressions. We got our punishment in the most sanguinary and expensive war of modern times."

But the empire has always had more supporters than opponents. By 1895 we had filled up our section of North America. We had tried twice —and failed—to conquer Canada. We had taken everything that we wanted from Mexico. Where next? Well, there was the Caribbean at our front door and the vast Pacific at our back. Enter the Four Horsemen— Mahan, Adams, Roosevelt, and Lodge.

The original republic was thought out carefully, and openly, in *The Federalist Papers:* We were not going to have a monarchy and we were not going to have a democracy. And to this day we have had neither. For two hundred years we have had an oligarchical system in which men of property can do well and the others are on their own. Or, as Brooks Adams put it, the sole problem of our ruling class is whether to coerce or to bribe the powerless majority. The so-called Great Society bribed; today coercion is very much in the air. Happily, our neoconservative Mongoloids favor only authoritarian and never totalitarian means of coercion.

Unlike the republic, the empire was worked out largely in secret. Captain Mahan, in a series of lectures delivered at the Naval War College, compared the United States with England. Each was essentially an island state that could prevail in the world only through sea power. England had already proved his thesis. Now the United States must do the same. We must build a great navy in order to acquire overseas possessions. Since great navies are expensive, the wealth of new colonies must be used to pay for our fleets. In fact, the more colonies acquired, the more ships; the more ships, the more empire. Mahan's thesis is agreeably circular. He showed how small England had ended up with most of Africa and all of southern Asia, thanks to sea power. He thought that we should do the same. The Caribbean was our first and easiest target. Then on to the Pacific Ocean, with all its islands. And, finally, to China, which was breaking up as a political entity.

Theodore Roosevelt and Brooks Adams were tremendously excited by this prospect. At the time Roosevelt was a mere police commissioner in New York City, but he had dreams of imperial glory. "He wants to be," snarled Henry Adams, "our Dutch-American Napoleon." Roosevelt began to maneuver his way toward the heart of power, sea power. With Lodge's help, he got himself appointed assistant secretary of the navy, under a weak secretary and a mild president. Now he was in place to modernize the fleet and to acquire colonies. Hawaii was annexed. Then a part of Samoa. Finally, colonial Cuba, somehow, had to be liberated from Spain's tyranny. At the Naval War College, Roosevelt declared, "To prepare for war is the most effectual means to promote peace." How familiar that sounds! But since the United States had no enemies as of June 1897, a contemporary might have remarked that since we were already at peace with everyone, why prepare for war? Today, of course, we are what he dreamed we would be, a nation armed to the teeth and hostile to everyone. But what with Roosevelt was a design to acquire an empire is for us a means to transfer money from the Treasury to the various defense industries, which in turn pay for the elections of Congress and president.

Our turn-of-the-century imperialists may have been wrong, and I think they were. But they were intelligent men with a plan, and the plan worked. Aided by Lodge in the Senate, Brooks Adams in the press, Admiral Mahan at the Naval War College, the young assistant secretary of the navy began to build up the fleet and look for enemies. After all, as Brooks Adams proclaimed, "war is the solvent." But war with whom? And for what? And where? At one point England seemed a likely enemy. There was a boundary dispute over Venezuela, which meant that we could invoke the all-purpose Monroe Doctrine (the invention of John Quincy Adams, Brooks's grandfather). But as we might have lost such a war, nothing happened. Nevertheless, Roosevelt kept on beating his drum: "No triumph of peace," he shouted, "can equal the armed triumph of war." Also: "We must take Hawaii in the interests of the white race." Even Henry Adams, who found T.R. tiresome and Brooks, his own brother, brilliant but mad, suddenly declared, "In another fifty years . . . the white race will have to reconquer the tropics by war and nomadic invasion, or be shut up north of the 50th parallel." And so at century's end, our most distinguished ancestral voices were not prophesying but praying for war.

An American warship, the *Maine,* blew up in Havana harbor. We held Spain responsible; thus, we got what John Hay called "a splendid little war." We would liberate Cuba, drive Spain from the Caribbean. As for the Pacific, even before the *Maine* was sunk, Roosevelt had ordered Commodore Dewey and his fleet to the Spanish Philippines—just in case. Spain promptly collapsed, and we inherited its Pacific and Caribbean colonies. Admiral Mahan's plan was working triumphantly.

In time we allowed Cuba the appearance of freedom while holding on to Puerto Rico. Then President William McKinley, after an in-depth talk with God, decided that we should also keep the Philippines, in order, he said, to Christianize them. When reminded that the Filipinos were Roman Catholics, the president said, Exactly. We must Christianize them. Although Philippine nationalists had been our allies against Spain, we promptly betrayed them and their leader, Emilio Aguinaldo. As a result it took us several years to conquer the Philippines, and tens of thousands of Filipinos died that our empire might grow.

The war was the making of Theodore Roosevelt. Surrounded by the flower of the American press, he led a group of so-called Rough Riders up a very small hill in Cuba. As a result of this proto-photo opportunity he became a national hero, governor of New York, McKinley's running mate and, when McKinley was killed in 1901, president.

Not everyone liked the new empire. After Manila, Mark Twain thought that the stars and bars of the American flag should be replaced by a skull and crossbones. He also said, "We cannot maintain an empire in the

Orient and maintain a republic in America." He was right, of course. But as he was only a writer who said funny things, he was ignored. The compulsively vigorous Roosevelt defended our war against the Philippine population, and he attacked the likes of Twain. "Every argument that can be made for the Filipinos could be made for the Apaches," he explained, with his lovely gift for analogy. "And every word that can be said for Aguinaldo could be said for Sitting Bull. As peace, order and prosperity followed our expansion over the land of the Indians, so they will follow us in the Philippines."

Despite the criticism of the few, the Four Horsemen had pulled it off. The United States was a world empire. And one of the horsemen not only got to be president but for his pious meddling in the Russo-Japanese conflict, our greatest apostle of war was awarded the Nobel Peace Prize. One must never underestimate Scandinavian wit.

Empires are restless organisms. They must constantly renew themselves; should an empire start leaking energy, it will die. Not for nothing were the Adams brothers fascinated by entropy. By energy. By force. Brooks Adams, as usual, said the unsayable. "Laws are a necessity," he declared. "Laws are made by the strongest, and they must and shall be obeyed." Oliver Wendell Holmes, Jr., thought this a wonderful observation, while the philosopher William James came to a similar conclusion, which can also be detected, like an invisible dynamo, at the heart of the novels of his brother Henry.

According to Brooks Adams, "The most difficult problem of modern times is unquestionably how to protect property under popular governments." The Four Horsemen fretted a lot about this. They need not have. We have never had a popular government in the sense that they feared, nor are we in any danger now. Our only political party has two right wings, one called Republican, the other Democratic. But Henry Adams figured all that out back in the 1890s. "We have a single system," he wrote, and "in that system the only question is the price at which the proletariat is to be bought and sold, the bread and circuses." But none of this was for public consumption. Publicly, the Four Horsemen and their outriders spoke of the American mission to bring to all the world freedom and peace, through slavery and war if necessary. Privately, their constant fear was that the weak masses might combine one day against the strong few, their natural leaders, and take away their money. As early as the election of 1876 socialism had been targeted as a vast evil that must never be allowed to corrupt simple American persons. When Christianity was invoked as the natural enemy of those who might limit the rich and their games, the combination of cross and dollar sign proved—and proves—irresistible.

During the first decade of our disagreeable century, the great world fact was the internal collapse of China. Who could pick up the pieces? Britain grabbed Kowloon; Russia was busy in the north; the Kaiser's fleet prowled the China coast; Japan was modernizing itself and biding its time. Although Theodore Roosevelt lived and died a dedicated racist, the Japanese puzzled him. After they sank the Russian fleet, Roosevelt decided that they were to be respected and feared even though they were our racial inferiors. For those Americans who served in the Second World War, it was an article of faith—as of 1941 anyway—that the Japanese could never win a modern war. Because of their slant eyes, they would not be able to master aircraft. Then they sank our fleet at Pearl Harbor.

Jingoism aside, Brooks Adams was a good analyst. In the 1890s he wrote: "Russia, to survive, must undergo a social revolution internally and/or expand externally. She will try to move into Shansi Province, richest prize in the world. Should Russia and Germany combine . . ." That was the nightmare of the Four Horsemen. At a time when simpler folk feared the rise of Germany alone, Brooks Adams saw the world ultimately polarized between Russia and the United States, with China as the common prize. American maritime power versus Russia's landmass. That is why, quite seriously, he wanted to extend the Monroe Doctrine to the Pacific Ocean. For him, "war [was] the ultimate form of economic competition."

=

We are now at the end of the twentieth century. England, France, and Germany have all disappeared from the imperial stage. China is now reassembling itself, and Confucius, greatest of political thinkers, is again at the center of the Middle Kingdom. Japan has the world money power and wants a landmass; China now seems ready to go into business with its ancient enemy. Wars of the sort that the Four Horsemen enjoyed are, if no longer possible, no longer practical. Today's conquests are shifts of currency by computer and the manufacture of those things that people everywhere are willing to buy.

I have said very little about writers because writers have figured very little in our imperial story. The founders of both republic and empire wrote well: Jefferson and Hamilton, Lincoln and Grant, T.R. and the Adamses.

Today public figures can no longer write their own speeches or books, and there is some evidence that they can't read them either.

Yet at the dawn of the empire, for a brief instant, our *professional* writers tried to make a difference. Upton Sinclair and company attacked the excesses of the ruling class. Theodore Roosevelt coined the word "muckraking" to describe what they were doing. He did not mean the word as praise. Since then a few of our writers have written on public themes, but as they were not taken seriously, they have ended by not taking themselves seriously, at least as citizens of a republic. After all, most writers are paid by universities, and it is not wise to be thought critical of a garrison state which spends so much money on so many campuses.

When Confucius was asked what would be the first thing that he would do if he were to lead the state—his never-to-be-fulfilled dream—he said *rectify the language.* This is wise. This is subtle. As societies grow decadent, the language grows decadent, too. Words are used to disguise, not to illuminate, action: You liberate a city by destroying it. Words are used to confuse, so that at election time people will solemnly vote against their own interests. Finally, words must be so twisted as to justify an empire that has now ceased to exist, much less make sense. Is rectification of our system possible for us? Henry Adams thought not. In 1910 he wrote: "The whole fabric of society will go to wrack if we really lay hands of reform on our rotten institutions." Then he added, "From top to bottom the whole system is a fraud, all of us know it, laborers and capitalists alike, and all of us are consenting parties to it." Since then, consent has grown frayed; and we have become poor, and our people sullen.

To maintain a thirty-five-year arms race it is necessary to have a fearsome enemy. Not since the invention of the Wizard of Oz have American publicists created anything quite so demented as the idea that the Soviet Union is a monolithic, omnipotent empire with tentacles everywhere on earth, intent on our destruction, which will surely take place unless we constantly imitate it with our war machine and its secret services.

In actual fact, the Soviet Union is a Second World country with a First World military capacity. Frighten the Russians sufficiently and they might blow us up. By the same token, as our republic now begins to crack under the vast expense of maintaining a mindless imperial force, we might try to blow them up. Particularly if we had a president who really was a twice-born Christian and believed that the good folks would all go to heaven (where they were headed anyway) and the bad folks would go where *they* belong. Fortunately, to date, we have had only hypocrites in the White House. But you never can tell.*

Even worse than the not-very-likely prospect of a nuclear war—deliberate or by accident—is the economic collapse of our society because too many of our resources have been wasted on the military. The Pentagon is like a black hole; what goes in is forever lost to us, and no new wealth is created. Hence, our cities, whose centers are unlivable; our crime rate, the highest in the Western world; a public education system that has given up . . . you know the litany.

There is now only one way out. The time has come for the United States to make common cause with the Soviet Union. The bringing together of the Soviet landmass (with all its natural resources) and our island empire (with all its technological resources) would be of great benefit to each society, not to mention the world. Also, to recall the wisdom of the Four Horsemen who gave us our empire, the Soviet Union and our section of North America combined would be a match, industrially and technologically, for the Sino-Japanese axis that will dominate the future just as Japan dominates world trade today. But where the horsemen thought of war as the supreme solvent, we now know that war is worse than useless. Therefore, the alliance of the two great powers of the Northern Hemisphere will double the strength of each and give us, working together, an opportunity to survive, economically, in a highly centralized Asiatic world.†

THE NATION
*January 11, 1986*

---

*I had not yet read Halsell's *Prophecy and Politics* (see p. 102 *et seq.*).

†The suggestion that the United States and the USSR join forces set alarm bells ringing in Freedom's Land. The Israel lobby, in particular, attacked me with such ferocity that I felt obliged to respond, cheerily. (See the following essay.)

# CHAPTER 10

# A CHEERFUL RESPONSE

**R**ecently, Norman Mailer and I chatted together at the Royale Theatre in New York, under the auspices of PEN American Center. Part of what I said was reprinted in *The Nation* on January 11, 1986. I gave a bit of a history lesson about our empire's genesis, and I brooded on its terminus last fall, when Tokyo took over from New York as the world's economic center.

My conclusion: For America to survive economically in the coming Sino-Japanese world, an alliance with the Soviet Union is a necessity. After all, the white race is a minority race with many well-deserved enemies, and if the two great powers of the Northern Hemisphere don't band together, we are going to end up as farmers—or, worse, mere entertainment—for the more than one billion grimly efficient Asiatics.* In principle, Mailer agreed.

As expected, that wonderful, wacky couple, Norman (Poddy) Podhoretz and his wife, Midge Decter, checked in. The Lunts of the right wing (Israeli fifth column division), they are now, in their old age, more and more like refugees from a Woody Allen film: *The Purple Prose of West End Avenue.*

Poddy was the first to respond. He is the editor of *Commentary* (circulation 55,000 and allegedly falling; paid for by the American Jewish Committee). He is best known—and by me loved—for his autobiographical "novel," *Making It,* in which he tells us that he has made it because he has become editor of *Commentary* and might one day be a guest at the White House, as he has already been a guest of Huntington Hartford in Nassau. Over the years, Poddy has, like his employers, the AJC, moved from those liberal positions traditionally occupied by American Jews (and me) to the far right of American politics. The reason for that is simple. In order to get Treasury money for Israel (last year five billion dollars), pro-Israel lobbyists must see to it that America's "the Russians are coming" squads are in place so that they can continue to frighten the American people into spending enormous sums for "defense," which also means the support of Israel in its never-ending wars against just about everyone. To make sure that nearly two thirds of the federal budget goes to the Pentagon and Israel, it is necessary for the pro-Israel lobbyists to make common cause with our lunatic right. Hence, the virulent propaganda.

Poddy denounced Mailer and me in the pages of *The New York Post.* According to him, we belong to that mindless majority of pinko intellectuals who actually think that the nation spends too much on the Pentagon and not enough on, say, education. Since sustained argument is not really his bag, he must fall back on the *ad hominem* attack, a right-wing specialty —and, of course, on our flag, which he wears like a designer caftan because "the blessings of freedom and prosperity are greater and more widely shared [here] than in any country known to human history." Poddy should

---

*Again, I was attacked as a racist, invoking the "Yellow Peril." Simultaneously, the Japanese premier announced that the United States was a failure because there were too many inferior races in our heterodox land, while one of his cabinet ministers predicted that, in the next century, the United States would be Japan's farm, and Western Europe its boutique.

visit those Western European countries whose per capita income is higher than ours. All in all, Poddy is a silly billy.

Significantly, the one Yiddish word that has gained universal acceptance in this country is *chutzpah.* Example: In 1960, Mr. and Mrs. Podhoretz were in upstate New York where I used to live. I was trying out a play at the Hyde Park Playhouse; the play was set during the Civil War. "Why," asked Poddy, "are you writing a play about, of all things, the Civil War?" I explained to him that my mother's family had fought for the Confederacy and my father's for the Union, and that the Civil War was—and is —to the United States what the Trojan War was to the Greeks, the great single tragic event that continues to give resonance to our Republic.

"Well, to me," said Poddy, "the Civil War is as remote and as irrelevant as the War of the Roses." I realized then that he was not planning to become an "assimilated American," to use the old-fashioned terminology; but, rather, his first loyalty would always be to Israel. Yet he and Midge stay on among us, in order to make propaganda and raise money for Israel —a country they don't seem eager to live in. Jewish joke, circa 1900: A Zionist is someone who wants to ship other people off to Palestine.

Midge was next to strike. But before she launched her attack, in something called *Contentions,* she put on her thinking cap and actually read what I wrote. I give her high marks for that. Unfortunately, she found my history lesson hard going. But then, like most of our Israeli fifth columnists, Midge isn't much interested in what the *goyim* were up to before Ellis Island. She also likes the *ad hominem* attack. When I noted that our writers seldom speak out on matters of war and peace because so many of them are paid for by universities that receive money from the garrison state, Midge tartly retorted, *"He,* after all, is not paid by a university but by those great centers of independence, the film companies." Since my last Hollywood film, *The Best Man,* was made in 1964, I have been "paid" by that American public that buys my books about the American past, a subject of no demonstrable interest to Midge and Poddy and their friends.

Midge was amazed by my description of how we seized territories from Mexico, including California; annexed Hawaii and Puerto Rico and, of course, the Philippines, where we slaughtered between 100,000 and 200,-000 of the inhabitants. Interesting note: American imperialists froth if the figures for those murdered are ever in excess of 60,000 men, women, and children, the acceptable statistical minimum for genocide. Then Midge, with that magisterial gooniness that marks her polemical style, told us, "that three of these conquered territories are now states of the United States, and a fourth an independent republic, is evidently beside the point —as, we cannot resist remarking . . ."

Oh, Midge, resist. Resist! Don't you get the point? We stole other people's land. We murdered many of the inhabitants. We imposed our religion—and rule—on the survivors. General Grant was ashamed of what we did to Mexico, and so am I. Mark Twain was ashamed of what we did in the Philippines, and so am I. Midge is not because in the Middle East another predatory people is busy stealing other people's land in the name of an alien theocracy. She is a propagandist for these predators (paid for?), and that is what all this nonsense is about.

Since spades may not be called spades in freedom's land, let me spell it all out. In order to get military and economic support for Israel, a small number of American Jews,* who should know better, have made common cause with every sort of reactionary and anti-Semitic group in the United States, from the corridors of the Pentagon to the TV studios of the evangelical Jesus Christers. To show that their hearts are in the far-right place, they call themselves neoconservatives and attack the likes of Mailer and me, all in the interest of supporting the likes of Sharon and Greater Israel as opposed to the Peace Now Israelis whom they disdain. There is real madness here; mischief too.

"Well, one thing is clear in all this muddle," writes Midge, adrift in her tautological sea, "Mr. Vidal does not like his country." Poor Midge. Of course I like my country. After all, I'm its current biographer. But now that we're really leveling with each other, I've got to tell you I don't much like your country, which is Israel.

Although there is nothing wrong with being a lobbyist for a foreign power, one is supposed to register with the Justice Department. Also, I should think that tact would require a certain forbearance when it comes to the politics of the host country. But tact is unknown to the Podhoretzes. Joyously they revel in the politics of hate, with plangent attacks on blacks and/or fags and/or liberals, trying, always, to outdo those moral majoritarians who will, as Armageddon draws near, either convert all the Jews, just as the Good Book says, or kill them.

---

*This sentence has since been carefully revised by publicists like W. Safire and M. Peretz and C. Krauthammer to mean "all Jews," thus demonstrating my "virulent" anti-Semitism. Well, ours is a sectarian society.

All in all, the latest Podhoretz diatribes have finally convinced me that the time has come for the United States to stop all aid not only to Israel but to Jordan, Egypt, and the rest of the Arab world. The Middle Easterners would then be obliged to make peace, or blow one another up, or whatever. In any case, we would be well out of it. After all, the theological and territorial quarrels of Israel and Islam are as remote to 225 million Americans as—what else?—the Wars of the Roses.

THE NATION
*March 22, 1986*

# CHAPTER 11

# OLLIE

Lieutenant Colonel Oliver L. North (U.S.M.C.) has now metastasized in the national psyche rather the way that Tom Sawyer did more than a century ago. Like Tom, Ollie is essentially fictional; like Tom, Ollie is an American archetype: the con man as Peck's Bad Boy. It is hardly possible for any of us not to succumb, if only momentarily, to Ollie's boyish charm, as he hurries back and forth across our television sets, on his way, or so one gathers from the twinkle in his eye, to some top-secret *Contra* massage parlor. Actually my own favorite image of him is from the past: He has come, a mere boy, in uniform—direct from the battlefield—to put the case for the Vietnam War on a right-wing television program. The enraptured host is actually salivating at so much gung-ho martial spirit. Although I was, as always, briefly stricken, one detail bothered me. Why did he keep his garrison cap on? In the army we took them off indoors. Could it be that Ollie was deliberately playing a part even then? Could it be that he was not absolutely entirely sincere? Perish, as they say, the thought. He is a marine.

Much is made by the present administration of the marines to whom, in my day, we used to go tell it to. Since a number of rogues in high places are former marines, we are daily reminded of the corps's bravery and of its motto, *Semper fidelis* (always faithful), faithful particularly to those in high places. Now the real marines are indeed brave, that is, the enlisted men. On the other hand, I betray no secret when I say that those of us who served in the army in the Pacific during the Second World War regarded marine officers as, by and large, a bunch of dangerous boneheads, exuberantly careless with the lives of their men. Certainly they managed to decimate my generation with their legendary frontal assault, and if the recent off-the-wall ramblings of their retiring commander (General P. X. Kelly) archetypal, their collective IQ has not risen in the last forty years. So let us never forget that Ollie is not really a marine at home in Montezuma's hall; he is a *marine officer,* and should be kept on a tight leash along with gutsy Don Regan and pastryman Bud McFarlane.

In the coming days, Ollie will be the nation's number one daytime television star. There will be incredible suspense. Will he be *fidelis* to the president who let him off the leash to commit so many astonishing crimes? Will he be the strong silent sort like G. Gordon Liddy, who held his tongue so that he could later find it, most profitably, on the lecture circuit? Or will Ollie just go ahead and shred Ron and Nancy and Galanos and all those who drove him to crime? Tune in. This is high drama. It is also simply appalling in its implications.

Thirty years ago I wrote that should the United States ever have a dictator, it would not be a spellbinding autocrat like Douglas MacArthur; rather it would be someone really nice and folksy like Arthur Godfrey, a popular radio-TV pitchman of the era. In due course, big money, out to make even bigger bucks, cold-bloodedly hired an Arthur Godfrey to act the part of president. And we went along with him—or at least half of that bemused 50 percent of the electorate which bothers to vote in presidential elections did. Luckily, age and incompetence have saved us from a dictatorship, and the actor himself will soon be gone. But, for a moment, it was a very close thing indeed: A president deliberately tried to overthrow the constitution and place himself outside those laws he had sworn faithfully to execute. In retrospect, all this will seem pretty funny. Of course, Ollie will do time; he will also discover God yet again, be born a third time, and have a book written for him. He will be a celebrity forever and will enjoy the friendship of Pat Boone. On the other hand, we, the TV audience (and that is really all that we are—passive viewers and active consumers), will be living on in a republic that no longer works, its political system burnt out and its resources wasted during the reign of an actor whom we allowed so unwisely to step off the screen and into the White House.

Perhaps the most startling aspect of this whole affair has been the fact that no one seems particularly troubled. Congress is thrilled by the attention but its members refuse to lift the lid on anything important like, let us say, the CIA. But then the CIA is now totally unaccountable to anyone and Congress dares not ask such questions as: Were arms flown by the agency to the *Contras* in Nicaragua? And were those planes then filled with cocaine for the return journey? Of course only a communist would ask such a question. Meanwhile, marines are casually sacrificed in Lebanon by a government with no morality and an officer corps with no sense; the president compulsively tells lies on television as he has done throughout his entire political career and no one minds because he has such a nice smile.

The last best hope of earth, two trillion dollars in debt, is spinning out of control, and all we can do is stare at a flickering cathode-ray tube as Ollie "answers" questions on TV while the press, resolutely irrelevant as ever, asks politicians if they have committed adultery. From V-J Day 1945 to this has been, my fellow countrymen, a perfect nightmare.

NEWSWEEK
*July 13, 1987*


[N.B.: The true significance of Ollie was missed by all at the time, including me. There are two governments of the United States: the more or less secret National Security State* (National Security Council, Pentagon, CIA, etc.) and the cosmetic "constitutional" government of Congress, the judiciary and the ongoing, never-ending, issueless presidential election. In the constant presence of a benign crisis manager from Langley, Ollie tried to tell the Senate that he worked for the real government to which they were irrelevant, while Reagan's easygoing vagueness in the

*See next chapter.

matter derived from the president's dual function. Although he is the chief irrelevancy, he is also, if he chooses to be, a player in the actual government. He was very much at play in Nicaragua and Iran; but the cosmetic Congress dared not put a finger on him.

Several days after my piece in *Newsweek* appeared, the White House correspondent for *Time* magazine rang me. I've known him slightly for a long time. He is called Hugh Sidey; and he has yet to meet a president he could not worship. He had been at Camp David with President and Mrs. Reagan, and the President had said, "with a twinkle in his eye," how inaccurate Vidal is (good to know that he reads *Newsweek*). Apparently in my book about Lincoln, I show Lincoln watching the dawn from his office. But, said Reagan, you can't see the sun rise from the office. Sidey had been going through the book with a researcher: There was (how do they say at *Time?*) an edge of panic in his voice. We can't find the scene, he said. Because, I said, there was no such scene in the book: Lincoln did not get up as early as Reagan. I also reminded him—and the president— that Lincoln's office was at the southeast end of the second floor of the White House, with a fine view of the Potomac as well as of sunrises and sunsets. The present office, which has no view, was only built in 1904. Sidey reported in the next issue of *Time* the president's aria about how wrong I was "because I had Lincoln seeing something he couldn't have seen from the White House." The very stuff of history.]

# CHAPTER 12

# THE NATIONAL
# SECURITY STATE

Every now and then, usually while shaving, I realize that I have lived through nearly one third of the history of the United States, which proves not how old I am but how young the Republic is. The American empire, which started officially in 1898 with our acquisition of the Philippines, came to a peak in the year 1945, while I was still part of that army which had won us the political and economic mastery of two hemispheres. If anyone had said to me then that the whole thing would be lost in my lifetime, I would have said it is not possible to lose so much so quickly without an atomic catastrophe, at least. But lose it we have.

Yet, in hindsight, I can see that our ending was implicit in our beginning. When Japan surrendered, the United States was faced with a choice:

Either disarm, as we had done in the past, and enjoy the prosperity that comes from releasing so much wealth and energy to the private sector, or maintain ourselves on a full military basis, which would mean a tight control not only over our allies and such conquered provinces as West Germany, Italy, and Japan but over the economic—which is to say the political—lives of the American people. As Charles E. Wilson, a business-man and politician of the day, said as early as 1944, "Instead of looking to disarmament and unpreparedness as a safeguard against war, a thoroughly discredited doctrine, let us try the opposite: full preparedness according to a continuing plan."

The accidental president, Harry Truman, bought this notion. Although Truman campaigned in 1948 as an heir to Roosevelt's New Deal, he had a "continuing plan." Henry Wallace was onto it, as early as: "Yesterday, March 12, 1947, marked a turning point in American history, [for] it is not a Greek crisis that we face, it is an American crisis. Yesterday, President Truman . . . proposed, in effect, America police Russia's every border. There is no regime too reactionary for us provided it stands in Russia's expansionist path. There is no country too remote to serve as the scene of a contest which may widen until it becomes a world war." But how to impose this? The Republican leadership did not like the state to be the master of the country's economic life while, of the Democrats, only a few geopoliticians, like Dean Acheson, found thrilling the prospect of a military state, to be justified in the name of a holy war against something called communism in general and Russia in particular. The fact that the Soviet Union was no military or economic threat to us was immaterial. It must be made to appear threatening so that the continuing plan could be set in motion in order to create that National Security State in which we have been living for the past forty years.*

What is the National Security State? Well, it began, officially, with the National Security Act of 1947; it was then implemented in January 1950 when the National Security Council produced a blueprint for a new kind

*For those interested in the details, I recommend H. R. Shapiro's *Democracy in America*, the only political history of the United States from British shires to present deficits. Needless to say, this masterly work, fourteen years in the making, is published privately by Manhattan Communication, 496 LaGuardia Place, Suite 406, New York, NY 10012. The present volume is only half the whole and lacks scholarly apparatus (index, bibliography) but not scholarship.

of country, unlike anything that the United States had ever known before. This document, known as NSC-68 for short, and declassified only in 1975, committed—and still, fitfully, commits—us to the following program: First, never negotiate, ever, with Russia. This could not last forever; but the obligatory bad faith of U.S.-U.S.S.R. meetings still serves the continuing plan. Second, develop the hydrogen bomb so that when the Russians finally develop an atomic bomb we will still not have to deal with that enemy without which the National Security State cannot exist. Third, rapidly build up conventional forces. Fourth, put through a large increase in taxes to pay for all of this. Fifth, mobilize the entire American society to fight this terrible specter of communism. Sixth, set up a strong alliance system, directed by the United States (this became NATO). Seventh, make the people of Russia our allies, through propaganda and CIA derring-do, in this holy adventure—hence the justification for all sorts of secret services that are in no way responsible to the Congress that funds them, and so in violation of the old Constitution.

Needless to say, the blueprint, the continuing plan, was not openly discussed at the time. But, one by one, the major political players of the two parties came around. Senator Arthur Vandenburg, Republican, told Truman that if he really wanted all those weapons and all those high taxes to pay for them, he had better "scare hell out of the American people." Truman obliged, with a series of speeches beginning October 23, 1947, about the Red Menace endangering France and Italy; he also instituted loyalty oaths for federal employees; and his attorney general (December 4, 1947) published a list of dissident organizations. The climate of fear has been maintained, more or less zealously, by Truman's successors, with the brief exception of Dwight Eisenhower, who in a belated fit of conscience at the end of his presidency warned us against the military-industrial complex that had, by then, established permanent control over the state.

The cynicism of this coup d'etat was breathtaking. Officially we were doing nothing but trying to preserve freedom for ourselves and our allies from a ruthless enemy that was everywhere, monolithic and all-powerful. Actually, the real enemy were those National Security Statesmen who had so dexterously hijacked the country, establishing military conscription in peacetime, overthrowing governments that did not please them, and finally keeping all but the very rich docile and jittery by imposing income taxes that theoretically went as high as 90 percent. That is quite an achievement in a country at peace.

We can date from January 1950 the strict governmental control of our economy and the gradual erosion of our liberties, all in order to benefit the economic interest of what is never, to put it tactfully, a very large group —defense spending is money but not labor intensive. Fortunately, all bad things must come to an end. Our huge indebtedness has made the maintenance of the empire a nightmare; and the day Japan stops buying our Treasury bonds, the troops and the missiles will all come home to a highly restless population.*

Now that I have defined the gloomy prospect, what solutions do I have? I shall make five proposals. First, limit presidential election campaigns to eight weeks. That is what most civilized countries do, and all democratic ones are obliged to do. Allow no paid political ads. We might then entice that half of the electorate which never votes to vote.

Second, the budget: The press and the politicians constantly falsify the revenues and the disbursements of the federal government. How? By wrongly counting Social Security contributions and expenditures as a part of the federal budget. Social Security is an independent, slightly profitable income-transferring trust fund, which should be factored out of federal revenue and federal spending. Why do the press and the politicians conspire to give us this distorted view of the budget? Because neither they nor their owners want the public to know how much of its tax money goes for a war that does not exist. As a result Federal Reserve chairman Alan Greenspan could say last March, and with a straight face, that there are only two options for a serious attack on the deficit. One is to raise taxes. The other is to reduce the entitlement programs like Social Security and Medicare. He did not mention the defense budget. He did not acknowledge that the so-called entitlements come from a special fund. But then, he is a disciple of Ayn Rand.

In actual fact, close to 90 percent of the disbursements of the federal government go for what is laughingly known as "defense." This is how: In 1986 the gross revenue of the government was $794 billion. Of that amount, $294 billion were Social Security contributions, which should be subtracted from the money available to the National Security State. That leaves $500 billion. Of the $500 billion, $286 billion go to defense; $12 billion for foreign arms to our client states; $8 billion to $9 billion to energy, which means means, largely, nuclear weapons; $27 billion for

*See Appendix.

veterans' benefits, the sad and constant reminder of the ongoing empire's recklessness; and, finally, $142 billion for interest on loans that were spent, over the past forty years, to keep the National Security State at war, hot or cold. So, of 1986's $500 billion in revenue, $475 billion was spent on National Security business. Of that amount, we will never know how much was "kicked back" through political action committees and so-called soft money to subsidize candidates and elections. Other federal spending, incidentally, came to $177 billion in 1986 (guarding presidential candidates, cleaning the White House), which was about the size of the deficit, since only $358 billion was collected in taxes.

It is obvious that if we are to avoid an economic collapse, defense spending must be drastically reduced. But it is hard to reduce a budget that the people are never told about. The first politician who realizes why those politicians who appear to run against the government always win, could not only win himself but be in a position to rid us of the National Security State—which is what people truly hate. "Internal Improvements" was the slogan of Henry Clay's popular movement. A neo-Clayite could sweep the country if he wanted seriously to restore the internal plant of the country rather than invade Honduras or bob expensively about the Persian Gulf or overthrow a duly elected government in Nicaragua while running drugs (admittedly, the CIA's only margin of profit).

Third, as part of our general retrenchment, we should withdraw from NATO. Western Europe is richer and more populous than America. If it cannot defend itself from an enemy who seems to be falling apart even faster than we are, then there is nothing that we, proud invaders of Grenada, can effectively do. I would stop all military aid to the Middle East. This would oblige the hardliners in Israel to make peace with the Palestinians. We have supported Israel for forty years. No other minority in the history of the United States has ever extorted so much Treasury money for its Holy Land as the Israeli lobby, and it has done this by making a common cause with the National Security State. Each supports the other. I would have us cease to pay for either.

Fourth, we read each day about the horrors of drug abuse, the murder of policemen, the involvement of our own government in drug running, and so on. We are all aware that organized crime has never been richer nor the society more demoralized. What is the solution? I would repeal every prohibition against the sale and use of drugs, because it is these prohibitions that have caused the national corruption, not to mention most of the addiction. Since the American memory has a span of about three days, I will remind you that in 1919 alcohol was prohibited in the United States. In 1933 Prohibition was repealed because not only had organized crime expanded enormously but so had alcoholism. What did not work then does not work now. But we never learn, which is part of our national charm. Repeal would mean that there is no money for anyone in selling drugs. That's the end of the playground pusher. That's the end of organized crime, which has already diversified and is doing very nicely in banking, films, and dry cleaning. Eventually, repeal will mean the end of mass drug addiction. As there will always be alcoholics, there will always be drug addicts, but not to today's extent. It will be safe to walk the streets because the poor will not rob you to pay for their habit.*

Fifth, two years ago I described how the American empire ended the day the money power shifted from New York to Tokyo and we became, for the first time in seventy-one years, a debtor nation. Since then, we have become the largest debtor country in history. I suggested a number of things that might be done, some of which I've again mentioned. But, above all, I see our economic survival inextricably bound up with that of our neighbor in the Northern Hemisphere, the Soviet Union. Some sort of alliance must be made between us so that together we will be able to compete with Japan and, in due course, China. As the two klutzes of the north, each unable to build a car anyone wants to drive, we deserve each other. In a speech at Gorbachev's anti-nuclear forum in Moscow, I quoted a Japanese minister of trade who said that Japan would still be number one in the next century. Then, tactlessly he said that the United States will be Japan's farm and Western Europe its boutique. A Russian got up and asked, "What did he say about us?" I said that they were not mentioned but, if they did not get their act together, they would end up as ski instructors. It is my impression that the Russians are eager to be Americans, but, thanks to the brainwashing of the National Security State's continuing plan, Americans have a built-in horror of the Evil Empire,

---

*I called for the legalization of drugs pretty much in these same words on the op-ed page of *The New York Times*, September 26, 1970. Today more and more voices are joining mine (e.g., *The Economist*, April 2, 1985).

which the press and the politicians have kept going for forty years.*
Happily, our National Security State is in the red, in more ways than one.
Time for a change?

THE NATION
*June 4, 1988*

---

*The press, which should know better, is of no help. The Iran-*Contra* hearings was a
sudden dramatic confrontation between the real government of the United States, as
represented by Ollie North et al., and the cosmetic government. Ollie told us as much. But
no one got the point.

# CHAPTER 13

# MONGOLIA!

In August, Moscow's weather is like that of Bangor, Maine; the cool wind has begun to smell of snow while the dark blue sky is marred with school-of-Tiepolo clouds. Last August the rowan trees were overloaded with clusters of red berries. "Rowanberries in August mean a hard winter," said the literary critic as he showed me the view from the Kremlin terrace. "But after the hard winter," I said, sententious as Mao, "there will come the spring." He nodded. "How true!" As we pondered the insignificance of what neither had said, a baker's dozen of ornithologists loped into view. Moscow was acting as host to a world ornithological congress. To a man, ornithologists are tall, slender, and bearded so that they can stand motion-less for hours, imitating kindly trees, as they watch for birds. Since they are staying at our group's hotel, we have dubbed them the tweet-tweets.

The critic asked, "Have you read *Gorky Park?*" I said that I had not because I have made it a rule only to read novels by Nobel Prize winners. That way one will never read a bad book. I told him the plot of Pearl Buck's *This Proud Heart.* He told me the plot of *Gorky Park.* "It's a really good bad book," he said. "You know, everyone's making such heavy weather about it here. I can't think why. It's wonderfully silly. An American gunman loose in Moscow!" He chuckled. "It's so surrealist." I said that they should publish it as an example of American surrealism, with a learned commentary explaining the jokes.

As we chatted, two Russian soldiers walked by us. One was in uniform; the other wore blue jeans and a T-shirt emblazoned with the words THE UNITED STATES MILITARY ACADEMY, WEST POINT. The literary critic smiled. "Could an American soldier wear a Kremlin T-shirt?" I explained to him, patiently, I hope, the difference between the free and the unfree worlds. Abashed, he changed the subject to, where was I going next? When I said, "Ulan Bator," he laughed. When I wanted to know what was so funny, he said, "I thought you said you were going to Ulan Bator." When I told him that that was exactly where I was going, to the capital of the Mongolian People's Republic (sometimes known as Outer Mongolia), he looked very grave indeed. "It is said," he whispered so that the ubiquitous KGB would not overhear us, "that the British and French embassies have a spy at the airport and that anyone who looks promising is approached—oh, very furtively—and asked if he plays bridge. You did not hear this from me," he added.

At midnight the plane leaves Moscow for Ulan Bator, with stops at Omsk and Irkutsk (in Siberia). The trip takes ten hours; there is a five-hour time difference between Moscow and Ulan Bator (U.B. to us fans). Moscow Aeroflot planes have a tendency to be on time, but the ceilings are too low for claustrophobes, and there is a curious smell of sour cream throughout the aircraft. Contrary to legend, the stewardesses are agreeable, at least on the Siberian run.

Our party included an English-born, Nairobi-based representative of the United Nations Environment Programme—White Hunter, his name. A representative of the World Wildlife Fund International who turned out to be a closet tweet-tweet—and was so named. And the photographer, Snaps. We were accompanied by the youthful Boris Petrovich, who has taught himself American English through the study of cassettes of what appears to have been every American film ever made. We had all met at the Rossya Hotel in Moscow. According to the Russians, it is the largest hotel in the world. Whether or not this is true, the Rossya's charm is not unlike that of New York's Attica Prison. In the Soviet Union the foreigner is seldom without a low-level anxiety, which can, suddenly, develop into wall-climbing paranoia. *Where are the visas?* To which the inevitable Russian answer, "No problem," is ominous indeed.

Now our little group was being hurtled through the Siberian skies to a part of Outer Mongolia where no white—or, for that matter, black—Westerner had ever been before, or as one of our men at the American Embassy put it: "You will be the first American ever to set foot in that part of the Gobi Desert." I asked for my instructions. After all, those of us who believe in freedom must never not be busy. When I suggested that I might destabilize the Mongolian government while I was there, one of our men was slightly rattled. "Actually," he said, "no American has ever been there because there isn't anything there." My fierce patriotism was seriously tried by this insouciance. "Then why," I asked, "am I going?" He said he hadn't a clue. Why *was* I going?

It all came back to me on the night flight to Ulan Bator. The World Wildlife Fund has taken to sending writers around the world to record places where the ecology is out of joint. My task was a bit the reverse. I was to report on the national park that the Mongolian government is creating in the Gobi in order to keep pristine the environment so that flora and fauna can proliferate in a perfect balance with the environment.

As I stared out the porthole window at my own reflection (or was it Graham Greene's? The vodka bottle seemed familiar), my mind was a-whirl with the intense briefings that I had been subjected to. For instance, is the People's Republic of Mongolia part of the Soviet Union? No. It is an independent socialist nation, grateful for the "disinterested" aid that it gets from the other socialist nations. When did it come into being? Sixty years ago, when the Chinese were ejected and their puppet, the Living Buddha, was shorn of his powers and the twenty-eight-year-old Damdiny Sükh, known as Ulan Bator (Red Hero in Mongolian), took charge of the state, with disinterested Soviet aid. Meanwhile, back at the Kremlin, Vladimir Ilyich Ulyanov Lenin was not entirely thrilled. Classic Marxism requires that a state evolve from feudalism to monarchy to capitalism and then to communism. As of 1920, whatever had been going on in Mongolia for two millennia, it was not capitalism. The people were nomadic. Every now and then, in an offhand way, they'd conquer the world. Genghis Khan ruled from the Danube to the Pacific Ocean, and some twelve hundred years ago, according to one account, Mongol tribes crossed from Asia to North America via the Bering Strait, making the Western Hemisphere a sort of Mongol colony. Lenin knitted his brow and came up with the following concept: "With the aid of the proletariat of the advanced countries, backward countries can go over to the Soviet system and, through certain stages of development, to communism, without having to pass through the capitalist stage." So it came to pass. In sixty years an illiterate population has become totally literate, life expectancies have increased, industries and mining have taken the place of the old nomadic way of life, and there is a boom in population. "Sixty percent of the population," said Boris Petrovich, "is under sixteen years of age." Tweet-tweet looked grim. "So much the worse for them," he said. Boris Petrovich said, "But, gosh, they need people here. Why, they've only got one and a half million people to one and a half million square kilometers. That's not enough people to feed themselves with." As the environmental aspect was carefully explained to Boris Petrovich, his eyes lost their usual keenness. "Should I," he asked me, changing the subject, "buy Lauren Bacall's book?"

Jet lag and culture shock greeted us at the airport, where blue asters had broken through the landing strip. But no one was asked to play bridge, because we were whisked aboard an Air Mongolia plane and flown five more hours to the provincial capital of Gobi Altai, the southwestern province of Mongolia. At the foot of the Altai range of mountains is the town of Altai. Here we spent the night in a two-story hotel on the main street, whose streetlamps did not turn on. Opposite the hotel is the police station. At the end of the street is a new hospital of raw cement.

We were given dinner by the deputy chairman of the province, the Soviet director of the park, and the deputy minister of forestry (under whose jurisdiction is the near-treeless Gobi), as well as two ministerial officials assigned to the United Nations Environment Programme. Toasts were drunk as dishes of mutton came and went. Money is no longer flowing from the UN, White Hunter pointed out. The Reagan administration is cutting back. The Soviet Union is making a fair contribution to the fund, but—such is the Soviet sense of fun—the money is in unconvertible rubles. This means that the Soviet contribution can be spent only in the Soviet sphere. Hence, the Gobi park.

Although Mongolia smells of mutton fat, the Mongols smell not at all, even though the Russians go on about the great trouble they have getting them to bathe. Men and women are equally handsome: tall, narrow-waisted, with strong white teeth. Some wear the national tunic with sash and boots; others wear the international uniform of blue jeans. "Why," I asked one of our Mongolian colleagues, "are there no bald men here?" He was startled by the question. "The old men shave their heads," he said, as if this was an answer. Even so, there are no bald men to be seen anywhere. Our group came to the conclusion that over the millennia bald babies were exposed at birth.

As the evening ended, I had a sense of what the English call *déjà vu.* I had been in this company before. But where? It came to me: in my grandfather's state of Oklahoma, on one of the Indian reservations. Physically, the Mongolians are dead ringers for the Cherokees, whose nation my grandfather represented as an attorney in an effort to get some money for the land that the American government had stolen from them. All in all, the Russians are doing rather better by their Mongols than we are doing by ours.

I proposed a toast to Kublai Khan, "China's great Mongol emperor, who opened up a peaceful discourse between East and West." The Mongols at table were amused. The Russians less so. "You know," said one of the ministerials, "we are making a number of movies about Mongolian history." I did not ask if any of these films would deal with the 250-year Mongol occupation of Russia. The Russians still complain of their suffering during the Mongol occupation. "Now," said the ministerial, "we are making a movie about American Indians." When I asked what the theme was, I got a vague answer. "Oh, the . . . connections. You'll see."

The next day there was rain in the Gobi. Something unheard of, we were told. In fact, there had been a flood a few days before, and many people were said to have been drowned. Due to bad weather, the plane would not take us to the encampment. So we set out on a gray afternoon in jeeps and Land Rovers. There is no road, only a more or less agreed-upon trail.

═══

As we left Altai, we saw a bit of the town that Snaps and I had not been allowed to see earlier that morning, when we had set out to record the real life of the Mongols, who live in what the Russians call a *yurta* and the owners call a *ger:* a round tent, ingeniously made of felt, with a removable flap across the top to let out smoke. In winter the fire is lit in the morning for cooking; then it goes out until sundown, when it is lit again for the evening meal. Apparently the *yurta* retains warmth in winter and is cool in summer. At Altai, every hundred or so *yurtas* are surrounded by wooden fences, "to hold back the drifts of snow in winter," said a Russian, or "to keep them in their particular collective," said a cynical non-Russian. Whatever, the wooden fences have curious binary devices on them: "king's ring and queen's ring," I was told by a Mongol—and no more.

Every time Snaps and I were close to penetrating one of the enclosures, a policeman would indicate that we should go back to the hotel. Meanwhile, the children would gather around until Snaps snapped; then they would shriek *nyet* and scamper off, only to return a moment later with many giggles. The older people quite liked being photographed, particularly the men on their ponies, whose faces—the ponies'—are out of prehistory, pendulous-lipped and sly of slanted eye. In costume, women wear boots; not in costume, they wear high heels as they stride over the dusty graveled plain, simulating the camel's gait.

*The Gobi Desert* by Mildred Cable with Francesca French is an invaluable look at central Asia in the twenties and thirties by two lady missionaries who traveled the trade routes, taught the Word, practiced medicine.* "The Mongol's home is his tent, and his nomadic life is the expression of a compelling instinct. A house is intolerable to him, and even the restricting sense of an enclosing city wall is unbearable." One wonders what today's Mongols think, cooped up in their enclosures. "They hate the new housing," said one official. "They put their animals and belongings in the apartment houses, and then they stay in their *yurtas.*" Others told me that, in general, the people are content, acclimatized to this bad century. "The Mongol lives in and for the present, and looks neither backward toward his ancestors nor forward to his descendants."

"Snaps, one word is worth a thousand pictures," I said. "Which word?" he asked. "That would be telling," I told him. But now comes the time when I must come to Snaps's aid and through the living word transmit to the reader's eye the wonder that is Mongolia when the monsoons are almost done with and the heat has dropped after July's 1 1 3 degrees Fahrenheit and lizards cook in Gobi.

*Frederic Prokosch relied heavily on the two ladies for *The Seven Who Fled.*

=====

We are in a jeep, lurching over rough terrain. The driver is young, wears a denim jacket, grins as he crashes over boulders. Picture now a gray streaked sky. In the distance a dun-colored mountain range, smooth and rounded the way old earth is. We are not yet in the Gobi proper. There is water. Herds of yaks and camels cross the horizon. But once past this watered plain, the Gobi Desert begins—only it is not a proper desert. Sand is the exception, not the rule. Black and brown gravel is strewn across the plain. Occasional white salt slicks vary the monotony. All sorts of shy plants grow after a rain or near one of the rare springs. Actually, there is water under a lot of the Gobi, in some places only a few feet beneath the surface. For those who missed out on the journeys to the moon, the Gobi is the next best thing.

"The word Gobi," authority tells us (*Géographie Universelle,* P. Vidal de la Blache et L. Gallois), "is not the proper name of a geographical area, but a common expression used by Mongols to designate a definite order of geographical features. These are wide, shallow basins in which the smooth rocky bottom is filled with sand, pebbles, or, more often, with gravel." *L'autre* Vidal tells us that, properly speaking, the Gobi covers a distance of 3,600 miles, "from the Pamirs to the confines of Manchuria." But Outer Mongolia's Gobi, together with that part of the Gobi inside China to our south and west, is the desert's heart, once crossed by the old silk route that connected the Middle Kingdom with the West.

We arrive in darkness at Tsogt, a small town on whose edge is the fenced-in administrative center of the park. We slept in spacious *yurtas,* worthy of the great Khan. In the dining *yurta* a feast of mutton had been prepared. We were joined by several Russian specialists connected with the park. One was a zoologist, given to wearing green camouflage outfits with a most rakish hat. Another had spent a winter in New York City, where "every square meter costs one million dollars."

Next day, at second or third light, we were shown a fuzzy film of all the fauna that the park contained, from wild Bactrian camels to wild bears to the celebrated snow leopard and, of course, the ubiquitous goat. But once the Gobi is entered, there are few herds to be seen, and only the occasional tweet, usually a kite or a variety of low-flying brown-and-white jay. As befits a World Wildlife Funder, Tweet-tweet was becoming unnaturally excited. Snaps, too, was in his heaven. Bliss to be in Gobi, almost.

After the film we boarded a plane that I had last flown in in 1935, and flew south across the Gobi, which I had last seen in the pages of the old *Life* magazine, circa 1935, as portrayed by Margaret Bourke-White. Time kept warping until I noticed that Snaps was furtively vomiting into his camera case; others were also queasy. When I suggested that air be admitted to the cabin, I was greeted with 1935 stares of disbelief. So we returned to base. We were then loaded into jeeps and crossed a low mountain range to the park itself.

On a high hill with dark mountains behind, the Gobi stretches as far as anyone could wish, its flatness broken by the odd mountain, set island-like in the surrounding gravel. I got out of the jeep to commune with the silence. The driver started to pluck at small dark-green clumps of what turned out to be chives. We ate chives and looked at the view, and I proceeded to exercise the historical imagination and conjured up Genghis Khan on that famous day when he set his standard of nine yak tails high atop Gupta, and the Golden Horde began its conquest of Europe. "Hey" —I heard the Americanized voice of Boris Petrovich—"did any of you guys see *The Little Foxes* with Elizabeth Taylor?" A chorus of noes did not faze him. "Well, why not?" It was Tweet-tweet who answered him. "If you have gone to the theater seriously all your life," he said sternly, "there are plays that you know in advance that you will not be caught dead at." But Tweet-tweet had not reckoned with the Russian sense of fair play. "How can you say that when you wouldn't even go *see* her in the play? I mean, so she was crucified by the reviewers . . ." Thus, put in our place, we descended into Gobi. Thoughts of Taylor's fleshy splendor had restored Genghis to wraithdom and dispersed the Horde.

We stopped at an oasis, a bright strip of ragged green in the dark shining gravel. Water bubbles up from the earth and makes a deep narrow stream down a low hill to a fenced-in place where a Mongol grows vegetables for the camp. The water is cool and pure, and the Mongols with us stare at it for a time and smile; then they lie down on their bellies and drink deeply. We all do. In fact, it is hard to get enough water in Gobi. Is this psychological or physiological? The Mongol gardener showed me his plantation. "The melons don't grow very large," he apologized, holding up a golf ball of a melon. "It is Gobi, you see." I tried to explain to him that if he were to weed his patch, the vegetables would grow larger, but in that lunar landscape I suspect that the weeds are as much a delight to him as the melons.

As we lurched across the desert to the Yendiger Mountains, we passed an empty village where nomads used to winter. Whether or not they are still allowed in the park is a moot point. No straight answer was available. We were told that certain sections of the park are furrowed off—literally, a furrow is plowed and, except for the park rangers, no human being may cross the furrow unless he wants to be detained for poaching. Are there many poachers? A few . . .

At the deserted village, each jeep took a different route toward the dark mountains in the distance. En route, the jeep that I was traveling in broke down four times. Long after the others had arrived at camp, our group was comfortably seated on a malachite-green rock, sipping whisky from the bottle and watching the sun pull itself together for a Gobi Special sunset, never to be forgotten. Tweet-tweet said that in the Galapagos Islands Tom Stoppard had worked out a numeric scale with which to measure the tasteless horror of each successive night's overwrought sunset. But I defended our Gobi Special. For once, Mother Nature was the soul of discreet good taste. Particularly the northern sky, where clouds like so many plumes of Navarre had been dipped in the most subtle shade of Du Barry gray, while the pale orange of the southern sky did not cloy. True, there was a *pink* afterglow in the east. But then perfection has never been Mother Nature's ideal.

The jeep functional, we drove between dark brown rocks along the bottom of what looked to be an ancient riverbed until we came to a turn in the ravine, and there was the campsite. In a row: one *yurta,* a dozen pup tents, a truck that contained a generator. "This is the first electricity ever to shine in this part of Gobi," said the Soviet director. As the Mongol lads strung electric lines from tent to tent, Snaps, with narrowed eyes and camera poised, waited. "You never know," he whispered, "when you'll get a shot of electrified Mongol. *Tremendous* market for that, actually."

We were told that close to camp there is a famous watering hole where, at sundown, the snow leopard lies down, as it were, with the wild ass. But we had missed sundown. Nevertheless, ever game, our party walked halfway to the hole before settling among rocks on the ridge to fortify ourselves with alien spirits against the black desert night that had fallen with a crash about us. As we drank, we were joined by a large friendly goat. Overhead, the stars (so much more satisfactory than the ones beneath our feet) shone dully: Rain clouds were interfering with the Gobi's usual surefire light show. I found the Dipper; it was in the wrong place. There was a sharp difference of agreement on the position of Orion's Belt. Shooting stars made me think, comfortably, of war. I showed Boris Petrovich what looked to be one of the Great Republic's newest satellites. "Keeping watch over the Soviet Union," I said. "Unless," he said, "it is one of our missiles on its way to Washington. But, seriously," he added, "don't you agree that Elizabeth Taylor was a first-rate *movie* actress? You know, like Susan Hayward."

First light seized us from our pup tents, where we had slept upon the desert floor, inhaling the dust of millennia. As I prepared for a new day of adventure, sinuses aflame, there was a terrible cry, then a sob, a gasp —silence. Our friend of the evening before, the goat, was now to be our dinner.

We checked out the watering hole, which turned out to be a muddy place in the rocks; there were no signs of beasts. Again we were on the move, this time southeasterly toward the Mount Mother system. The heat was intense. We glimpsed a wild ass, wildly running up ahead of us. Some gazelles skittered in the distance. The countryside was almost always horizontal but never pleasingly flat. To drive over such terrain is like riding a Wild West bronco. As we penetrated deeper into the preserve, vegetation ceased. What thornwood there was no longer contained greenery. Thornwood—with camel and goat dung—provides the nomads with their fuel. We were told that poachers are more apt to steal the wood in the preserve than the animals.

Suddenly, all of our jeeps converged on the same spot, close to the steep dark-red Khatan Khairkhan, an island of rock rising from a dry sea. The drivers gathered around a circle of white sand some six feet in diameter. Three spurts of icy water bubbled at the circle's center. Again, the happy smiles. Mongols stare at water rather the way northerners stare at fires. Then each of us tried the water. It tasted like Badois. Camel and wild-ass dung in the immediate vicinity testified to its excellent, even curative, mineral qualities.

Halfway up the red mountain, we made camp at the mouth of a ravine lined with huge, smooth red rocks. Glacial? Remains of a sea that had long since gone away? No geologist was at hand to tell us, but in the heights above the ravine were the Seven Cauldrons of Khatan Khairkhan, where, amongst saksaul groves and elm trees, the waters have made seven rock basins, in which Tweet-tweet and White Hunter disported themselves while Snaps recorded the splendors of nature. The author, winded halfway up, returned to camp and read Mme. de La Fayette's *La Princesse de Clèves.*

That night our friend the goat was served in the famous Mongolian hot pot. Red-hot rocks are dropped into metal pots containing whatever animal has been sacrificed to man's need. The result is baked to a T. As usual, I ate tomatoes, cucumbers, and bread. We drank to the Golden Horde, now divided in three parts: Outer Mongolia, which is autonomous, thanks to the "disinterested" Soviet Union's presence; Inner Mongolia, which is part of China and filling up with highly interested Chinese; and Siberia, which contains a large Mongolian population. Since functioning monasteries are not allowed in China or Siberia, practicing Buddhists come to Ulan Bator, where there are a large school, a lamasery, and the Living Buddha. This particular avatar is not the result of the usual search for the exact incarnation practiced in ancient times. He was simply selected to carry on.

Even rarer than a functioning lamasery in Mongolia is Przhevalski's horse. These horses exist in zoos around the world, but whether or not they are still to be found in Gobi is a subject of much discussion. Some think that there are a few in the Chinese part of the Gobi; some think that they are extinct there. In any case, the Great Gobi National Park plans to reintroduce—from the zoos—Przhevalski's horse to its original habitat. We drank to the Przhevalski horse. We drank to the plane that was to pick us up the next morning when we returned to base. "Will it really be there?" I asked. "No problem."

At dawn we lurched across the desert beneath a lowering sky. At Tsogt there was no plane. "No problem." We would drive four or five hours to Altai. Along the way we saw the marks that our tires had made on the way down. "In Gobi, tracks may last fifty years," one of the Russians said.

At the Altai airport low-level anxiety went swiftly to high: The plane for Ulan Bator might not take off. Bad weather. The deputy minister of forestry made a ministerial scene, and the plane left on time. There was not a cloud on the route. We arrived at dusk. The road from the airport to the city passes beneath not one but two huge painted arches. From the second arch, Ulan Bator in its plain circled by mountains looks very large indeed. Four hundred thousand people live and have their being beneath a comforting industrial smog. As well as the usual fenced-off *yurtas,* there are high-rise apartment houses, an opera house, a movie palace, functioning streetlamps, and rather more neon than one sees in, say, Rome. Although our mood was gala as we settled in at the Ulan Bator Hotel, low-level anxiety never ceased entirely to hum. Would the visas for the Soviet Union be ready in time? Had the plane reservations for Moscow and the West been confirmed? Would we get back the passports that we had surrendered upon arrival?

===

The next day, our questions all answered with "No problem," we saw the sights of Ulan Bator. A museum with a room devoted to odd-shaped dinosaur eggs, not to mention the skeletons of the dinosaurs that had laid them. Every public place was crowded. A convention of Mongol experts was in town; there was also a delegation of Buddhists, paying their respects to the Living Buddha, who would be, his secretary told me, too busy with the faithful to receive us that day. Undaunted, Snaps and I made our way to the Buddhist enclosure, where we found several temples packed with aged priests and youthful acolytes with shaved heads. As the priests read aloud from strips of paper on which are printed Sanskrit and Tibetan texts, their voices blend together like so many bees in a hive while incense makes blue the air and bells tinkle at odd intervals to punctuate the still-living texts. In a golden robe, the Living Buddha sat on a dais. As the faithful circled him in an unending stream, he maintained a costive frown. Outside, aged costumed Mongols of both sexes sat about the enclosure, at a millennium's remove from cement block and Aeroflot.

The United Kingdom's man in Ulan Bator, James Paterson, received us at the British Embassy. Outside, a suspicious policeman stands guard with a walkie-talkie, keeping close watch not only on the ambassador and his visitors but on the various Mongols who paused in front of the embassy to look at the color photographs, under glass, of the wedding of the Prince and Princess of Wales. The Mongols would study the pictures carefully and then, suddenly, smile beatifically. How very like, I could practically hear them say to themselves, our own imperial family—the Khans of yesteryear!

Paterson is tall and tweedy with a charming wife (in central Asia all of us write like the late Somerset Maugham). "I am allowed to jog," he said. "But permission must be got to make trips." Since he knew that I was asking myself the one question that visitors to U.B. ask themselves whenever they meet a noncommunist ambassador (there are four, from Britain, France, Canada, and India)—What on earth did you *do* to be sent here? —he brought up the subject and laughed, I think, merrily. He was raised in China; he was fascinated by the Mongol world—unlike the French ambassador who, according to diplomats in Moscow, used to go about Ulan Bator muttering, "I am here because they fear me at the Quai d'Orsay." When I asked Paterson where the French ambassador was, I was told, "He is no longer here." Tact, like holly at Christmas, festooned the modest sitting room, where a much-fingered, month-old *Economist* rested on the coffee table.

A reception was given us by the minister of forestry. He is a heavyset man with gray hair and a face much like that of the old drawings of Kublai Khan. He hoped that we had enjoyed the visit to the park. He hoped that there would be more money from the United Nations, but if there should be no more, he quite understood. White Hunter found this a bit ominous, as he favors further UN funding of the park. Tourism was discussed: A new guest complex would be built at Tsogt. The plans look handsome. Room for only eighteen people—plainly, a serious place for visiting scientists. Elsewhere, hunters are catered for.

Tweet-tweet spoke eloquently of the Wildlife Fund's work around the world. "Under its president, Prince Philip," he intoned. The Mongol translator stopped. "Who?" Tweet-tweet repeated the name, adding, "The husband of our queen." The translator could not have been more gracious. "The husband of *whose* queen?" he asked. Tweet-tweet went on to say that if it were not for the politicians, there would be world peace and cooperation, and the environment would be saved. I noticed that the minister's highly scrutable Oriental face, so unlike our veiled Occidental ones, was registering dismay. I interrupted. "As one politician to another," I said, "even though I have just lost an election, having polled only a half-million votes"—roughly a third of the population of Mongolia, I thought, in a sudden frenzy of demophilia—"I am as peace-loving as, I am sure, His Excellency is." I got a wink from the minister, and after dinner a powerful pinch of snuff. Even in Mongolia, we pols must stick together in a world made dangerous for us by well-meaning Tweet-tweets.

The next day all was in order; there was indeed no problem. The ten-hour trip took place in daylight. As we stretched our legs in Omsk, White Hunter noticed a handsome blond girl beyond the airport railings. He turned to Boris Petrovich. "What are the girls like here?" Boris Petrovich shook his head. "Well, I was only here once, when I was on the junior basketball team. We played everywhere." White Hunter said, "You mean you didn't make out?" Boris Petrovich looked shocked. "Well, gosh,

I was only sixteen." I told him that in the United States many males at sixteen have not only passed their sexual peak but are burned-out cases. Boris Petrovich's eyes glittered. "I'll bet there are some movies on that," he said. "You know, that soft-porn stuff on cassettes."

Before our party separated at the Moscow airport, we agreed that the Great Gobi National Park was a serious affair and not a front for Soviet missiles or, worse, a hunters' paradise with Gobi bears and snow leopards as the lure. Snaps was thrilled with the Buddhist pictures; less thrilled with the Gobi, "of an ugliness not to be reproduced"; pleased with the pictures of the people, though we had failed to penetrate a single *yurta*. White Hunter had hopes that the United Nations would raise enough money to keep the park going. Tweet-tweet was satisfied that wildlife was being tended to. Meanwhile, Boris Petrovich darted between the two groups— one headed for London, one for Rome.

As I was leaving the reception area, he made a small speech about the necessity of good Soviet-American relations, the importance of world peace, the necessity of cooperation on environmental matters. Then he lowered his voice. "I have a question to ask you." He looked about to see if we were being overheard. Thus, I thought to myself, Philby was re-cruited. Swiftly, I made my decision. If I were to sell out the free world, I must be well paid. I would want a *dacha* on the Baltic, near Riga. I would want . . . "How tall," asked Boris Petrovich, "is Paul Newman, really?"

VANITY FAIR
*March 1983*

# CHAPTER 14

# AT HOME
# IN A ROMAN STREET

For twenty years I have rented a small penthouse on top of the moldering seventeenth-century Origo Palace in the middle of what bureaucratic Romans call the Historic Center and everyone else calls Old Rome. The palace is at the northwest corner of a busy square that has all the charm of New York City's Columbus Circle, minus Huntington Hartford's masterpiece, and plus, below street level, three classical temples, home to a colony of cats, a perennial—no, millennial—reminder that this precinct was once sacred to the goddess Isis, and the cat was, and is, her creature. In a nearby street there is a large marble foot on a pedestal, all that is left of Isis' cult statue. Cats now sun themselves on her toes.

The west façade of the palace is set in a two-thousand-year-old north-south Roman street that starts a half-dozen blocks to the north in what of Mars (where the Roman army used to parade and now ˌˌrades), continues on to the Pantheon and then to us. We live ˌ was once the vestibule to a huge complex of baths, libraries, ˌncert halls, theaters and, of course, the Pantheon, all built by one Marcus Agrippa, the John D. Rockefeller of his day, who wanted to celebrate his wealth and the emperor Augustus' glory, in about that order.

The penthouse is a small, square, rickety, twentieth-century addition to the palace; it is built around a squalid inner court, more than compensated for by two huge terraces at right angles to one another. From the south terrace we can see a corner of the Victor Emmanuel monument, a snowy-white wedding cake in the form of an antique Remington Rand typewriter, a bit of the Campidoglio, the Aventine Hill, the Synagogue, the dome of San Carlo and, directly below us, the eighteenth-century Teatro Argentina, where *The Barber of Seville* was booed on opening night while Rossini sat next door at Bernasconi's eating pastry. The pastry is still good at Bernasconi's, and the theater still functions.

From the west terrace, Sant' Andrea della Valle (Act i, *Tosca*) fills the sky to the left. We are so close to it that we can identify the wild flowers that grow out of cracks in the dome and lantern. Next, we can see, in the distance, like a gray-ridged soccer ball, Saint Peter's; then Sant' Agnese in the Piazza Navona; and, finally, best of all, the fantastic, twisted spire of Sant' Ivo alla Sapienza, Borromini's literally off-the-sky masterpiece.

In summer, when the red sun starts to drop behind Saint Peter's, birds suddenly appear—real birds, swifts, as opposed to the pigeons that use the terraces as a convention hall. From sunset to dark, the swifts do Jonathan Livingston Seagull free falls and glides with great panache. In winter, they vanish. Although Roman winters are not severe, last January a heavy snow fell on Rome and the single lemon tree on the terrace outside my bedroom window was covered with two inches of snow, framing each gold lemon in white.

Question I most hear: Why have you spent almost a third of your life in this Roman apartment? I quote Howard Hughes. When asked why he had ended up a long-nailed recluse in a sealed hotel room, he croaked with perfect candor: "I just sort of drifted into it." That's almost always the real answer to everything. But there are, of course, a thousand other reasons. Although I have a house in the unfashionable Hollywood Hills, and my subject, as a writer, is the United States, I have never had a proper human-scale village life anywhere on earth except in this old Roman street.

In Los Angeles we live in our cars, en route to houses where a pool is a pool is a pool and there are only three caterers and you shall have no other. A car trip to Chalet Gourmet on the Sunset Strip is a chore not an adventure. But a trip down our street is a trip indeed.

By and large, the shops are exactly like the shops of two thousand years ago, as preserved at Pompeii and Ostia: a single deep room with a wide door that can be shuttered and a counter at the back. Produce is displayed on benches or tables on the sidewalk or in the doorway. Fresh food in season is all-important here, and we talk a lot about food. As I write, we are sweating out the first peas. No one will eat a frozen one deliberately. Sex and politics are not obsessive; but health care is. We are all hypochondriacs. In fact, Italians buy more pills per capita than any other nationality. Luckily, they usually forget to take them. In our pharmacy with its eighteenth-century rococo boiserie, there is a comfortable chair where you sit while the pharmacist takes your blood pressure, not once but, properly, twice. I trust him more than any doctor. We all do.

I know every shopkeeper in this street, and just about every old resident. We seldom have names for one another, but everyone knows everything about everyone else, and we—the older crowd, of course—study each other closely for signs of debility. We are all diagnosticians. The vegetable man's tremor is worse, we say to one another at the butcher's. We discuss Parkinson's among the Tuscan sausages. The carpenter goes by, green of face—he has been drunk for a week. We feel sorry for the wife. *Peccato* — "a shame." But the daughter is married to the hardware-store owner and pregnant again. Will she need a second cesarean?

The herb shop has been doing business for over a century: dark wooden paneling and drawers, porcelain apothecary jars with gilt Latin inscriptions. Two old brothers—not old when I first came—preside over this two-thousand-year-old anthology of herbal remedies and pleasures. An old woman suddenly turns to me, in a state of ecstasy. "I am ninety years old," she says, "and everything in the street's changed except this place. It's the same! The same!" That, I fear, is the retrograde joy of our village life.

Even our lunatics are always the same. For decades now, the flower woman goes out each day in the bus to the cemetery to steal flowers from new graves; then she returns to the street and sits in the doorway of a deconsecrated church and makes up bouquets (as I write, daffodils, tulips, and mimosa). We are worried lately about her loss of the last set of dentures. True, they did not fit, but she now looks really awful. She has also, overambitiously, acquired more plastic bags than she can carry at one time. This is worrying.

Then there is the small man in the three-piece suit with the homburg, whose brim is always curled up like Chaplin's bowler. As he makes his daily progress down the street, he looks very worried. Suddenly he will come up to you and ask the time. "What time is it?" he murmurs urgently. You tell him. He nods three times; patters off. He has never been heard to say anything else.

Beneath us in the palace, a mother and son live. She is a charming lady, somewhat bent now from a decade of sleeping in a chair so that she can watch over her son, who was sent home from the sort of institution that Governor Reagan shut down in California. At the full moon, he howls; at the dark of the moon, he storms our door, shouting for us to release the beautiful women covered with jewels locked inside. Currently, he has a full beard and looks like Karl Marx.

Next to the palace is a hole in the wall: the most popular *fruttateria* in town. Like swifts at sundown, motorcycled adolescents park on the sidewalk and swig fruit drinks. Efforts to get them on drugs or alcohol have so far failed: This is an old city.

Literature? Two blocks to our north, back of the Pantheon, Thomas Mann lived and wrote *Buddenbrooks.* Nearby, George Eliot stayed at the Minerva Hotel. Ariosto lived in Pantheon Square; Stendhal was close to us. I myself have written at least a part of every one of my books from *Washington, D.C.,* to *Lincoln* in this flat. The last chapters of *Lincoln* were composed on the dining room table.

Italo Calvino now lives at the north of the street, and we *cher confrère* one another when we meet. Then we move on. Yes, we are all growing old. But a baby's being born to the wife of the hardware-store owner, while a half-dozen babies of a few years ago are now men and women. So—plenty more where we came from. That is the lesson of the street. Meanwhile, what time is it? Free the bejeweled ladies held captive! Daffodils, tulips, and mimosa! What time is it? The same.

ARCHITECTURAL DIGEST

*October 1985*

# PART II

# CHAPTER 15

# THE BOOKCHAT
# OF HENRY JAMES

On the evening of January 12, 1905, President and Mrs. Theodore Roosevelt held a reception for the diplomatic corps. After the reception, a limited number of grandees were given a dinner; among those so distinguished was Henry James, who was staying across the street at the house of Henry Adams. The reception had been boycotted by Adams himself, who found it impossible to finish a sentence once the voluble president was wound up. But Adams sent over his houseguests, James, John La Farge, and Augustus Saint-Gaudens.

The confrontation between Master and Sovereign contained all the elements of high comedy. Each detested the other. James regarded Roosevelt as "a dangerous and ominous jingo" as well as "the mere monstrous embodiment of unprecedented and resounding noise" while Theodore

Rex, as the Adams circle dubbed him, regarded the novelist as "a miserable little snob" and, worse, "effete." As it turned out, snob and jingo were each on his best behavior that night, and James, in a letter to Mary Cadwalader Jones, noted that the president was "a really extraordinary creature for native intensity, veracity and *bonhomie.*" What TR thought of his guest on that occasion is not recorded, but he could never have been approving of James, who had settled in England, had never roughed it, had never ridden, roughly, up Kettle Hill (to be renamed San Juan, since no one could be the hero of anything so homely as a kettle).

===

But the true high comedy of that January evening was that the two great men were meeting not as literary lion and president but as book reviewer and author reviewed. Seven years earlier, James had given Roosevelt (an indefatigable writer of echoing banality) a very bad review in the English paper *Literature.* Although reviews were not signed in those days, concerned authors could almost always find out who had done them in, and if the wielder of the axe were a writer of James's fame, the secret could never have been kept for long.

James begins, blandly,

Mr. Theodore Roosevelt appears to propose—[the first verb is a hint of fun to come] in *American Ideals and Other Essays Social and Political*—to tighten the screws of the national consciousness as they have never been tightened before. The national consciousness for Mr. Theodore Roosevelt is, moreover, at the best a very fierce affair.

James then suggests that this approach is not only overwrought but vague.

It is "purely as an American," he constantly reminds us, that each of us must live and breathe. Breathing, indeed, is a trifle; it is purely as Americans that we must think, and all that is wanting to the author's demonstration is that he shall give us a receipt for the process. He labours, however . . . under the drollest confusion of mind.

All in all, TR was saintly to put such an un-American reviewer at his dinner table, separated from his own intensely American self by a single (American) lady. Of course, in April 1898, James could not have known that the author, a mere assistant secretary of the Navy, was glory-bound. Yet if he had, the Jamesian irony (so like that of his friends John Hay and Henry Adams, and so deeply deplored, in retrospect, by the President) could not resist serving up such quotes as,

"The politician who cheats or swindles, or the newspaperman who lies in any form, should be made to feel that he is an object of scorn for all honest men." That is luminous; but, none the less, "an educated man must not go into politics as such; he must go in simply as an American . . . or he will be upset by some other American with no education at all . . ." A better way perhaps than to barbarize the upset—already, surely, sufficiently unfortunate—would be to civilize the upsetter.

For James, whatever useful insights that politician Roosevelt might have are undone "by the puerility of his simplifications."

===

The Library of America has seen fit to publish in one volume all of James's book reviews on American and English writers, as well as a number of other meditations on literature. To read the book straight through (1413 pages of highly uneven bookchat) is to get to know Henry James in a way that no biographer, not even the estimable Leon Edel, the present editor, can ever capture. Here one can study the evolution of James's taste and mind.

As a critic, James began far too young. From age twenty-three to twenty-five, he was reviewing everything that came to hand for the *North American Review* and *The Nation.* He was still an American resident: He did not set out from the territory for old Europe until John Hay, then at the *New York Tribune,* sent him to Paris as a general correspondent (1875–1876). By 1878 he was settled in England, his domicile to the end.

In London, he wrote *French Poets and Novelists,* and a long study of Hawthorne. In 1878, "I had ceased to 'notice' books—that faculty seemed to diminish for me, perversely, as my acquaintance with books grew." Fortunately for the readers of this volume, in 1898 James became a householder. In need of money, he went back to book reviewing for a year or two and produced some of his most interesting pieces. Finally, in 1914, he wrote *The New Novel,* in which he threaded his way, as best he could, among the young Turks—H. G. Wells and Arnold Bennett and (they meet at last! the great tradition) D. H. Lawrence, whose *Sons and Lovers* James remarks "hang(s) in the dusty rear of Wells and Bennett."

≡

There is a lifelong prejudice in James against the slice-of-life novel as opposed to the consciously shaped work of art. (Yet, paradoxically, he is enthralled by Balzac, on whom he was lecturing in 1905.) In that sense, he is the snob that Theodore Rex called him. Although he is most comfortably at home in fairly high society, his true subject is displaced, classless, innocent Americans with money, at sea in old Europe which, at the beginning of his career, he saw as beguiling and dangerous and, at the end, quite the reverse: Old Europe was no match for young America's furious energy and ruthless, mindless exertion of force. But the milieu of *Sons and Lovers* depressed him, as did that of Thomas Hardy, whose village oafs he quotes at length in a review of *Far from the Madding Crowd.*

James, justifiably, hated dialect novels, American or English. Hardy's "inexhaustible faculty for spinning smart dialogue makes him forget that dialogue in a story is after all but episode. . . ." The book "is inordinately diffuse, and, as a piece of narrative, singularly inartistic. The author has little sense of proportion, and almost none of composition." Worse, the book is much too long (this from James the First not yet Old Pretender), thanks to the tradition of the three-volume novel. "Mr. Hardy has gone astray very cleverly, and his superficial novel is a really curious imitation of something better."

Yet with George Eliot, whom he admires, he notes of *Silas Marner,* "Here, as in all George Eliot's books, there is a middle life and a low life; and here, as usual, I prefer the low life." This is James, aged twenty-three, indicating that Eliot does not feel quite at home in middle life much less high life. But twenty years later, a wiser James sums up the great novelist:

What *is* remarkable, extraordinary—and the process remains inscrutable and mysterious—is that this quiet, anxious, sedentary, serious, invalidical English lady, without animal spirits, without adventures or sensations, should have made us believe that nothing in the world was alien to her; should have produced such rich, deep, masterly pictures of the multiform life of man.

In the notorious case of Walt Whitman one can observe James's evolution from disdainful, supercilious, but observant youth to mystified, awed admirer. Of *Drum-Taps* he writes (1865),

It has been a melancholy task to read this book; and it is a still more melancholy one to write about it. . . . It exhibits the effort of an essentially prosaic mind [and] frequent capitals are the only marks of verse in Mr. Whitman's writing . . . As a general principle, we know of no circumstance more likely to impugn a writer's earnestness than the adoption of an anomalous style. He must have something very original to say if none of the old vehicles will carry his thoughts. Of course, he *may* be surprisingly original. Still, presumption is against him. . . . This volume is an offense against art.

He scolds Whitman for crowning himself the national poet: "You cannot entertain and exhibit ideas; but, as we have seen, you are prepared to incarnate them." This was the point, of course, to Whitman; but young James can only groan, "What would be bald nonsense, and dreary platitudes in anyone else becomes sublimity in you." A quarter century later, Whitman has become "the good Walt." Of *Calamus* (Whitman's highly adhesive letters to the working-class lad Pete Doyle): "There is not even by accident a line with a hint of style—it is all flat, familiar, affectionate, illiterate colloquy" yet "the record remains, by a mysterious marvel, a thing positively delightful. If we can ever find out why, it must be another time. The riddle meanwhile is a neat one for the sphinx of democracy to offer." When the riddle was "solved" by Dr. Kinsey in 1948, the Republic had a nervous breakdown, which continues to this day.

===

One is constantly surprised by the spaciousness of James's sympathies as he got older. In time, the vulgarity of Whitman was seen for what it is, the nation itself made flesh. Edith Wharton in *A Backward Glance* writes,

It was a joy to me to discover that James thought [Whitman] the greatest of American poets. *Leaves of Grass* was put into his hands, and all that evening we sat rapt while he wandered from "The Song of Myself" to "When Lilacs Last in the Dooryard Bloom'd."

On the other hand, no sentiment was ever exempt from his critical irony, and James could not resist exclaiming, at the reading's end, "Oh, yes, a great genius; undoubtedly a very great genius! Only one cannot help deploring his too-extensive acquaintance with foreign languages." Like the late Tennessee Williams, Whitman loved foreign phrases and usually got them wrong.

The fact that one is never told just how James's heroes make their money was neither coyness nor disdain: It was simply a blank, as he confessed in 1898: "Those who know [business] are not the men to paint it; those who might attempt it are not the men who know it." One wonders what his friend the author of *The Rise of Silas Lapham* thought of the alleged absence in our literature of the businessman—of "the magnificent theme *en disponibilité.*"

James was very much interested in "the real world"; and not without a certain shrewdness in political matters. Surprisingly, he reviews in *The Nation* (1875) Charles Nordhoff's *The Communistic Societies of the United States, from Personal Visit and Observation, Etc.*, a book once again in print. Nordhoff was a Prussian-born American journalist who covered the Civil War for the *New York Herald.* In the 1870s, he decided to investigate applied communism in the United States, as demonstrated by the Oneida, Amana, Mount Lebanon, and Shaker groups. "Hitherto," Nordhoff writes, "very little, indeed almost nothing definite and precise, has been made known concerning these societies; and Communism remains loudly but very vaguely spoken of, by friends as well as enemies, and is commonly either a word of terror or contempt in the public prints." *Tout ça change,* as the good Walt might have said.

For over a century, communism has been the necessary enemy of our republic's ruling oligarchy. Yet before 1917, communism was not associated with totalitarianism or Russian imperialism or the iron rule of a *nomenklatura.* Communism was simply an economic theory, having to do with greater efficiency in production as a result of making those who did the work the owners. James grasps this principle rather better than most of his contemporaries, and he commends Nordhoff for his ability to show us

communistic life from the point of view of an adversary to trades-unions, and to see whether in the United States, with their vast area for free experiments in this line, it might not offer a better promise to workingmen than mere coalitions to increase wages and shorten the hours of labor.

Although he thinks Nordhoff (probably a closet German socialist) tends to "dip his pen into rose-color," James is intrigued by the material efficiency of the societies. He is also appalled by their social customs: Some are celibate, some swap mates. "One is struck, throughout Mr. Nordhoff's book, with the existence in human nature of lurking and unsuspected strata, as it were, of asceticism, of the capacity for taking a grim satisfaction in dreariness." Then James adds with characteristic sly irony: "Remember that there are in America many domestic circles in which, as compared with the dreariness of private life, the dreariness of Shakerism seems like boisterous gaiety."

Predictably, James deplores the "attempt to organize and glorify the detestable tendency toward the complete effacement of privacy in life and thought everywhere so rampant with us nowadays." Would that he could move among us today and revel in our government's call for obligatory blood and urine tests. "But [lack of privacy] is the worst fact chronicled in Mr. Nordhoff's volume, which, for the rest, seems to establish fairly that, under certain conditions and with strictly rational hopes, communism in America may be a paying experiment." Now that I have revived these lines, James, already banned in certain public libraries for pornography (*The Turn of the Screw*, what else?), can now be banned as a communist. A small price, all in all, to pay for freedom.

As the complete Henry James is to be republished in the Library of America, it is amusing to read what he has to say of the other novelists in the series, also, more to the point, what he does *not* have to say. For instance, there is no mention of Jack London, whose best work was done before James died in 1916. Although the inner life of a dog in the Arctic circle might not have appealed to the Master, James might have found a good deal to ponder in *The Sea Wolf* and *The Iron Heel*. Stephen Crane appears in his letters (and his life; he liked him, not her) but there is no reference to Crane anywhere in the flow, the torrent, of names like Alger, Bazley, Channing, Fletcher, Gannett, Sedley, Spofford, Whitney . . .

James's study of Hawthorne is famous; it is also full of evasive high praise: James did not care for romance; yet Hawthorne's one "real" novel, *The Blithedale Romance,* which is not, to me, a romance at all, is to James notable for its "absence of satire . . . of its not aiming in the least at satire." I thought the whole thing a splendid send-up of Brook Farm, and Zenobia a truly comic character. In any case, Hawthorne is the only American novelist to whom James pays full homage.

He does do justice to his friend Howells. He certainly applauds Howells's ability for "definite notation"; yet he doesn't much care for Howells's ladies. But Howells is not writing about the drawing room; he writes about men, work, business. Bartley Hubbard is a splendid invention—the newspaperman as inventor—while the story of Silas Lapham does for the paint business what Balzac so magically did for paper. James (writing for lady readers?) looks elsewhere.

Fenimore Cooper is mentioned, blandly, twice, while Melville is dismissed in the following line: "the charming *Putnam* [magazine] of faraway years—the early fifties . . . the prose, as mild and easy as an Indian summer in the woods, of Herman Melville, of George William Curtis and 'Ik Marvel.' "

Mark Twain, with whom Henry James was forced so titanically to contest in the pages of Van Wyck Brooks (James lost), is mentioned only once: "In the day of Mark Twain there is no harm in being reminded that the absence of drollery may, at a stretch, be compensated by the presence of sublimity." So much for the Redskin Chief from the Paleface Prince. Finally, James praises his friend Mrs. Wharton, with the no longer acceptable but perfectly apt characterization: "of the masculine conclusion tending to crown the feminine observation."

=====

James is on happier ground when dealing with English and French writers. As for the Russians, except for Turgenev, whom he knew, they seem to have made no impression. There is a perfunctory nod to Tolstoy (1914) in a survey of the new novel. Tolstoy is "the great Russian" whose influence can be detected in the world of Wells and Bennett. The name Dostoevsky is added to a list of deliberately disparate writers. Admittedly, by then (1897) James had ceased to be a working reviewer as opposed to being an occasional writer of "London Notes" for *Harper's,* with a tendency "to pass judgment in parenthesis," something he maintained that the critic by him admired, Matthew Arnold, never did.

Henry James's admiration of the never entirely fashionable and often despised Balzac is to his eternal credit as a critic. On the other hand, his attitude to Flaubert, whom he knew, is very odd indeed. He thought that Flaubert (whom he could see all 'round, he once declared) had produced a single masterpiece; and that that was that. He seems not to have got the point to *Sentimental Education*, the first truly "modern novel," which demonstrated for the first time in literature the fact that life is simply drift; and though *Bouvard and Pécuchet* is unfinished, the notion is still splendid if droll (James, who was, in life, the essence of drollery, did not much care for levity in the novel, *tant pis*).

It is always easy to make fun of book reviewers, and what we take now to be, in our superior future time, their mistakes. But he *is* wrongheaded when he writes (1876): "Putting aside Mme. Sand, it is hard to see who, among the French purveyors of more or less ingenious fiction, is more accomplished than [M. Octave Feuillet]. There are writers who began with better things—Flaubert, Gustave Droz, and Victor Cherbuliez—but they have lately done worse, whereas M. Feuillet never falls below himself." Flaubert had been lately doing such "worse" things as publishing *Sentimental Education* (1869) and *The Temptation of Saint Anthony* (1874), while *Three Tales* would be published the next year. James had read one of them:

Gustave Flaubert has written a story about the devotion of a servant-girl to a parrot, and the production, highly finished as it is, cannot, on the whole, be called a success. We are perfectly free to call it flat, but I think it might have been interesting; and I, for my part, am extremely glad he should have written it; it is a contribution to our knowledge of what can be done—or what cannot. Ivan Turgenev has written a tale about a deaf and dumb serf and a lap-dog, and the thing is touching, loving, a little masterpiece. He struck the note of life where Flaubert missed it—he flew in the face of a presumption and achieved a victory.

James is never on thinner ice than when he goes on about "presumptions," as if the lovely art was nothing but constant presuming. In *The Art of Fiction* (1884), he is more open: "There is no impression of life, no manner of seeing it and feeling it, to which the plan of the novel may not offer a place; you have only to remember that talents so dissimilar as those of Alexandre Dumas and Jane Austen, Charles Dickens and Gustave

Flaubert have worked in this field with equal glory." *Equal* is not the right word; but *glory* is.

The usually generous James cannot entirely accept Flaubert, the one contemporary writer whose dedication to his art was comparable to his own. Although James goes on and on about the greatness of *Madame Bovary,* he cannot, simultaneously, resist undermining it:

Nothing will ever prevent Flaubert's heroine from having been an extremely minor specimen, even of the possibilities of her own type, a twopenny lady, in truth, of an experience so limited that some of her chords, it is clear, can never be sounded at all. It is a mistake, in other words, to speak of any feminine nature as consummately exhibited, that is exhibited in so small a number of its possible relations. Give it three or four others, we feel moved to say—"then we can talk."

Plainly, Flaubert's version of a "twopenny lady" is not the portrait of a lady of the sort that James could happily "talk" about. I suspect, finally, that James not only did not like Flaubert's writing but that he had serious moral reservations about French literature in general: "There are other subjects," he wrote plaintively, "than those of the eternal triangle of the husband, the wife and the lover." Among critics, James is hardly a master; rather, he is a master of the novel who makes asides that are, often, luminous; as often, not.

===

In the spring of 1948, I was received in Paris by André Gide at 1 *bis* Rue Vaneau. I spent a pleasant hour with the Master and John Lehmann, my English publisher. We talked of literature, of national differences, of changing fashions, of James. Then Gide (the proud translator of Conrad) asked, "What is it that you Americans—and English—see in Henry James?" I could only stammer idiocies in my schoolboy French. Ironically, now, nearly forty years later, I find myself explaining to the young that there was once a famous French writer named André Gide. Fashions change but, as George Santayana remarked, "it would be insufferable if they did not." Each generation has its own likes and dislikes and ignorances.

In our postliterary time, it is hard to believe that once upon a time a life could be devoted to the perfecting of an art form, and that of all the art forms the novel was the most—exigent, to use a modest word. Today the novel is either a commodity that anyone can put together, or it is an artifact, which means nothing or anything or everything, depending on one's literary theory. No longer can it be said of a writer, as James said of Hawthorne in 1905: "The grand sign of being a classic is that when you have 'passed,' as they say at examinations, you have passed; you have become one once for all; you have taken your degree and may be left to the light and the ages." In our exciting world the only light cast is cast by the cathode-ray tube; and the idea of "the ages" is, at best, moot— mute?

THE NEW YORK REVIEW OF BOOKS
*November 6, 1986*

# CHAPTER 16

# WILLIAM DEAN HOWELLS

1

On May 1, 1886, American workers in general and Chicago's workers in particular decided that the eight-hour workday was an idea whose time had come. Workers demonstrated, and a number of factories were struck. Management responded in kind. At McCormick Reaper strikers were replaced by "scabs." On May 3, when the scabs left the factory at the end of a long traditional workday, they were mobbed by the strikers. Chicago's police promptly opened fire and America's gilded age looked to be cracking open.

The next night, in Haymarket Square, the anarchists held a meeting presided over by the mayor of Chicago. A thousand workers listened to many thousands of highly incendiary words. But all was orderly until His

Honor went home; then the police "dispersed" the meeting with that tact which has ever marked Hog City's law-enforcement officers. At one point, someone (never identified) threw a bomb; a number of policemen and workers were killed or wounded. Subsequently, there were numerous arrests and in-depth grillings.

Finally, more or less at random, eight men were indicted for "conspiracy to murder." There was no hard evidence of any kind. One man was not even in town that day while another was home playing cards. By and large, the great conservative Republic felt no compassion for anarchists, even the ones who had taken up the revolutionary game of bridge; worse, an eight-hour workday would drive a stake through the economy's heart.

On August 20, a prejudiced judge and jury found seven of the eight men guilty of murder in the first degree; the eighth man (who had not been in town that night) got fifteen years in the slammer because he had a big mouth. The anarchists' counsel, Judge Roger A. Pryor, then appealed the verdict to the Supreme Court.

$$=$$

During the short hot summer of 1886, the case was much discussed. The peculiar arbitrariness of condemning to death men whom no one had seen commit a crime but who had been heard, at one time or another, to use "incendiary and seditious language" was duly noted in bookish circles. Yet no intellectual of the slightest national importance spoke up. Of America's famous men of letters, Mark Twain maintained his habitual silence on any issue where he might, even for an instant, lose the love of the folks. Henry James was in London, somewhat shaken by the recent failure of not only *The Bostonians* but *The Princess Casamassima*. The sad young man of *The Princess Casamassima* is an anarchist, who has had, like James himself that year, "more news of life than he knew what to do with." Although Henry Adams's education was being conducted that summer in Japan, he had made, the previous year, an interesting comment on the American political system—or lack of one:

Where no real principle divides us . . . some queer mechanical balance holds the two parties even, so that changes of great numbers of voters leave no trace in the sum total. I suspect the law will someday be formulated that in democratic societies, parties tend to an equilibrium.

As the original entropy man, Adams had to explain, somehow, the election of the Democrat Grover Cleveland in 1884, after a quarter-century of Republican abolitionist virtue and exuberant greed.

Of the Republic's major literary and intellectual figures (the division was not so clearly drawn then between town, as it were, and gown), only one took a public stand. At forty-nine, William Dean Howells was the author of that year's charming "realistic" novel, *Indian Summer;* he was also easily the busiest and smoothest of America's men of letters. Years before, he had come out of Ohio to conquer the world of literature; and had succeeded. He had been the first outlander to be editor of the *Atlantic Monthly.* In the year of the Haymarket Square riot, he had shifted the literary capital of the country from Boston to New York when he took over *Harper's Monthly,* for which he wrote a column called "The Editor's Study"; and a thousand other things as well. That summer Howells had been reading Tolstoy. In fact, Tolstoy was making a socialist out of him; and Howells was appalled by Chicago's judge, jury, and press. He was also turning out his column, a hasty affair by his own best standards but positively lapidary by ours.

---

In the September 1886 issue of *Harper's,* Howells, who had done so much to bring Turgenev and Tolstoy to the attention of American readers, decided to do the same for Dostoevsky, whose *Crime and Punishment* was then available only in a French translation. Since Howells had left school at fifteen, he had been able to become very learned indeed. He had taught himself Latin and Greek; learned Spanish, German, Italian, and French. He read many books in many languages, and he knew many things. He also wrote many books; and many of those books are of the first rank. He was different from us. Look at Dean run! Look at Dean read! Look-say what Dean writes!

While the Haymarket Square riots were causing Howells to question the basis of the American "democracy," he was describing a Russian writer who had been arrested for what he had written and sent off to Siberia where he was taken out to be shot but not shot—the kind of fun still to be found to this very day south of our borders where the dominoes roam. As Howells proceeded most shrewdly to explain Dostoevsky to American readers, he rather absently dynamited his own reputation for the next century. Although he admired Dostoevsky's art, he could find little

similarity between the officially happy, shadowless United States and the
dark Byzantine cruelties of czarist Russia:

It is one of the reflections suggested by Dostoevsky's book that whoever struck a
note so profoundly tragic in American fiction would do a false and mistaken thing.
. . . Whatever their deserts, very few American novelists have been led out to be
shot, or finally expelled to the rigors of a winter at Duluth. . . . We invite our
novelists, therefore, to concern themselves with the more smiling aspects of life,
which are the more American, and to seek the universal in the individual rather
than the social interests. It is worth while even at the risk of being called common-
place, to be true to our well-to-do actualities.

This was meant to be a plea for realism. But it sounded like an invitation
to ignore the sort of thing that was happening in Chicago. Ironists are
often inadvertent victims of their own irony.

≡

On November 2, 1887, the Supreme Court denied the anarchists' appeal.
On November 4, Howells canvased his literary peers. What to do? The
dedicated abolitionist of thirty years earlier, George William Curtis, whose
lecture *Political Infidelity* was a touchstone of political virtue, and the
noble John Greenleaf Whittier agreed that something must be done; but
they were damned if they were going to do it. So the belletrist who had
just enjoined the nation's scribblers to address themselves to the smiling
aspects of a near-perfect land hurled his own grenade at the courts.

In an open letter to the *New York Tribune* (published with deep reluctance by the ineffable Whitelaw Reid) Howells addressed all right-thinking
persons to join with him in petitioning the governor of Illinois to commute
the sentences. No respectable American man of letters had taken on the
American system since Thomas Paine, who was neither American nor
respectable. Of the Supreme Court, Howells wrote, it "simply affirmed the
legality of the forms under which the Chicago court proceeded; it did not
affirm the propriety of trying for murder men fairly indictable for conspiracy alone . . ." The men had been originally convicted of "constructive
conspiracy to commit murder," a star-chamberish offense, based on their
fiery language, and never proved to be relevant to the actual events in
Haymarket Square. In any case, he made the point that the Supreme
Court

by no means approved the principle of punishing them because of their frantic opinions, for a crime which they were not shown to have committed. The justice or injustice of their sentence was not before the highest tribunal of our law, and unhappily could not be got there. That question must remain for history, which judges the judgment of courts, to deal with; and I, for one, cannot doubt what the decision of history will be.

Howells said that the remaining few days before the men were executed should be used to persuade the governor to show mercy. In the course of the next week the national press attacked Howells, which is what the American system has a national press for.

On November 11, four of the men, wearing what look like surgical gowns, were hanged. Of the others, one had committed suicide and two had had their sentences commuted. On November 12, Howells, undaunted by the national hysteria now directed as much against him as against the enemies of property, wrote another public letter:

It seems of course almost a pity to mix a note of regret with the hymn of thanksgiving for blood growing up from thousands of newspapers all over the land this morning; but I reflect that though I write amidst this joyful noise, my letter cannot reach the public before Monday at the earliest, and cannot therefore be regarded as an indecent interruption of the Te Deum.

By that time journalism will not have ceased, but history will have at least begun. All over the world where civilized men can think and feel, they are even now asking themselves, For what, really, did those four men die so bravely? Why did one other die so miserably? Next week the journalistic theory that they died so because they were desperate murderers will have grown even more insufficient than it is now for the minds and hearts of dispassionate inquirers, and history will make the answer to which she must adhere for all time, *They died in the prime of the first Republic the world has ever known, for their opinions' sake* [original emphasis].

Howells then proceeds to make the case against the state's attorney general and the judge and the shrieking press. It is a devastating attack: "I have wished to deal with facts. One of these is that we had a political execution in Chicago yesterday. The sooner we realize this, the better for us." As polemic, Howells's letter is more devastating and eloquent than Emile Zola's *J'accuse;* as a defense of the right to express unpopular opinions, it is the equal of what we mistakenly take to be the thrust of Milton's *Areopagitica.*

Unfortunately, the letter was not published in the year 1887. Eventually, the manuscript was found in an envelope addressed to Whitelaw Reid. The piece had been revised three times. It is possible that a copy had been sent to Reid who had not published it; it is possible that Howells had had second thoughts about the possibilities of libel actions from judge and state's attorney general; it is possible that he was scared off by the general outcry against him. After all, he had not only a great career to worry about but an ill wife and a dying daughter. Whatever the reason, Howells let his great moment slip by. Even so, the letter-not-sent reveals a powerful mind affronted by "one of those spasms of paroxysmal righteousness to which our Anglo-Saxon race is peculiarly subject . . ." He also grimly notes that this "trial by passion, by terror, by prejudice, by hate, by newspaper" had ended with a result that has won "the approval of the entire nation."

I suspect that the cautious lifetime careerist advised the Tolstoyan socialist to cool it. Howells was in enough trouble already. After all, he was the most successful magazine editor in the country; he was a best-selling novelist. He could not afford to lose a public made up mostly of ladies. So he was heard no more on the subject. But at least he, alone of the country's writers, had asked, publicly, on November 4, 1887, that justice be done.

Howells, a master of irony, would no doubt have found ironic in the extreme his subsequent reputation as a synonym for middle-brow pusillanimity. After all, it was he who was the spiritual father of Dreiser (whom he did nothing for, curiously enough) and of Stephen Crane and Harold Frederic and Frank Norris, for whom he did a very great deal. He managed to be the friend and confidant of both Henry James and Mark Twain, quite a trick. He himself wrote a half-dozen of the Republic's best novels. He was learned, witty, and generous.

Howells lived far too long. Shortly before his death at the age of eighty-four, he wrote his old friend Henry James: "I am comparatively a dead cult with my statues cut down and the grass growing over me in the pale moonlight." By then he had been dismissed by the likes of Sinclair Lewis as a dully beaming happy writer. But then Lewis knew as little of the American literary near-past as today's writers know, say, of Lewis. If Lewis had read Howells at all, he would have detected in the work of this

American realist a darkness sufficiently sable for even the most lost-and-found of literary generations or, as Howells wrote James two years after the Haymarket Square riots: "After fifty years of optimistic content with 'civilization' and its ability to come out all right in the end, I now abhor it, and feel that it is coming out all wrong in the end unless it bases itself on a real equality." What that last phrase means is anyone's guess. He is a spiritual rather than a practical socialist. It is interesting that the letter was written in the same year that Edward Bellamy's *Looking Backward: 2000–1887* was published. The ideas of Robert Owen that Howells had absorbed from his father (later a Swedenborgian like Henry James, Sr.) were now commingled with the theories of Henry George, the tracts of William Morris, and, always, Tolstoy. Howells thought that there must be a path through the political jungle of a republic that had just hanged four men for their opinions; he never found it. But as a novelist he was making a path for himself and for others, and he called it realism.

2

On Thanksgiving Day 1858, the twenty-one-year-old Howells was received at the court of the nineteen-year-old first lady of Ohio, Kate Chase, a handsome ambitious motherless girl who acted as hostess to her father the governor, Salmon P. Chase, a handsome ambitious wifeless man who was, in Abraham Lincoln's thoughtful phrase, "on the subject of the Presidency, a little insane."

Howells had grown up in Ohio;* his father was an itinerant newspaper editor and publisher. He himself was a trained printer as well as an ambitious but not insane poet. Under the influence of Heine, he wrote a number of poems; one was published in the *Atlantic Monthly*. He was big in Cleveland. Howells and Kate got on well; she teased him for his social awkwardness; he charmed her as he charmed almost everyone. Although he wrote about the doings of the Ohio legislature for the Cincinnati *Gazette,* he preferred the company of cultivated ladies to that of politicians. A passionate autodidact, he tended to prefer the company of books

---

*The two principal biographies of Howells are Edwin H. Cady's magisterial two-volume study (*The Road to Realism* and *The Realist at War*) and Kenneth S. Lynn's shrewd *William Dean Howells*. Needless to say, they are out of print. Or were. I am told that this review helped get Cady back in print. Lynn is still out.

to people. But through Kate he met future presidents and was served at table by his first butler.

In a sense the Chase connection was the making of Howells. When Lincoln won the Republican presidential nomination in 1860, Howells was chosen, somewhat improbably, to write a campaign biography of the candidate. Characteristically, Howells sent a friend to Springfield to chat with the subject of his book; he himself never met Lincoln. He then cobbled together a book that Lincoln did not think too bad. One suspects that he did not think it too good, either. Shortly before the president was shot, he withdrew the book for the second time from the Library of Congress: nice that he did not have a copy of it on the coffee table in the Blue Room, but then Lincoln was so unlike, in so many ways, our own recent sovereigns.

Once Lincoln was president, Chase became secretary of the treasury. Chase proposed that the campaign biographer be rewarded with a consulate. But nothing happened until Howells himself went to Washington where he found an ally in Lincoln's very young and highly literary second secretary, John Hay, who, with the first secretary, John Nicolay, finally got Howells the consulate at Venice.

It is odd to think that a writer as curiously American as Howells should have been shaped by the Most Serene Republic at a bad moment in that ancient polity's history—the Austrian occupation—rather than by the United States at the most dramatic moment in that polity's history: the Civil War. Odd, also, that Howells managed, like the other two major writers of his generation, to stay out of the war. Neither Mark Twain nor Henry James rushed to the colors.

=

Since Howells had practically no official work to do, he learned Italian and perfected his German and French. He turned out poems that did not get printed in the *Atlantic*. "Not one of the MSS you have sent us," wrote the editor, "swims our seas." So Howells went off the deep end, into prose. He wrote Venetian sketches of great charm; he was always to be a good —even original—travel writer. Where the previous generation of Irving and Hawthorne had tended to love far too dearly a ruined castle wall, Howells gave the reader not only the accustomed romantic wall but the laundry drying on it, too. The Boston *Advertiser* published him.

Then came the turning point, as Howells termed it, in his life. He had acquired a charming if garrulous wife, who talked even more than Mark Twain's wife, or as Twain put it, when Elinor Howells entered a room "dialogue ceased and monologue inherited its assets and continued the business at the old stand." Howells wrote a serious study of the Italian theater called "Recent Italian Comedy," which he sent to the *North American Review,* the most prestigious of American papers, coedited by his friend James Russell Lowell and Charles Eliot Norton. At the time, Boston and Cambridge were in the throes of advanced Italophilia. Longfellow was translating Dante; and all the ladies spoke of Michelangelo. Lowell accepted the essay. Howells was now on his way, as a *serious* writer.

After nearly four years in Venice, which he did not much care for, Howells returned to New York. With a book of sketches called *Venetian Life* at the printers, he went job hunting. He was promptly hired by E. L. Godkin to help edit *The Nation.* Not long after, he was hired by the *Atlantic Monthly* as assistant to the editor; then from 1871 to 1881 he was editor in chief. In Boston, Howells was now at the heart of an American literary establishment which had no way of knowing that what looked to be eternal noon was actually Indian summer—for New England.

Just before Howells had gone to Venice, he had made the rounds of New England's literary personages. He had met Holmes and Hawthorne whom he had liked; and Emerson whom he had not. Now, at the *Atlantic,* every distinguished writer came his editorial way; and soon he himself would be one of them. But what sort of writer was he to be? Poetry was plainly not his métier. Journalism was always easy for him, but he was ambitious. That left the novel, an art form which was not yet entirely "right." The American product of the 1860s was even less "aesthetic" than the English and neither was up to the French, who were, alas, sexually vicious, or to the Russians, who were still largely untranslated except for the Paris-based Turgenev. At this interesting moment, Howells had one advantage denied his contemporaries, always excepting Henry James. He could read—and he had read—the new Europeans in the original. He went to school to Zola and Flaubert. Realism was in the European air, but how much reality could Americans endure? Out of the tension between the adventurousness of Flaubert and the edgy reticence of Hawthorne came the novels of William Dean Howells.

From Heine, Howells had learned the power of the plain style. Mark Twain had also learned the same lesson—from life. Whereas the previous generation of Melville and Hawthorne had inclined to elevated, even "poetic" prose, Twain and Howells and James the First were relatively straightforward in their prose and quotidian in their effects—no fauns with pointed ears need apply. In fact, when Howells first met Hawthorne, he shyly pointed to a copy of *The Blithedale Romance* and told the great man that that was his own favorite of the master's works. Hawthorne appeared pleased; and said, "The Germans like it, too."

But realism, for Howells, had its limits. He had grown up in a happy if somewhat uncertain environment: His father was constantly changing jobs, houses, religions. For a writer, Howells himself was more than usually a dedicated hypochondriac whose adolescence was shadowed by the certainty that he had contracted rabies which would surface in time to kill him at sixteen. Like most serious hypochondriacs, he enjoyed full rude health until he was eighty. But there were nervous collapses. Also, early in life, Howells had developed a deep aversion to sexual irregularity, which meant any form of sexuality outside marriage. When his mother befriended a knocked-up seamstress, the twelve-year-old Howells refused to pass her so much as the salt at table.

In Venice he could not get over the fact that there could be no social intercourse of any kind with unmarried girls (unlike the fun to be had with The American Girl, soon to be celebrated not only by Henry James but by Howells himself), while every married woman seemed bent on flinging even the purest of young bachelors into the sack. Doubtless, he kept himself chaste until marriage. But he railed a good deal against European decadence, to the amusement of the instinctively more worldly, if perhaps less operative Henry ("Oh, my aching back!") James, who used to tease him about the latest descriptions of whorehouses to be found in French fiction. Nevertheless, for a writer who was to remain an influence well into the twentieth century, an aversion to irregular sexuality was not apt to endear him to a later generation which, once it could put sex into the novel, proceeded to leave out almost everything else. Where the late-nineteenth-century realistic novel might be said to deal with social climbing, the twentieth-century novel has dealt with sexual climbing, an activity rather easier to do than to write about.

═══

The Library of America now brings us four of Howells's novels written between 1875 and 1886. Before the publications of these four novels,

Howells had already published his first novel *Their Wedding Journey* (1871); his second novel *A Chance Acquaintance* (1873); as well as sketches of Italy, people, and yet another personage. Elinor Mead Howells was a cousin of President Rutherford (known to all good Democrats as Rather-fraud) B. Hayes. So the campaign biographer of Lincoln, duly and dutifully and dully, wrote a book called *Sketch of the Life and Character of Rutherford B. Hayes* (1876). Thanks to Cousin Hayes, Howells was now able to reward those who had helped him. James Russell Lowell was sent to London as American ambassador.

Of the books written before *A Foregone Conclusion* (the first of the four now reissued), the ever-polite but never fraudulent Turgenev wrote Howells in 1874:

Accept my best thanks for the gracious gift of your delightful book *Their Wedding Journey,* which I have read with the same pleasure experienced before in reading *A Chance Acquaintance* and *Venetian Life.* Your literary physiognomy is a most sympathetic one; it is natural, simple and clear—and in the same time—it is full of unobtrusive poetry and fine humor. Then—I feel the peculiar American stamp on it—and that is not one of the least causes of my relishing so much your works.

This was written in English. In a sense, Turgenev is responding to Howells's championing of his own work (Howells had reviewed *Lisa* and *Rudin*) but he is also responding to a sympathetic confrere, a young writer whom he has influenced though not so much as has "the peculiar American stamp." Unfortunately, Turgenev never lived to read the later books. It would be interesting to see what he might have made of *A Modern Instance,* a book as dark and, at times, as melodramatic as a novel by Zola, whose *L'Assommoir* Turgenev disliked.

$$=$$

*A Foregone Conclusion* (1875) has, as protagonist, the—what else?—American consul at Venice. The consul is a painter (young writers almost always make their protagonists artists who practice the one art that they themselves know nothing about: It's the light, you see, in Cimabue). The consul attracts a young priest, Don Ippolito, who wants to emigrate to America and become an inventor. It is no accident that practically the first building in Washington to be completed in imperial marble splendor was the Patent Office. Don Ippolito is a sort of Italian Major Hoople. The inventions don't really work but he keeps on because "Heaven only knows what kind of inventor's Utopia our poor, patent-ridden country appeared to him in those dreams of his, and I can but dimly figure it to myself." Here the auctorial "I" masquerades as the "I" of the consul, Ferris, who is otherwise presented in the objective third person. Howells has not entirely learned Turgenev's lesson: stay out of the narrative. Let the characters move the narration and the reader. Howells's native American garrulousness—and tendentiousness—occasionally breaks in.

Enter, inexorably, middle-aged American lady and daughter—Mrs. Vervain and Florida. This was four years before Howells's friend sicked *Daisy Miller* on to a ravished world. But then The American Girl was to be a Howells theme, just as it was to be James's and, later, and in a much tougher way, Mrs. Wharton's. As every writer then knew, the readers of novels were mostly women, and they liked to read about the vicissitudes of young women, preferably ladies. But while James would eventually transmute his American girls into something that Euripides himself might find homely (e.g., Maggie Verver), Howells tends, gently, to mock. Incidentally, I do not believe that it has ever before been noted that the portrait of Florida is uncannily like Kate Chase.

It is a foregone conclusion that American girl and American mother ("the most extraordinary combination of perfect fool and perfect lady, I ever saw") will miss the point to Don Ippolito and Venice and Europe, and that he will miss the point to them. Don Ippolito falls in love with Florida. The Americans are horrified. How can a priest sworn to celibacy . . . ? Since they are Protestants, the enormity of his fall from Roman Catholic grace is all the greater. Although Don Ippolito is perfectly happy to give up the Church, they will not let him. Mother and daughter flee. As for Ferris, he has misunderstood not only Don Ippolito but Florida's response to him. Don Ippolito dies—with the comment to Ferris, "You would never see me as I was."

The consul goes home to the States and joins the army. Like so many other characters in the works of those writers who managed to stay out of the Civil War, Ferris has a splendid war: "Ferris's regiment was sent to a part of the southwest where he saw a good deal of fighting and fever and ague" (probably a lot easier than trying to get a job at the *Atlantic*). "At the end of two years, spent alternately in the field and the hospital, he was riding out near the camp one morning in unusual spirits, when two men in butternut fired at him: one had the mortification to miss him; the bullet of the other struck him in the arm. There was talk of amputation at first . . .' Pre-dictaphone and word processor, it was every writer's nightmare that he lose his writing arm. But, worse, Ferris is a painter: *he can never crosshatch again.* Broke, at a loose end, he shows an old picture at an exhibition. Florida sees the picture. They are reunited. Mrs. Vervain is dead. Florida is rich. Ferris is poor. What is to be done?

===

It is here that the avant-garde realism of Howells shoves forward the whole art of the popular American novel: "It was fortunate for Ferris, since he could not work, that she had money; in exalted moments he had thought this a barrier to their marriage; yet he could not recall anyone who had refused the hand of a beautiful girl because of the accident of her wealth, and in the end, he silenced his scruples." This is highly satisfying.

Then Howells, perhaps a bit nervous at just how far he has gone in the direction of realism, tosses a bone of, as it were, marzipan to the lady-reader: "It might be said that in many other ways he was not her equal; but one ought to reflect how very few men are worthy of their wives in any sense." Sighs of relief from many a hammock and boudoir! How well he knows the human heart.

Howells smiles at the end; but the smile is aslant, while the point to the tragedy (not Ferris's, for he had none, but that of Don Ippolito) is that, during the subsequent years of Ferris's marriage, Don Ippolito "has at last ceased to be even the memory of a man with a passionate love and a mortal sorrow. Perhaps this final effect in the mind of him who has realized the happiness of which the poor priest vainly dreamed is not the least tragic phase of the tragedy of Don Ippolito."

This coda is unexpectedly harsh—and not at all smiling. A priest ought not to fall in love. It is a foregone conclusion that if you violate the rules governing sexuality, society will get you, as Mrs. Wharton would demonstrate so much more subtly in *The Age of Innocence;* and Henry James would subtly deny since he knew, in a way that Howells did not, that the forbidden cake could be both safely eaten and kept. It is an odd irony that the donnée on which James based *The Ambassadors* was a remark that the fifty-seven-year-old Howells made to a friend in Paris: No matter what, one ought to have one's life; that it was too late for him, personally, but for someone young . . ." Don't, at any rate, make *my* mistake," Howells said. "Live!"

═══

Kenneth S. Lynn has put the case, persuasively to my mind, that the "happy endings" of so many of Howells's novels are deliberately "hollow" or ironic. After all, it was Howells who had fashioned the, to Edith Wharton, "lapidary phrase": Americans want tragedies with happy endings. There are times when Howells's conclusion—let's end with a marriage and live happily ever after—carry more formidable weight than the sometimes too-lacquered tragic codas of James: "We shall never be again as we were." The fact is that people are almost always exactly as they were; and they will be so again and again, given half a chance.

At forty-four, the highly experienced man of letters began his most ambitious novel, *A Modern Instance*. Although the story starts in a New England village, the drama is acted out in the Boston of Howells's professional life, and the very unusual protagonist is a newspaperman on the make who charms everyone and hoodwinks a few; he also puts on too much weight, steals another man's story, and makes suffer the innocent young village heiress whom he marries. In a sense, Howells is sending himself up; or some dark side of himself. Although Bartley Hubbard is nowhere in Howells's class as a writer, much less standard-bearer for Western civilization, he is a man who gets what he wants through personal charm, hard work, and the ability to write recklessly and scandalously for newspapers in a way that the young William Randolph Hearst would capitalize on at century's end, thus making possible today's antipodean "popular" press, currently best exemplified by London's giggly newspapers.

Unlike Howells, or the Howells that we think we know, Bartley is sexually active; he is not about to make the Howells-Strether mistake. He *lives* until he is murdered by a man whom he may have libeled in a western newspaper. It would have been more convincing if an angry husband had been responsible for doing him in, but there were conventions that Howells felt obliged to observe, as his detractors, among them Leslie Fiedler, like to remind us. Mr. Fiedler writes:

Only in *A Modern Instance,* written in 1882 [*sic:* 1881], does Howells deal for once with a radically unhappy marriage; and here he adapts the genteel-sentimental pattern which had substituted the bad husband (his Bartley Hubbard has "no more moral nature than a baseball") for the Seducer, the long-suffering wife for the Persecuted Maiden or fallen woman.*

Mr. Fiedler, of course, is—or was in 1960—deeply into "the reality of dream and nightmare, fantasy and fear," and for him Howells is "the author of flawlessly polite, high-minded, well-written studies of untragic, essentially eventless life in New England—the antiseptic upper-middle-brow romance. Yet his forty books [*sic:* he means novels, of which Howells wrote thirty-five; there are close to one hundred books], in which there are no seductions and only rare moments of violence, are too restrictedly 'realistic', too . . . ," *et cetera.*

Mr. Fiedler gets himself a bit off the hook by putting those quotes around the word realistic. After all, Howells had developed an aesthetic of the novel: and if he preferred to shoot Bartley offstage, why not? The classic tragedians did the same. He also inclined to Turgenev's view that the real drama is in the usual. Obviously, this is not the way of the romantic writer but it is a no less valid way of apprehending reality than that of Melville or Faulkner, two writers Howells would have called "romancers," about as much a term of compliment with him as "too unrestrictedly 'realistic' " is to Mr. Fiedler. Without rehashing the tired Redskin versus Paleface debate of the 1940s, it should be noted that there is something wrong with a critical bias that insists upon, above all else, "dream and nightmare, fantasy and fear" but then when faced with the genuine article in, say, the books of William Burroughs or James Purdy or Paul Bowles starts to back off, nervously, lighting candles to The Family and all the other life-enhancing if unsmiling aspects of American life that do *not* cause AIDS or social unrest.

===

Whatever our romantic critics may say, Bartley Hubbard is an archetypal American figure, caught for the first time by Howells: the amiable, easygoing bastard, who thinks nothing of taking what belongs to another. Cer-

---

*Leslie Fiedler, *Love and Death in the American Novel* (New York: Criterion Books, 1960; Stein and Day, 1975).

tainly Mark Twain experienced the shock of recognition when he read the book: "You didn't intend Bartley for me but he *is* me just the same . . .' " James, more literary, thought the character derived from Tito, in the one (to me) close-to-bad novel of George Eliot, *Romola.* In later years Howells said that he himself was the model. Who was what makes no difference. There is only one Bartley Hubbard, and he appears for the first time in the pages of a remarkable novel that opened the way to Dreiser and to all those other realists who were to see the United States plain. The fact that there are no overt sexual scenes in Howells ("no palpitating divans," as he put it) does not mean that sexual passion is not a powerful motor to many of the situations, as in life. On the other hand, the fact that there are other motors—ambition, greed, love of power, simply extend the author's range and make him more interesting to read than most writers.

In this novel, Howells is interesting on the rise of journalism as a "serious" occupation. "There had not yet begun to be that talk of journalism as a profession which has since prevailed with our collegians . . ." There is also a crucial drunk scene in which Bartley blots his copybook with Boston; not to mention with his wife. It is curious how often Howells shows a protagonist who gets disastrously drunk and starts then to fall. Mark Twain had a dark suspicion that Howells always had *him* in mind when he wrote these scenes. But for Mr. Fiedler, "drunkenness is used as a chief symbol for the husband's betrayal of the wife." Arguably, it would have been better (and certainly more manly) if Bartley had cornholed the Irish maid in full view of wife and child, but would a scene so powerful, even *existential,* add in any way to the delicate moral balances that Howells is trying to make?

After all, Howells is illuminating a new character in American fiction, if not life, who, as "he wrote more than ever in the paper . . . discovered in himself that dual life, of which every one who sins or sorrows is sooner or later aware: that strange separation of the intellectual activity from the suffering of the soul, by which the mind toils on in a sort of ironical indifference to the pangs that wring the heart; the realization that in some ways his brain can get on perfectly well without his conscience." This is worthy of the author of *Sentimental Education;* it is also the kind of insight about post-Christian man that Flaubert so often adverted to, indirectly, in his own novels and head-on in his letters.

≡

*The Rise of Silas Lapham* (1885) begins with Bartley Hubbard brought back to life. It is, obviously, some years earlier than the end of *A Modern Instance*. Bartley is interviewing a self-made man called Silas Lapham who has made a fortune out of paint. Lapham is the familiar diamond in the rough, New England Jonathan style. He has two pretty daughters, a sensible wife, a comfortable house; and a growing fortune, faced with all the usual hazards. Howells makes the paint business quite as interesting as Balzac made paper making. This is not entirely a full-hearted compliment to either; nevertheless, each is a novelist fascinated by the way the real world works; and each makes it interesting to read about.

In a sense, Silas Lapham's rise is not unlike that of William Dean Howells: from a small town to Boston back street to Beacon Street on the Back Bay. But en route to the great address there are many lesser houses and Howells is at his best when he goes house hunting—and building. In fact, one suspects that, like Edith Wharton later, he would have made a splendid architect and interior decorator. In a fine comic scene, a tactful architect (plainly the author himself) guides Lapham to Good Taste. " 'Of course,' resumed the architect, 'I know there has been a great craze for black walnut. But it's an ugly wood . . .' " All over the United States there must have been feminine gasps as stricken eyes were raised from the page to focus on the middle distance where quantities of once-beauteous black shone dully by gaslight; but worse was to come: ". . . and for a drawing room there is really nothing like white paint. We should want to introduce a little gold here and there. Perhaps we might run a painted frieze round under the cornice—garlands of roses on a gold ground; it would tell wonderfully in a white room." From that moment on, no more was black walnut seen again in the parlors of the Republic, while the sale of white paint soared; gold, too.

The rise of Lapham's house on Beacon Hill is, in a sense, the plot of the book, as well as the obvious symbol of worldly success. Howells makes us see and feel and smell the house as it slowly takes shape. Simultaneously, a young man called Tom Corey wants to work for Lapham. Since Corey belongs to the old patriciate, Lapham finds it hard to believe Corey is serious. But the young man is sincere; he really likes the old man. He must also work to live. There are romantic exchanges between him and the two daughters; there is an amiable mix-up. Finally, Tom says that it is Penelope not her sister whom he wants to marry. Mr. and Mrs. Lapham are bemused. In the world of the Coreys they are a proto–Maggie and Jiggs couple.

Corey takes Lapham to a grand dinner party where the old man gets drunk and chats rather too much. It is the same scene, in a sense, as Bartley's fall in the earlier novel but where Bartley could not have minded less the impression he made, Lapham is deeply humiliated; and the fall begins. He loses his money; the new house burns down; by then, the house is an even more poignant character than Lapham, and the reader mourns the white-and-gold drawing room gone to ash. But there is a happy enough ending. Maggie and Jiggs return to the Vermont village of their origin (which they should never have left?) while Corey marries Penelope.

It would be easy to point out traits in Penelope's character which finally reconciled all her husband's family and endeared her to them. These things continually happen in novels; and the Coreys, as they had always promised themselves to do, made the best, and not the worst, of Tom's marriage. . . . But the differences remained uneffaced, if not uneffaceable, between the Coreys and Tom Corey's wife.

The young couple move from Boston. Then Howells shifts from the specific to the general:

It is certain that our manners and customs go for more in life than our qualities. The price that we pay for civilization is the fine yet impassable differentiation of these. Perhaps we pay too much; but it will not be possible to persuade those who have the difference in their favor that this is so. They may be right; and at any rate the blank misgiving, the recurring sense of disappointment to which the young people's departure left the Coreys is to be considered. That was the end of their son and brother for them; they felt that; and they were not mean or unamiable people.

This strikes me as a subtle and wise reading of the world—no, not *a* world but *the* world; and quite the equal of James or Hardy.

Whether or not this sort of careful social reading is still of interest to the few people who read novels voluntarily is not really relevant. But then today's "serious" novel, when it is not reinventing itself as an artifact of words and signs, seldom deals with the world at all. One is no longer shown a businessman making money or his wife climbing up or down the social ladder. As most of our novelists now teach school, they tend to tell us what it is like to be a schoolteacher, and since schoolteachers have been taught to teach others to write only about what they know, they tell us what they know about, too, which is next to nothing about the way the rest of the population of the Republic lives.

In a sense, if they are realists, they are acting in good faith. If you don't know something about the paint business you had better not choose a protagonist who manufactures paint. Today, if the son of an Ohio newspaper editor would like to be a novelist, he would not quit school at fifteen to become a printer, and then learn six languages and do his best to read all the great literary figures of the present as well as of the past so that he could introduce, say, Barthes or Gadda to the American public while writing his own novels based on a close scrutiny of as many classes of society as he can get to know. Rather, he would graduate from high school; go on to a university and take a creative writing course; get an M.A. for having submitted a novel (about the son of an Ohio editor who grew up in a small town *and found out about sex* and wants to be a writer and so goes to a university where he submits, etc.).

Then, if he is truly serious about a truly serious literary career, he will become a teacher. With luck, he will obtain tenure. In the summers and on sabbatical, he will write novels that others like himself will want to teach just as he, obligingly, teaches their novels. He will visit other campuses as a lecturer and he will talk about his books and about those books written by other teachers to an audience made up of ambitious young people who intend to write novels to be taught by one another to the rising generation and so on and on. What tends to be left out of these works is the world. World gone, no voluntary readers. No voluntary readers, no literature—only creative writing courses and English studies, activities marginal (to put it tactfully) to civilization.*

3

Civilization was very much on Howells's mind when he came to write *Indian Summer* (1886). He deals, once more, with Americans in Italy. But

*I know that this passage will be said to have said that no one who teaches school has ever written a good novel. Read it again.

this time there are no Don Ippolitos. The principals are all Americans in Florence. A middle-aged man, Theodore Colville, meets, again, Mrs. Bowen, a lady who once did not marry him when he wanted to marry her. She married a congressman. She has a young daughter, Effie. She is a widow.

Colville started life as an architect, a suitable occupation for a Howells character; then he shifted to newspaper publishing, an equally suitable profession. In Des Vaches, Indiana, he published, successfully, the *Democrat-Republican* newspaper. Although he lost a race for Congress, he has received from former political opponents "fulsome" praise. Like most American writers Howells never learned the meaning of the word *fulsome.* Colville then sold his newspaper and went to Europe because "he wanted to get away, to get far away, and with the abrupt and total change in his humor he reverted to a period in his life when journalism and politics and the ambition of Congress were things undreamed of." He had been young in Italy, with a Ruskinian interest in architecture; he had loved and been rejected by Evelina—now the widow Bowen. He looks at Florence: "It is a city superficially so well known that it affects one somewhat like a collection of views of itself: they are from the most striking points, of course, but one has examined them before, and is disposed to be critical of them." The same goes for people one has known when young.

Mrs. Bowen has a beautiful young friend named Imogene. Colville decides that he is in love with Imogene, and they drift toward marriage. There are numerous misunderstandings. Finally, it is Mrs. Bowen not Imogene who is in love with Colville. The drama of the three of them (a shadowy young clergyman named Morton is an undelineated fourth) is rendered beautifully. There are many unanticipated turns to what could easily have been a simpleminded romantic novella.

When Colville is confronted with the thought of his own great age (forty-one), he is told by a very old American expatriate:

At forty, one has still a great part of youth before him—perhaps the richest and sweetest part. By that time the turmoil of ideas and sensations is over; we see clearly and feel consciously. We are in a sort of quiet in which we peacefully enjoy. We have enlarged our perspective sufficiently to perceive things in their true proportion and relation; we are no longer tormented with the lurking fear of death, which darkens and imbitters our earlier years; we have got into the habit of life; we have often been ailing and we have not died . . .

Finally, "we are put into the world to be of it." Thus, Howells strikes the
Tolstoyan note. Yes, he is also smiling. But even as *Indian Summer* was
being published, its author was attacking the state of Illinois for the
murder of four workmen. He also sends himself up in the pages of his own
novel. A Mrs. Amsden finds Colville and Imogene and Effie together after
an emotional storm. Mrs. Amsden remarks that they form an interesting,
even dramatic group:

"Oh, call us a passage from a modern novel," suggested Colville, "if you're in a
romantic mood. One of Mr. James's."
    "Don't you think we ought to be rather more of the great world for that? I
hardly feel up to Mr. James. I should have said Howells. Only nothing happens
in that case."

For this beguiling modesty Howells no doubt dug even deeper the grave
for his reputation. How can an American novelist who is ironic about
himself ever be great? In a nation that has developed to a high art advertising, the creator who refuses to advertise himself is immediately suspected
of having no product worth selling. Actually, Howells is fascinated with
the interior drama of his characters, and quite a lot happens—to the reader
as well as to the characters who are, finally, suitably paired: Imogene and
Mr. Morton, Colville and Mrs. Bowen.
    The Library of America has served William Dean Howells well. Al-
though the spiritual father of the library, Edmund Wilson, did not want
this project ever to fall into the hands of the Modern Language Association, all four of the novels in the present volume bear the proud emblem
of that association. One can only assume that there are now fewer scholars
outside academe's groves than within. I found no misprints; but there are
eccentricities.
    In *A Modern Instance* (p. 474) we read of "the presidential canvas of
the summer"; then (p. 485) we read "But the political canvass . . ." Now
a tent is made of canvas and an election is a canvass of votes. It is true
that the secondary spelling of "canvass" is "canvas" and so allowable;
nevertheless, it is disturbing to find the same word spelled two ways within
eleven pages. On page 3 the variant spelling "ancles" is used for "ankles."
On page 747 Howells writes "party-colored statues" when, surely, "parti-
colored" was nineteenth-century common usage as opposed to the

Chaucerian English "party." Of course, as the editors tell us, "In nineteenth-century writings, for example, a word might be spelled in more than one way, even in the same work, and such variations might be carried into print."

Anyway, none of this is serious. There are no disfiguring footnotes. The notes at the back are for the most part helpful translations of foreign phrases in the text. The chronology of Howells's life is faultless but, perhaps, skimpy. For those who are obliged for career reasons to read Howells, this is a useful book. For those who are still able to read novels for pleasure, this is a marvelous book.

For some years I have been haunted by a story of Howells and that most civilized of all our presidents, James A. Garfield. In the early 1870s Howells and his father paid a call on Garfield. As they sat on Garfield's veranda, young Howells began to talk about poetry and about the poets that he had met in Boston and New York. Suddenly, Garfield told him to stop. Then Garfield went to the edge of the veranda and shouted to his Ohio neighbors. "Come over here! He's telling about Holmes, and Longfellow, and Lowell, and Whittier!" So the neighbors gathered around in the dusk; then Garfield said to Howells, "Now go on."

Today we take it for granted that no living president will ever have heard the name of any living poet. This is not, necessarily, an unbearable loss. But it is unbearable to have lost those Ohio neighbors who actually read books of poetry and wanted to know about the poets.

For thirty years bookchat writers have accused me of having written that the novel is dead. I wrote no such thing but bookchat writers have the same difficulty extracting meaning from writing as presidents do. What I wrote was, "After some three hundred years the novel in English has lost the general reader (or rather the general reader has lost the novel), and I propose that he will not again recover his old enthusiasm." Since 1956, the audience for the serious (or whatever this year's adjective is) novel has continued to shrink. Arguably, the readers that are left are for the most part involuntary ones, obliged by the schools to read novels that they often have little taste for. The fact that a novelist like Howells—or even Bellow —is probably no longer accessible to much of anyone would be bearable if one felt that the sense of alternative worlds or visions or—all right, Leslie

—nightmares, fantasies, fears could be obtained in some other way. But movies are no substitute while television is, literally, narcotizing: The human eye was not designed to stare at a light for any length of time. Popular prose fictions are still marketed with TV and movie tie-ins, but even the writers or word processors of these books find it harder and harder to write simply enough for people who don't really know how to read.

Obviously, there is a great deal wrong with our educational system, as President Reagan recently, and rather gratuitously, noted. After all, an educated electorate would not have elected him president. It is generally agreed that things started to go wrong with the schools after the First World War. The past was taught less and less, and Latin and Greek ceased to be compulsory. Languages were either not taught or taught so badly that they might just as well not have been taught at all while American history books grew more and more mendacious, as Frances Fitzgerald so nicely described,* and even basic geography is now a nonsubject. Yet the average "educated" American has been made to believe that, somehow, the United States must lead the world even though hardly anyone has any information at all about those countries we are meant to lead. Worse, we have very little information about our own country and its past. That is why it is not really possible to compare a writer like Howells with any living American writer because Howells thought that it was a good thing to know as much as possible about his own country as well as other countries while our writers today, in common with the presidents and paint manufacturers, live in a present without past among signs whose meanings are uninterpretable.

≡

Edmund Wilson's practical response was to come up with the idea of making readily available the better part of American literature; hence, the Library of America. It is a step in the right direction. But will this library attract voluntary readers? Ultimately—and paradoxically—that will depend on the schools.

Since no one quite knows what a university ought to do, perhaps *that* should be the subject of our educational system. What variety of things should *all* educated people know? What is it that we don't know that we

*America Revised* (New York: Atlantic–Little, Brown, 1979).

need to know? Naturally, there is a certain risk in holding up a mirror to the system itself (something the realistic novelist always used to do) because one is apt to see, glaring back, the face of Caliban or, worse, plain glass reflecting glass. But something must now be done because Herzen's terrible truth is absolutely true: "The end of each generation is itself."

THE NEW YORK REVIEW OF BOOKS
*October 27, 1983*

# CHAPTER 17

# THE GOLDEN BOWL
# OF HENRY JAMES

1

A century ago, Mrs. Henry Adams confided to her diary: "It is high time Harry James was ordered home by his family. He is too good a fellow to be spoiled by injudicious old ladies in London—and in the long run they would like him all the better for knowing and living in his own country. He had better go to Cheyenne and run a hog ranch. The savage notices of his Hawthorne in American papers, all of which he brings me to read, are silly and overshoot the mark in their bitterness, but for all that he had better not hang around Europe much longer if he wants to make a lasting literary reputation." That same year the egregious Bret Harte observed, sadly, that Henry James "looks, acts, thinks like an Englishman and writes like an Englishman."

But the thirty-seven-year-old James was undeterred by public or private charges of un-Americanism; he had every intention of living the rest of a long and productive life in England. Since he was, in the phrase of his older brother William, like all the Jameses a native only of the James family, the Wyoming pig farmer that might have been preferred rooting, as it were (Oh, as it were!—one of his favorite phrases: a challenge to the reader to say, As it were *not?*), for those truffles that are to be found not beneath ancient oak trees in an old country but in his own marvelous and original consciousness. James did nothing like an Englishman—or an American. He was a great fact in himself, a new world, a *terra incognita* that he would devote all his days to mapping for the rest of us. In 1880 James's American critics saw only the fussy bachelor expatriate, growing fat from too much dining out; none detected the sea change that was being undergone by what had been, until then, an essentially realistic American novelist whose subject had been Americans in Europe, of whom the most notorious was one Daisy Miller, eponymous heroine of his first celebrated novel (1878).

But by 1880, James was no longer able—or willing?—to render American characters with the same sureness of touch. For him, the novel must now be something other than the faithful detailing of familiar types engaged in mating rituals against carefully noted backgrounds. Let the Goncourts and the Zolas do that sort of thing. James would go further, much as Flaubert had tried to do; he would take the usual matter of realism and heighten it; and he would try to create something that no writer in English had ever thought it possible to do with a form as inherently loose and malleable as the novel: He would aim at perfection. While James's critics were complaining that he was no longer American and could never be English, James was writing *The Portrait of a Lady,* as nearly perfect a work as a novel can be. From 1881, James was the master of the novel in English in a way that no one had ever been before; or has ever been since. Even that Puritan divine, F. R. Leavis, thought *The Portrait* "one of the great novels of the English language."

═══

Over the next twenty years, as James's novels got longer and longer, they became, simultaneously and oddly, more concentrated. There are fewer and fewer characters (usually Americans in a European setting but Americans at some psychic distance from the great republic) while the backgrounds are barely sketched in. What indeed *are* the spoils of the house Poynton? James never tells us what the "old things" are that mother and son fight for to the death. Balzac would have given us a catalogue, and most novelists would have indicated something other than an impression of a vague interior perfection. As James more and more mastered his curious art, he relied more and more on the thing *not* said for his essential dramas; in the process, the books become somewhat closer to theater than to the novel-tradition that had gone before him. Famously, James made a law of the single viewpoint; and then constantly broke it. In theory, the auctorial "I" of the traditional novel was to be banished so that the story might unfold much like a play except that the interpretation of scenes (in other words, who is thinking what) would be confined to a single observer if not for an entire book, at least for the scene at hand. Although James had sworn to uphold forever his own Draconian law, on the first page of *The Ambassadors,* where we meet Strether, the principal consciousness of the story and the point of view from which events are to be seen and judged, there is a startling interference by the author, Mr. James himself, who states, firmly: "The principle I have just mentioned . . ." Fortunately, no more principles are mentioned by the atavistic "I."

There is the familiar joke about the three styles of Henry James: James the First, James the Second, and the Old Pretender. Yet there are indeed three reigns in the master's imagined kingdom. James I is the traditional nineteenth-century novelist, busy with the usual comings and goings of the ordinary fiction writer; James II is the disciplined precise realist whose apotheosis is *The Portrait of a Lady.* From 1890 to 1895 there is a break in the royal line: James turns to the theater; and most beautifully fails. Next comes the restoration. James returns in triumph to the novel—still James II (for purposes of simile, Charles II as well); and then, at the end, the third James, the Old Pretender, the magician who, unlike Prospero, breaks not his staff but a golden bowl.

═══

After 1895, there is a new heightening of effect in James's narratives; he has learned from the theater to eliminate the nonessential but, paradoxically, the style becomes more complex. The Old Pretender's elaborateness is due, I should think, to the fact that he had now taken to dictating his novels to a series of typewriter operators. Since James's conversational style was endlessly complex, humorous, unexpected—euphemistic where most people are direct and suddenly precise where avoidance or ellipsis is usual —the last three novels that he produced (*The Ambassadors,* 1903; *The*

*Wings of the Dove,* 1902; and *The Golden Bowl,* 1904) can be said to belong as much to the oral tradition of narrative as to the written.

James was fifty-seven when he started *The Ambassadors* and sixty-one when he completed *The Golden Bowl.* In those five years he experienced a late flowering without precedent among novelists. But then he was more than usually content in his private life. He had moved out of London; and he had established himself at the mayoral Lamb House in Rye. If there is an eternal law of literature, a *pleasant* change of house for a writer will produce an efflorescence. Also, at sixty, James fell in love with a young man named Jocelyn Persse. A charming Anglo-Irish man-about-town, Persse was not at all literary; and somewhat bewildered that James should be in his thrall. But, for James, this attractive young extrovert must have been a great improvement over his predecessor in James's affection, Hendrik Andersen, the handsome sculptor of megalomaniac forms. Andersen had been trouble. Persse was good company: "I rejoice greatly in your breezy, heathery, grousy—and housey, I suppose—adventures and envy you, as always, your exquisite possession of the Art of Life which beats any Art of mine hollow." This "love affair" (with the Master, quotes are always necessary because we lack what Edith Wharton would call the significant data) had a most rejuvenating effect on James, and the first rapturous days with Persse coincided with the period in which he was writing *The Golden Bowl.*

=

A decade earlier (November 28, 1892) Henry James sketched in his note-book the first design for *The Golden Bowl:* ". . . a father and daughter —an only daughter. The daughter—American of course—is engaged to a young Englishman, and the father, a widower and still youngish, has sought in marriage at exactly the same time an American girl of very much the same age as his daughter. Say he has done it to console himself in his abandonment—to make up for the loss of the daughter, to whom he has been devoted. I see a little tale, *n'est-ce pas?*—in the idea that they all shall have married, as arranged, with this characteristic consequence—that the daughter fails to hold the affections of the young English husband, whose approximate mother-in-law the pretty young second wife of the father will now have become." James then touches upon the commercial aspect of the two marriages: "young Englishman" and "American girl" have each been bought. They had also known each other before but could not marry because each lacked money. Now "they spend as much of their time together as the others do, and for the very reason that the others spend it. The whole situation works in a kind of inevitable rotary way—in what would be called a vicious circle. The *subject* is really the pathetic simplicity and good faith of the father and daughter in their abandonment . . . he peculiarly paternal, she passionately filial." On Saint Valentine's Day 1895, James again adverts to the story which now demands to be written, though he fears "the adulterine element" might be too much for his friend William Dean Howells's *Harper's Magazine*. 'But may it not be simply a question of *handling* that?'

Seven years later, James was shown a present given the Lamb family by King George I: It is a golden bowl. The pieces have now begun to come together. James has just completed, in succession, *The Ambassadors* and *The Wings of the Dove*. Comfortably settled in the garden room at Lamb House (later to be inhabited by E. F. Benson's dread Miss Mapp and then the indomitable Lucia; later still, to be blown up in World War II), James wrote, in slightly more than a year, what he himself described to his American publisher as "distinctly the most done of my productions—the most composed and constructed and completed. . . . I hold the thing the solidest, as yet, of all my fictions." The "as yet" is splendid from a sixty-one-year-old writer. Actually, *The Golden Bowl* was to be the last novel that he lived to complete, and it has about it a kind of spaciousness—and even joy—that the other novels do not possess. In fact, *pace* F. R. Leavis, I do not think James has in any way lost his sense of life or let slip "his moral taste" (what a phrase!).

2

When I first read *The Golden Bowl*, I found Amerigo, the Prince, most sympathetic. I still do. I also found—and find—Charlotte the most sympathetic of the other characters; as a result, I don't think that her creator does her justice or, perhaps, he does her too much conventional justice, a black cloth on his head as he sentences her to a living death. But then James *appears* to accept entirely the code of the class into which he has placed both himself in life and the characters in his book. This means that the woman must always be made to suffer for sexual transgression while the man suffers not at all or, in the case of the Prince, very little—although the renewed and intensified closeness to Maggie may well be a rarefied punishment that James only hints at when, for the last time, he shuts the door to the golden cage on Husband and Wife Victrix. For once, in James, the heiress has indisputably won; and the other woman, the enchantress, is routed.

I barely noticed Adam Verver the first time I read the book. I saw him as an aged (at forty-seven!) proto–J. Paul Getty, out "to rifle the Golden Isles" in order to memorialize himself with a museum back home—typical tycoon behavior, I thought; and thought no more. But now that he could be my younger brother (and Maggie an exemplary niece), I regard him with new interest—not to mention suspicion. What is he up to? He is plainly sly; and greedy; and although the simultaneous possession and ingestion of confectionary is a recurrent James theme, my God, how this father and daughter manage to both keep and devour the whole great world itself! They buy the handsome Prince, a great name, *palazzi*, the works. They buy the brilliant Charlotte. But they do not know that the two beauties so triumphantly acquired are actually a magnificent pair, destined to be broken up by Maggie when she discovers the truth, and, much as Fanny Assingham smashes the golden bowl into three parts and pedestal, Maggie breaks the adulterine situation into three parts: Amerigo, Charlotte, and Adam (she is, plainly, pedestal). Then, adulterine world destroyed, Maggie sends Adam and Charlotte home to American City at the heart of the great republic.

Best of all, from Maggie's viewpoint, Charlotte does not know for certain even then that Maggie knows all—a real twist to the knife for in a James drama *not* to know is to be the sacrificial lamb. Once Mr. and Mrs. Adam Verver have gone forever, the Prince belongs absolutely to Maggie. One may or may not like Maggie (I don't like what she does or, indeed, what she is) but the resources that she brings to bear, first *to know* and then *to act*, are formidable. Yet there is a mystery in my second experience of the novel which was not present thirty years ago. What, finally, does Adam Verver know? And what, finally, does he do? Certainly father and daughter are so perfectly attuned that neither has to *tell* the other anything at all about the unexpected pair that they have acquired for their museum. But does Maggie lead him? Or does he manage her? Can it be that it is Adam who pulls all the strings, as befits the rich man who has produced a daughter and then bought her—and himself—a life that even he is obliged to admit is somewhat selfish in its perfection?

===

As one rereads James's lines in his notebook, the essentially rather banal short story that he had in mind has changed into a wonderfully luminous drama in which nothing is quite what it seems while James's pious allusion to the subject as "really the pathetic simplicity and good faith of the father and daughter in their abandonment" is plain nonsense. James is now giving us monsters on a divine scale.

I think the clue to the book is the somewhat, at first glance, over-obvious symbol of the golden bowl. Whatever the king's christening gift was made of, James's golden bowl proves to be made not of gold but of gilded crystal, not at all the same thing; yet the bowl is massy and looks to be gold. The bowl is first seen in a Bloomsbury shop by Charlotte, who wants to buy a wedding present for her friend Maggie. Charlotte cannot afford anything expensive, but then, as she remarks to her lover, Maggie's groom-to-be, " 'She's so modest,' she developed—'she doesn't miss things. I mean if you love her—or, rather, I should say, if she loves you. She lets it go.' " The Prince is puzzled by this use of *let,* one of James's two most potent verbs (the other is *know*): "She lets what—?" Charlotte expatiates on Maggie's loving character. She wants nothing but to be kind to those she believes in: "It's of herself that she asks efforts."

At first the bowl enchants Charlotte. But the shop owner overdoes it when he says that he has been saving it for a special customer. Charlotte knows then that there must be a flaw and says as much. The dealer rises to the challenge: "But if it's something you can't find out, isn't it as good as if it were nothing?" Charlotte wonders how—or if—one can give a present that one knows to be flawed. The dealer suggests that the flaw be noted to the recipient, as a sign of good faith. In any case, the bowl is a piece of solid crystal and crystal, unlike glass, does not break; but it can shatter 'on lines and by laws of its own'. Charlotte decides that she cannot afford the bowl; she joins Amerigo, who has been waiting for her in the street. He had seen the flaw at once. *"Per Dio,* I'm superstitious! A crack is a crack—and an omen's an omen."

For the moment, that is the end of the bowl itself. But James has now made the golden bowl emblematic, to use a Dickens word, of the relations between the lovers and their legal mates. To all appearances, the world of the two couples is a flawless rare crystal, all of a piece, beautifully gilded with American money. Of the four, the Prince is the first to detect the flaw; and though he wanted no part of the actual bowl, he himself slips easily into that adulterine situation which is the flaw in their lives. Charlotte refused to buy the bowl because she could not, simply, pay the price; yet she accepts the adultery—and pays the ultimate price.

In due course, Maggie acquires the bowl as a present for her father. Although she does not detect the flaw, the dealer believes himself mysteriously honor-bound to come to her house and tell her that the flaw is there. During his confession, he notices photographs of the Prince and Charlotte; tells Maggie that they were in his shop together. Thus, she learns that they knew each other before her marriage and, as she tells Fanny, "They went about together—they're known to have done it. And I don't mean only before—I mean after."

≡

As James's other triumph of knowledge gained through innocence was called *What Maisie Knew,* so this story might easily have been called *When Maggie Knew.* As the bowl is the symbol of the flawed marriages, so the line: "knowledge, knowledge was a fascination as well as a fear," stands as a sort of motto to this variation on one of our race's earliest stories, Adam and Eve and the forbidden fruit of knowledge which, once plucked, let the first human couple know both the joys of sex and the pain of its shadow, death. But if James was echoing in his last novel one of the first of all our stories, something is missing: the serpent-tempter. Is it Adam Verver? Or is he too passive to be so deliberate an agent? Actually, the shop owner is the agent of knowledge; but he is peripheral to the legend. Fanny Assingham has something slightly serpentine about her. Certainly, she is always in the know, but she is without malice. In fact, she prefers people *not* to know, and so she makes the splendid gesture of smashing the bowl and, presumably, the knowledge that the bowl has brought Maggie. But it is too late for that. Maggie moves into action. She sets out to rid herself of Charlotte because "I want a happiness without a hole in it. . . . The golden bowl—as it *was* to have been."

In the first of a series of splendid confrontations, Maggie tells the Prince that she knows. He, in turn, asks if Adam knows. "Find out for yourself!" she answers. Maggie is now having, as James colloquially puts it, "the time of her life—she knew it by the perpetual throb of this sense of possession, which was almost too violent either to recognize or to hide." Again, "possession." When the suspicious Charlotte confronts her in the garden (of Eden?) at Fawns, Maggie lies superbly; and keeps her enemy in ignorance, a worse state—for her—than even the United States. Finally, Maggie's great scene with her father is significant for what is not said. No word is spoken by either against Charlotte; nor is there any hint that all is not well with Amerigo and Maggie. But James's images of Maggie and Adam together in the garden—again the garden at Fawns (from the Latin *fons:* spring or source?)—are those of a husband and wife at the end or the beginning of some momentous change in their estate. The images are deliberately and precisely marital: "They were husband and wife—oh, so immensely!—as regards other persons." The reference here is to house party guests but the implication is that "other persons" include her husband and his wife. They speak of their social position and its ambiguities, of the changes that their marriages have made. She is a princess. He is the husband of a great lady of fashion. They speak of the beauty and selfishness of their old life.

Maggie remarks of her husband that "I'm selfish, so to speak, *for* him." Maggie's aria on the nature of jealousy (dependent in direct ratio on the degree of love expended) is somewhat mystifying because she may "seem often not to know quite *where* I am." But Adam appears to know exactly where he is: "I guess I've never been jealous." Maggie affirms that that is because he is "beyond everything. Nothing can pull *you* down." To which Adam responds, "Well, then, we make a pair. We're all right." Maggie reflects on the notion of sacrifice in love. The ambiguities are thick in the prose: Does she mean, at one point, the Prince or Charlotte or Adam himself? But when she says, "I sacrifice you," all the lines of the drama cross and, as they do, so great is the tension that James switches the point of view in mid-scene from daughter to father as James must, for an instant, glimpse Adam's response to this declaration: "He had said to himself, 'She'll break down and name Amerigo; she'll say it's to him she's sacrificing me; and it's by what that will give me—with so many other things too— that my suspicion will be clinched.' " Actually, this is supposed to be Maggie's view of what her father senses, but James has simply abandoned her in mid-consciousness for the source of her power, the father-consort. How Adam now acts will determine her future. He does not let her down. In fact, he is "practically *offering* himself, pressing himself upon her, as a sacrifice . . ." The deed is done. He will take Charlotte back to American City. He will leave the field to Maggie.

Adam has been sacrificed. But has he? This is the question that reverberates. Maggie finds herself adoring him for his stillness and his power; and for the fact "that he was always, marvellously, young—which couldn't but crown, at this juncture, his whole appeal to her imagination." She gives him the ultimate accolade: "I believe in you more than anyone." They are again as one, this superbly monstrous couple. "His hands came out, and while her own took them he drew her to his breast and held her. He held her hard and kept her long, and she let herself go; but it was an embrace that august and almost stern, produced, for its intimacy, no revulsion and broke into no inconsequence of tears."

Where Maggie leaves off and Adam begins is not answered. Certainly, incest—a true Jamesian "horror"—hovers about the two of them, though in a work as delicately balanced as this the sweaty deed itself seems irrelevant and unlikely. It is enough that two splendid monsters have triumphed yet again over everyone else and, best of all, over mere human nature. But then Maggie contains, literally, the old Adam. He is progenitor; and the first cause; *fons*.

It is Adam who places Charlotte in her cage—a favorite Jamesian image; now James adds the image of a noose and silken cord by which Adam leads her wherever he chooses—in this case to the great republic of which Fanny observes to Maggie: "I see the long miles of ocean and the dreadful great country, State after State—which have never seemed to me so big or so terrible. I see *them* at last, day by day and step by step, at the far end— and I see them never come back." It is as if a beautiful, wealthy, American young woman of today were doomed to spend her life entirely in London. But the victorious Maggie believes that Charlotte will probably find life back home "interesting" while she and her father are the real losers because they are now forever parted. But Fanny is on to her. Fanny gets Maggie to confess that what was done not only suits her ("I let him go") but was indeed no more than the successful execution of Adam's master plan: "Mrs. Assingham hesitated, but at last her bravery flared. 'Why not call it then frankly his complete success?'" Maggie agrees that that is all that is left for her to do.

At the end, Adam has brought together Maggie and Amerigo. James now throws all the switches in the last paragraph:

[Amerigo] tried, too clearly, to please her—to meet her in her own way; but with the result only that, close to her, her face kept before him, his hands holding her shoulders, his whole act enclosing her, he presently echoed: " 'See'? I see nothing *but* you." And the truth of it had, with this force, after a moment, so strangely lighted his eyes that, as for pity and dread of them, she buried her own in his breast.

The golden cage has shut on them both. She is both jailer and prisoner. She is both august and stern. In the book's last line the change of the word *dread* to *awe* would have made the story a tragedy. But James has aimed at something else—another and higher state for the novel (for life, too, that poor imitation of art with its inevitable human flaw): He has made gods of his characters; and turns them all to gold.

Years earlier, when James first saw the gilded Galerie d'Apollon in the palace of the Louvre, he had "an immense hallucination," a sense of cosmic consciousness; and over the years he often said that he could, all in all, take quite a lot of gold. At the end of Henry James's life, in a final delirium, he thought that he was the Emperor Napoleon; and as the Emperor, he gave detailed instructions for the redoing of the Tuileries and the Louvre: and died, head aswarm with golden and imperial visions. Fortunately, he had lived long enough to make for us *The Golden Bowl*, a work whose spirit is not imperial so much as it is ambitiously divine.

THE NEW YORK REVIEW OF BOOKS

*January 19, 1984*

# CHAPTER 18

# LOGAN PEARSALL SMITH LOVES THE ADVERB

Should the human race survive the twentieth of those wondrous centuries since shepherds quaked at the sight of God's birth in a Middle Eastern stable (all in all, a bad career move), our century will be noted more for what we managed to lose along the way than for what we acquired. Although the physical sciences took off, literally, and some rightly stuffed American men with nothing much to say lurched about the moon, sublunary population was allowed to get out of control to such an extent that much of the earth's good land was covered with cement in order to house the new arrivals while the waters of the globe are now so poisoned that on the just and the unjust alike pale acid rain everywhere softly falls. As we get more people, we lose "amenities" of every sort.

The century that began with a golden age in all the arts (or at least the golden twilight of one) is ending not so much without art as without the idea of art, while the written culture that was the core of every educational system since the fifth century B.C. is now being replaced by sounds and images electronically transmitted. As human society abandoned the oral tradition for the written text, the written culture is giving way to an audiovisual one. This is a radical change, to say the least, and none of us knows quite how to respond. Obviously the change cannot be all bad. On the other hand, what is to become of that written language which was for two millennia wisdom's only mold? What is to become of the priests of literature, as their temples are abandoned? What happens to the work of (now one strikes plangently the diminuendo!) Logan Pearsall Smith?

It is startling to think that someone like Pearsall Smith actually lived most of his life in our century. Entirely possessed by the idea of literature, Logan was besotted with language and "the lovely art of writing." As a result, he spent almost as much time searching for the right unhackneyed adjective to describe the moon (one of whose Latin names is Trivia) as any of that body's recent callers spent in getting there. He even belonged to something called the Society for Pure English, surely long since dispersed, along with its objective. Yet he was not a pedant; he believed in "Idiom before Grammar." Finally, like so many of us, in old age, Logan fell in love —with the adverb.

There is something heroic in all this. There is also something beautifully irrelevant to a culture where the idea of literature is being erased by the word processor while even its memory is less than green in the minds of those proud schoolteachers who are currently charting for themselves vast cosmogonies of words and signs in the vacuum of Academe. Logan actually thought that there was such a thing as good—even fine—writing. Today hardly anyone knows the difference between good and bad prose while those who do know had better keep quiet about it: Literary excellence is not only undemocratic but tends to subvert teacherly texts.

Logan Pearsall Smith was born October 18, 1865, the son of a wealthy Philadelphia Quaker who, rather abruptly, left the family glass business and became an evangelist, preaching the Higher Life. Then, as abruptly, inspired by venery, he quit preaching. Logan's mother became—and remained—a writer of best-selling uplifting books. Logan lost his own faith at eleven—vanished while up a cherry tree, he said. But he remained to the end of his days a Quaker at heart, modest, self-aware, self-mocking. Happily, he was as hard on others as on himself.

England delighted in the Smiths; and they in England. The family settled there. In due course, one daughter married Bertrand Russell; another married Bernard Berenson. One niece married Virginia Woolf's brother; another niece married Lytton Strachey's brother. After Harvard and Oxford, Logan married literature and lived happily ever after, with occasional lapses into a kind of madness, the inevitable fate of one who has been denied not only the word processor but the Apple home computer in which to encode Thoughts.

As a young man, Logan had known and delighted in Walt Whitman of nearby Camden, New Jersey (described in Logan's memoir *Unforgotten Years,* 1939); but most of his life was spent in England, where he worshipped Henry James; knew Bernard Shaw and the Webbs; was related to Bloomsbury. Since Logan had an income, he could follow his own literary pursuits: making anthologies of Milton and Shakespeare and Jeremy Taylor; collecting aphorisms by others; making up his own. He was a favorite of those, like James, whom he regarded as masters. He was less favorably regarded by others. Mrs. Woolf was actually unkind about Uncle Logan. But Logan held his own. He confessed, in a letter to her (November 2, 1932): "I may have mocked at Bloomsbury because mockery is my favorite pastime, and also perhaps (to take a darker view into that dark cabinet, the human heart) because I was not admitted to its conclaves." But then, he sweetly added, "I know from my own feeling how justly critics resent criticism, and mockers being mocked."

In 1913 Logan became a British subject. On March 2, 1946, he died and his former secretary, Cyril Connolly, wrote in *The New Statesman:* "Two weeks before his death a friend asked him half jokingly if he had discovered any meaning in life. 'Yes,' he replied, 'there is a meaning; at least for me, there is one thing that matters—to set a chime of words tinkling in the minds of a few fastidious people.' "

Logan devoted his life to getting his own sentences right. Edmund Wilson did not think he always succeeded; "in spite of his cult of writing . . . he [never] became a real master. His prose is rather pale and dead."

But the Anglophobe Wilson was not well disposed toward the Anglophilic Logan. Later, Wilson came to see the virtue of Logan the miniaturist, the creator of *Trivia.*

A lover of language, Logan was always on the lookout for sentences, phrases, *aperçus, pensées* (he found fascinating the fact that the last two words have no English equivalents); he delighted in the splendors of seventeenth-century English prose, particularly that of Jeremy Taylor. He wrote appreciatively of Montaigne, de Sévigné, and Sainte-Beuve. But he was at his best when he wrote of "fine writing" and the works of the English aphorists.

As a writer, Logan himself was very much school of America's own (now seldom read) Emerson who was at *his* best in "the detached—and the detachable—sentence." Logan quotes Emerson on literature (in *English Aphorists*): "People do not deserve to have good writing, they are so pleased with the bad." And, "In every work of genius we recognize our own rejected thoughts; they come back to us with a certain alienated majesty." And, of course, "Poets are not to be seen."

$$\equiv$$

During the years that Logan was writing about other people's writing and collecting other writers' phrases, he was himself working on his own library of miniature portraits, narratives, descriptions, and other "trivia." (In 1755 Samuel Johnson nicely defined the word *trivial* as "vile, worthless, vulgar, such as may be picked up in the highway.") Logan saw himself as the latest in a line that extends in French from La Rochefoucauld's *Maximes* and Pascal's *Pensées* to Jules Renard's notebooks ("I find that when I do not think of myself I do not think at all"). In English the line begins with Bacon and includes Chesterfield, Blake, Hazlitt, Emerson. Just what it is these writers do is hard to explain in English because we lack the words —in itself something of a giveaway. These sharp thrusts are not really maxims or wisecracks or thoughts; yet they are often indistinguishable from them. At one point, Logan uses the word "illuminations"; and he notes that for those "whom the spectacle of life as it is, stripped of its illusions, possesses an inexhaustible fascination, for such students of human nature there will always be a great attraction in these profound X-rays of observation, which reveal the bones beneath the flesh; these acute and penetrating phrases which puncture man's pretensions and bring him disenflated to the earth."

Logan Pearsall Smith joined the glittering line in 1902 when he published, privately, a truly slender volume, *Trivia,* "from the papers of one Anthony Woodhouse." He thought a pseudonym necessary. So did Mother. "It is certainly very quaint and interesting," wrote Hannah Smith, "but it is what I would suppose would be called very 'precious,' as it begins nowhere and ends nowhere and leads to nothing." The terminus that Hannah Smith could not see in her son's work was, of course, perfection—a matter of no consequence to a believer in the Higher Life. Fifteen years later, Constable republished *Trivia,* and its author became agreeably if not enormously famous on both sides of the Atlantic. In 1921 he published *More Trivia;* then came *Afterthoughts* and, in 1933, all of his illuminations were gathered into one volume, *All Trivia* (containing the never-before-published *Last Words*).

When *Unforgotten Years* was distributed by the Book-of-the-Month Club in 1939, Logan became popular. Although he liked to quote Aristippus of Cyrene ("I am taken by these things, but they do not take me in"), he was delighted. In 1895, Henry James had warned him that loneliness was the dedicated artist's lot. Now Logan was taken up by a new generation of writers and remembered anew by an old generation of hostesses or, as he wrote one of the former, Hugh Trevor-Roper (June 26, 1941): "I will admit a weakness for one cup of poison, that of social success, whose flavor, as far as I have tasted it, is delicious and which I have never known anyone resist to whom it has been proffered. *Power* is, I believe, even more poisonous and more delicious, but that I have never tasted."

But despite sprigs of laurel and windfall checks, he kept on writing and reading, "miscellaneously," more or less well served by a series of secretaries, of whom the most celebrated was Cyril Connolly and the most aggrieved Robert Gathorne-Hardy, later his biographer. Logan himself never ceased to serve the English language and its literature. In 1924, when the seventeen-year-old Dwight Macdonald wrote him an admiring letter about *Trivia,* Logan responded: '. . . I don't think I had any natural gift for writing. But the art of prose, unlike that of poetry, is one that can be learnt.' Also, "the amused observation of one's own self is a veritable gold mine whose surface has hardly yet been scratched." In 1945, he wrote Trevor-Roper, "My life has been spent in mooning over that little book [*All Trivia*], as it was my fantastic daydream to write a little book which should live on after my own unregretted departure."

≡

Edmund Wilson came around in 1950: "I always used to think *Trivia* overrated. A certain amount of it, to be sure; and yet there *is* something in it, something dry, independent, even tough. There are things which one took in at a glance when one first picked up the book and looked through it, and yet which ever since have stuck in one's mind . . . in dealing with incidents frankly infinitesimal [four *in*'s in six lines is a record, Mr. Wilson], somehow succeeds in [a fifth!] being impressively truthful . . ."

The French have a phrase, *l'esprit de l'escalier,* which means, literally, "the wit of the staircase," referring to all those marvelous things that you did *not* say at the party which now occur to you as you descend the staircase en route to the exit. Fortunately, Logan saw to it that his own staircase-musings were not only polished highly but memorialized for all time. Whatever he may or may not have said at the party, he certainly had ample time to get it right on the stairs.

For what is now close to forty years a number of Logan's lines or anecdotes or volumes-in-miniature have stuck in my mind. "The Ear-Trumpet," for instance. At table, a deaf lady asks Logan to repeat a phrase he has too proudly let drop, which is, to his horror, as he booms it over and over again, "the interstices of their lives." This story later reverberated for me in a Washington, D.C., drawing room when a deaf lady asked a solemn man his name and he replied, solemnly, "I am Senator Bourke C. Hickenlooper of Iowa." She then asked him to repeat his name, which he did. "Now I have it!" she said at last. "How deaf I've become!" She gave a contented laugh. "And to think that I thought that you said your name was Senator Bourke C. Hickenlooper of Iowa." Thus, Logan chimes for me down the radioactive dusted corridors of the twentieth century.

To the extent that there will always be a few voluntary readers, Logan ought always to have some of them. *All Trivia* is a whole library in miniature. He retells legends and composes entire novels and biographies in a page while producing eternal wisdom as well as life-enhancing malice in a series of phrases: "Those who set out to serve both God and Mammon soon discover that there is no God," or "If you want to be thought a liar, always tell the truth." Logan has also written if not his urn burial his demitasse burial when he contemplates his world as posterity is apt to see it: "a dusty set of old waxworks simpering inanely in the lumber-room of Time." But then, as he comments in *English Aphorists,* "On the whole [the aphorists] are a malicious lot; their object is not to extricate man from the mire of his condition, but rather to roll him more deeply in it. So much do they enjoy fishing in muddy waters, that they are not unwilling to pursue their sport even in their own bosoms." He made fun of himself; he also made fun of those critics who disliked fine writing, pointing out that they have nothing to fear from it, since "the fever of perfection is not catching. . . ." In any case, "If you write badly about good writing, however profound may be your convictions or emphatic your expressions of them, your style has a tiresome trick (as a wit once pointed out) of whispering 6Don't listen!' in your reader's ear."

Presciently, Logan feared the insect world and its possible analogy to ours. "I hate . . . their cold intelligence; their stereotyped, unremitting industry repels me." Long before the DNA code was discovered, Logan feared a predetermined universe where "we are forced like the insects and can't help it, to undergo all the metamorphoses preordained for our species." But this laconic master is making me garrulous. Read him and hear the chimes at two minutes, or whatever it is, to midnight. Listen.

THE NEW YORK REVIEW OF BOOKS

*March 29, 1984*

# CHAPTER 19

# OSCAR WILDE:
# ON THE SKIDS AGAIN

**M**ust one have a heart of stone to read *The Ballad of Reading Gaol* without laughing? (In life, practically no one ever gets to kill the thing he hates, much less loves.) And did not *De Profundis* plumb for all time the shallows of the most-reported love affair of the past hundred years, rivaling even that of Wallis and David, its every nuance (O Bosie!) known to all, while trembling rosy lips yet form, over and over again, those doom-laden syllables *The Cadogan Hotel?* Oscar Wilde. Yet again. Why?

In *Four Dubliners* (1987), Richard Ellman published essays on Yeats, Joyce, Wilde, and Beckett. "These four," he admits, "make a strange consortium. Yet resemblances of which they were unaware begin to appear." Certainly no one could detect these resemblances better than the late Professor Ellmann, who devoted much of a distinguished career to Joyce and Yeats. He tells us that at eighteen Yeats heard Wilde lecture, while Joyce, at twenty, met Yeats and called him too old. In 1928 young Beckett met Joyce and they became friends. . . . So much for the traffic; somewhat more to the point, "Wilde and Yeats reviewed each other's work with mutual regard, and sometimes exploited the same themes. Joyce memorialized Wilde as a heroic victim, and repeatedly quoted or referred to him in his writings later. Beckett was saturated in all their works. . . . Displaced, witty, complex, savage they companion each other." I wonder.

Since Ellman had already written magisterial works on two of the four, symmetry and sympathy plainly drew him to a third; hence, this latest biography of Wilde, this last biography of Ellmann, our time's best academic biographer. Although Ellmann was unusually intelligent, a quality seldom found in academe or, indeed, on Parnassus itself, Wilde does not quite suit his schema or his talent. Aside from the fact that the four Dubliners, as he acknowledges, "were chary of acknowledging their connection," I suspect that the controlling adjective here is "academic." To an academic of Ellmann's generation, explication is all.

The problem with Wilde is that he does not need explication or interpretation. He needs only to be read, or listened to. He plays no word games other than that most mechanical of verbal tricks: the paradox. When he rises to the sublime in poetry or prose there is so much purple all over the place that one longs for the clean astringencies of Swinburne.

On those occasions when Wilde is true master, the inventor of a perfect play about nothing and everything, we don't need to have the jokes explained. One simply laughs and wonders why no one else has ever been able to sustain for so long so flawlessly elegant a verbal riff. I would not like to rise in the academic world with a dissertation on Wilde's masterpiece and I suspect (but do not know) that hardly anyone has tried, particularly now that ever-easy Beckett's clamorous silences await, so temptingly, tenure seekers.

All in all, Wilde provides little occasion for Ellmann's formidable critical apparatus. Where Ellmann showed us new ways of looking at Yeats and, above all, at Joyce, he can do nothing more with Wilde than fit him into a historical context and tell, yet again, the profane story so well known to those who read. Is this worthwhile? I am not so sure. Ellmann does straighten out earlier versions of the gospel—or bad news, I suppose one should say. He rises to the essential prurience; and it is interesting to know that at thirty-one, after a lifetime of vigorous heterosexuality which had given him not only two children but syphilis, Wilde was seduced by Robert Ross, then aged seventeen, at Oxford. It is also interesting to know that Wilde, unlike Byron, Charlemagne, and Lassie, was not into buggery, preferring either oral sex or the Dover-sole kiss *cum* intercrural friction. What a one-time warden of all souls did for Lawrence, Ellmann now does for Wilde. Future generations will be in his—their—debt.

Future generations. Now let us be relevant, the essential task of the irrelevant (O Oscar!): *Will there be future generations?* The British press of the AIDSy eighties thinks not. According to the *Daily Mail,* the last man on earth died in 1986, clutching to his dehydrated bosom a portrait of Margaret Thatcher. According to the *New York Post* (an Australian newspaper whose editors are able to do simple sums), the human race will be dead by century's end due to rabid homos and drug takers (mostly black and Hispanic and viciously opposed to prayer in America's chaste bookless schools). Therefore, it is now necessary to trot out an Oscar Wilde suitable for our anxious plague-ridden times. In the four decades since the Second World War, Wilde has gradually become more and more a victim-hero of a hypocritical society whose most deeply cherished superstitions about sex were to be violently shaken, first, by the war, where the principal secret of the warrior male lodge was experienced by millions on a global scale and, second, by Dr. Alfred C. Kinsey, who reported that more than one third of the triumphant Butch Republic's male population had participated in the tribal mysteries. The revolution in consciousness attributed to the Beatles and other confusions of the 1960s actually took place in the 1940s: war and Kinsey, penicillin and the pill. As a result, Oscar Wilde ceased to be regarded as a criminal; he had been nothing worse than maladjusted to a society that was not worth adjusting to. Wilde himself became a symbol of mental if not of physical health: Ellmann pinpoints the when and how of the syphilis that killed him when every orifice, suddenly, hugely, voided in a Paris hotel room. The cumulative effect of Ellmann's Wilde may suit altogether too well the AIDSy Eighties.

Currently, our rulers are tightening the screws; too much sexual freedom is bad for production and, even worse, for consumption. Sex is now worse than mere sin; it is murderous. In the selfish pursuit of happiness another may die. One understands those paranoids who think that AIDS was deliberately cooked up in a laboratory, for the idea of plague is endlessly useful, transforming society-persecutor into society-protector: urine samples here, blood tests there. Come along. Sick behind that fence. Keep moving.

Although Ellmann certainly did not set out to recast Wilde for our dismal age, he was, like the rest of us, a part of the way we live now, and his Wilde is more cautionary tale than martyr-story. There is the obligatory Freudianism. *Cherchez la mère* is indulged in, legitimately, I suppose. Jane Wilde, self-dubbed Speranza Francesca, was, if not larger than life, a good deal larger than average. A Protestant, Lady Wilde kept a literary salon rather than saloon in Dublin, favored an independent Ireland, wrote thundering verse worthy of her son (anent child-nurture: "Alas! The Fates are cruel. / Behold Speranza making gruel!"). She loved sensation-making and came into her own at a treason trial in Dublin, where she was gaveled down by the judge as she tried to make herself, rather than the defendant, the fount of sedition. Later, she endured the trial for seduction, of her husband, Sir William, an oculist. Trials were, rather ominously, her ice cream. Son deeply admired mother and vice versa. But Ellmann controls himself: "However accommodating it is to see a maternal smothering of masculinity as having contributed to [Oscar's] homosexuality there is reason to be skeptical."

Although Ellmann has not worked out that homosexual is an adjective describing an act not a noun descriptive of a human being, he has been able to assemble data which he then tests against fashionable theory; in this case he finds theory wanting. Oscar was a brilliant creature neither more nor less "masculine" than anyone else. What he learned from his mother was not how to be a woman but the importance of being a Show-off and a Poet and a questioner of whatever quo was currently status. He also inherited her talent for bad poetry. In due course, he re-created himself as a celebrity (a terrible word that has been used in our sense since the mid-1800s), and he was well known long before he had actually done anything at all of note. The Anglo-Irish gift of the gab, combined with an actor's timing, made him noticeable at Oxford and unescapable in London's drawing rooms during the 1880s. He invented a brand-new voice for himself (the Irish brogue, no matter how Merrion Squared, was dispensed with), and Beerbohm reports on his "mezzo voice, uttering itself in leisurely fashion, with every variety of tone." He also took to gorgeous costumes that set off his large ungainly figure to splendid disadvantage. With the death of Sir William, he possessed a small inheritance, expensive tastes and no focused ambition other than poetry, a common disease of that day; also, as Yeats put it, "the enjoyment of his own spontaneity."

What is most interesting in Ellmann's account is the intellectual progress of Wilde. He is particularly good on Wilde's French connection, much of it unknown to me, though I once asked André Gide several searching questions about his friend, and Gide answered me at length. That was in 1948. I have now forgotten both questions and answers. But until I read Ellmann I did not know how well and for how long the two had known each other and what an impression Wilde ("Creation began when you were born. It will end on the day you die") had made on Gide's tormented passage through that strait gate that leads the few to life.

As a result of a collection of fairy tales, *The Happy Prince* (a revelation to at least one American child forty years later), Wilde became famous for writing as well as for showing off, and Paris stirred, as it sometimes will, for an Anglo (the Celtic distinction is unknown there). With the publication of the dialogue "The Decay of Lying," Wilde took note of a change of direction in literature, and the French were both startled and delighted that the cultural wind was coming from the wrong side of the channel. Ellmann writes,

In England decadence had always been tinged with self-mockery. By 1890, symbolism, not decadence, had the cry, as Wilde acknowledged in the preface to *Dorian Gray.* "All art is at once surface and symbol. Those who go beneath the surface do so at their peril. Those who read the symbol do so at their peril." These aphorisms were a bow to Stéphane Mallarmé, whom he had visited in February 1891, when he was writing the preface.

Wilde then proceeded to conquer Parisian literary life in much the same way that he had the drawing rooms of London and the lecture halls of the United States. Incidentally, Ellmann's list of the number of places where Wilde spoke is positively presidential. In hundreds of cities and towns he lectured on the Beautiful, with numerous household hints. In his two chats "The House Beautiful" and "The Decorative Arts," he foreshadowed today's how-to-do-it books. He was a sensation. My twelve-year-old grandfather (during Reconstruction, southern boys were bred early and often) recalled Wilde's performance (July 15, 1882) at the Opera House in Vicksburg, Mississippi: "He wore," and the old man's voice trembled, "a *girdle,* and he held a flower in his hand." Happily, my grandfather never knew that two weeks later Wilde was received by General Grant. (As I write these lines, I wonder *how* did he know that Wilde was wearing a girdle?)

The siege of Paris was swift, the victory total. Symbolism did not need to lay siege to Wilde; he surrendered to the modernist movement, now the world's oldest *vague,* whose long roar shows no sign of withdrawing. Wilde also appropriated Mallarmé's unfinished *Hérodiade* for his own *Salomé,* written in French for Bernhardt; but the play was admired. It is interesting just how learned the writers of the last century were: The educational system Greeked and Latined them; other languages came easily to them, cultures, too. Today's writers know very little about anything. But then those who teach cannot be taught.

During the enchantment of Paris, Wilde himself was, significantly, overwhelmed by Huysman's *A Rebours,* still a touchstone as late as the 1940s. The young Proust was impressive to Wilde because of his "enthusiasm for English literature, especially for Ruskin (whom he translated) and George Eliot . . ." But when Proust invited him to dinner, Wilde arrived before Proust: "I looked at the drawing room and at the end of it were your parents, my courage failed me." Wilde departed, after the thoughtful observation to M. and Mme. Proust: "How ugly your house is."

With the local cat-king, Edmond de Goncourt, Wilde was no less magisterial. In a newspaper piece, Goncourt had got all wrong Wilde's remarks about Swinburne, while Wilde himself was sneered at as "this individual of doubtful sex, with a ham actor's language, and tall stories." Wilde chose to ignore the personal attack in a letter that set straight the gossip: "In Swinburne's work we meet for the first time the cry of flesh tormented by desire and memory, joy and remorse, fecundity and sterility. The English public, as usual hypocritical, prudish, and philistine, has not known how to find the art in the work of art: it has searched for the man in it." *Tiens!* as Henry James liked to write in his notebook. The biographer has license to go a-hunting for the man; the critic not; the reader— why not just read what's written?

Wilde, the playwright, is duly recorded, duly celebrated. Ellmann has some nice greenroom gossip for those who like that sort of thing. It is interesting to know that when Beerbohm Tree addressed a "brilliant lady" on stage he did so with his back to the audience (a Bernhardt trick, too). But then when he had an epigram to launch, he would turn to face the audience, to their ravishment. For those who like such things, there is also a very great deal about Wilde's love affair with a boring boy-beauty called Bosie. At this late date it is no longer a story worth retelling, and if Ellmann has added anything new to it I did not notice. The trial. Prison. Exile. The usual. I suspect that one of the reasons we create fiction is to make sex exciting; the fictional meeting between Vautrin and Lucien de Rubempré at the coach house in Balzac's *Illusions Perdues* is one of the most erotic ever recorded. But details of the real Oscar and Bosie in bed together or in combination with bits and pieces of England's adenoidal trade, more gifted at blackmail than ganymedery, create for the reader neither tumescence nor moistness; rather, one's thoughts turn somberly to laundry and to the brutal horror of life in a world without dry cleaning.

Ellmann's literary criticism is better than his telling of the oft-told tale. He is particularly good on *Dorian Gray*, a book truly subversive of the society that produced it—and its author. He is interesting on Wilde's conversion to a kind of socialism. Of Wilde's essay "The Soul of Man Under Socialism," Ellmann tells us that it "is based on the paradox that we must not waste energy in sympathizing with those who suffer needlessly, and that only socialism can free us to cultivate our personalities. Charity is no use—the poor are . . . right to steal rather than to take alms." On the other hand, Wilde was wary of authoritarianism, so often socialism's common-law helpmeet. In the end, Wilde veered off into a kind of anarchy; and defined the enemy thus:

There are three sorts of despots. There is the despot who tyrannizes over the body. There is the despot who tyrannizes over the soul. There is the despot who tyrannizes over the soul *and* body alike. The first is called the Prince. The second is called the Pope. The third is called the People.

Joyce was impressed by this and borrowed it for *Ulysses*. Inadvertently (I suspect), Richard Ellmann does make it clear that for all the disorder of Wilde's life he was never, in the Wordsworthian sense, "neglectful of the universal heart."

Yeats thought Wilde a man of action, like Byron, who had got waylaid by literature. When this was repeated to Wilde, he made an offhand remark about the boredom of Parliament. But Yeats did sense in Wilde the energy of the actor: of one who acts, rather than of one who simply, bemusedly *is*—the artist. But whatever Wilde might or might not have done and been, he was an extremely good man and his desire to subvert a supremely bad society was virtuous. Cardinal Newman, writing of their common day, said, "The age is so very sluggish that it will not hear you unless you bawl—you must first tread on its toes, and then apologise." But behavior suitable for an ecclesiastical busybody is all wrong for Oscar Wilde, whose only mistake was to apologize for his good work and life.

THE TIMES (LONDON) LITERARY SUPPLEMENT
*October 2–8, 1987*

# CHAPTER 20

# PAUL BOWLES'S STORIES

Carson McCullers, Paul Bowles, Tennessee Williams are, at this moment at least, the three most interesting writers in the United States." A third of a century has passed since I wrote that sentence in a piece on contemporary American writing.

Later, when I reprinted those words, I felt obliged to add: "This was written in 1952. McCullers was a good and fashionable novelist of the day (I cannot say that I have any great desire to read her again). Paul Bowles was as little known then as he is now. His short stories are among the best ever written by an American. Tennessee Williams, etc. . . ." All in all, I still see no reason not to support my youthful judgment of Paul Bowles. As a short-story writer, he has had few equals in the second half of the twentieth century. Obvious question: If he is so good, why is he so little known?

Great American writers are supposed not only to live in the greatest country in the world (the United States, for those who came in late), but to write about that greatest of all human themes: *the American experience.* From the beginning of the Republic, this crude America First-ism has flourished. As a result, there is a strong tendency to misrepresent or undervalue our three finest novelists: Henry James (who lived in England), Edith Wharton (who lived in France), Vladimir Nabokov (who lived in Switzerland, and who wasn't much of an American anyway despite an unnatural passion for our motels, so lyrically rendered in *Lolita*).

Paul Bowles has lived most of his life in Morocco. He seldom writes about the United States. On the other hand, he has shrewd things to say about Americans confronted with strange cultures and . . . strange selves.

Born in 1911, Bowles was brought up in New York City and New England. He attended the University of Virginia. When he was seventeen, the Paris-based avant-garde magazine *transition* published some of his poems. Bowles went to Paris, met Gertrude Stein, was influenced by the Surrealists. He quit school to become a writer. Except for Poe, his writing derives not from the usual Anglo-American tradition but from such 'exotics' as Valéry, Roussel, Gide and, of course, the expatriate Miss Stein. Later, he was to put to his own uses oral Mexican and Moroccan folklore; he listened as much as he read.

I suspect that Bowles's apparent foreignness has limited the number of doctoral theses that ought by now to have been devoted to one whose art far exceeds that of . . . well, name the great American writers of our day (a list that was as different yesterday as it will be tomorrow). For the American academic, Bowles is still odd man out; he writes as if *Moby Dick* had never been written. Odder still, he is also a distinguished composer of music. In fact, he supported himself for many years by writing incidental music for such Broadway plays as *The Glass Menagerie*. It is curious that at a time when a number of serious critics have expressed the hope that literature might one day take on the attributes of the "highest" of all the arts, music, Bowles has been composing music as well as writing prose. I am certain that the first critic able to deal both with his music and his writing will find that Bowles's life work has been marvelous in a way not accessible to those of us who know only one or the other of the two art forms. Only Anthony Burgess knows enough to do him justice.

In 1972, Paul Bowles wrote a memoir called, *Without Stopping*. For those able to read between the lines, the book was pleasurable. For anyone else, it must have sounded a bit like Julius Caesar's account of the wars in Gaul. Although there is a good deal of information about various commanders and troop movements, we don't learn much about what the subject had in mind. But there are interesting asides, and the best sort of memoir is entirely to one side of the mere facts of a life.

We learn that Bowles originally wanted to be a writer, not a composer. But at a progressive school he had shown an aptitude for mathematics, cousin germane to music. Nevertheless, he preferred to arrange words rather than notes upon a page until Gertrude Stein read his poems. "She sat back and thought a moment. Then she said: 'Well, the only trouble with all this is that it isn't poetry.' " She found his images false; did not think much of his attempt to write in the Surreal manner, "without conscious intervention." Later, she asked him if he had rewritten the poems. When he said no, "She was triumphant. 'You see,' she cried. 'I told you you were no poet. A real poet, after one conversation, would have gone upstairs and at least tried to recast them, but you haven't even looked at them.' " Bowles stopped writing. He turned to music.

Between 1929 and 1945 he made a name as a composer. He married the odd, brilliant Jane Bowles. She was a writer. He was a composer. Together and separately, they were much admired. During the late thirties and forties they became central figures in the transatlantic (and Pan-American) world of the arts. Although unknown to the general public, the Bowleses were famous among those who were famous; and in some mysterious way the art grandees wanted, if not the admiration of the Bowleses (seldom bestowed), their tolerance.

They lived in Mexico (the unknown Tennessee Williams made a pilgrimage to their house in Acapulco); they lived in New York, sharing a house with W. H. Auden and Benjamin Britten. After the Second War they moved for good to Tangier where Paul Bowles still lives. Jane Bowles died in Spain in 1973.

In the spring of 1945, Charles Henri Ford asked Bowles to edit an issue of the magazine *View*. The subject was Central and South American culture. Bowles translated a number of Spanish writers; and wrote some texts of his own. In the course of "reading some ethnographic books with texts from the Arapesh or from the Tarahumara given in word-for-word translation . . . the desire came to me to invent my own myths, adopting the point of view of the primitive mind." He resorted to "the old Surrealist method of abandoning conscious control and writing whatever words came from the pen." The first of these stories was written "one rainy Sunday"; it is called "The Scorpion."

The story was well received, and Bowles went on writing. "The subject matter of the myths soon turned from 'primitive' to contemporary. . . . It was through this unexpected little gate that I crept back into the land of fiction writing. Long ago I had decided that the world was too complex for me ever to be able to write fiction; since I failed to understand life, I would not be able to find points of reference which the hypothetical reader might have in common with me." He did not entirely proceed through that small gate until he wrote "A Distant Episode" and found that if life was no more understandable to him than before, prose was. He now possessed the art to depict his dreams.

During the next thirty years Paul Bowles wrote thirty-nine short stories. They were published originally in three volumes: *The Delicate Prey*, 1950; *The Time of Friendship*, 1967; *Things Gone and Thing Still Here*, 1977. Even before the first collection was published, three of the stories caused a great stir in the literary world. "Pages from Cold Point," "The Delicate Prey," and "A Distant Episode" were immediately recognized as being unlike anything else in our literature. I have just reread the three stories, with some nervousness. After all these years, I wondered if they would still "work." In my youth I had admired D. H. Lawrence's novels. Now, I deeply dislike them. I was relieved to find that Bowles's art is still as disturbing as ever. I was surprised to note how the actual stories differ from my memory of them. I recalled a graphic description of a sixteen-year-old boy's seduction of his father on a hot summer night in Jamaica. Over the years, carnal details had built up in my memory like a coral reef. Yet on rereading "Pages from Cold Point," nothing (and everything) happens. In his memoirs Bowles refers, rather casually, to this story as something he wrote aboard ship from New York to Casablanca: "a long story about a hedonist . . ." It is a good deal more than that. Both "The Delicate Prey" and "A Distant Episode" create the same sense of strangeness and terror that they did the first time I read them. "The Delicate Prey" turns on a Gidean *acte gratuit:* The slicing off of the boy's penis is not only like the incident on the train in *Les Caves du Vatican* but also presages the driving of a nail through a skull in Bowles's novel *Let It Come Down*. "A Distant Episode" seems to me to be more than ever emblematic of the helplessness of an overcivilized sensibility (the professor's) when confronted with an alien culture. Captured by North African nomads, his tongue cut out, he is made into a clown, a toy. He is used to make his captors laugh. He *appears* to accept his fate. Something harsh is glimpsed in the lines of a story that is now plainer in its reverberations than it was when written. But then it is no longer news to anyone that the floor to this ramshackle civilization that we have built cannot bear much longer our weight. It was Bowles's genius to suggest the horrors which lie beneath that floor, as fragile, in its way, as the sky that shelters us from a devouring vastness.

The stories fall into rough categories. First: locale. Mexico and North Africa are the principal settings. Landscape is all-important in a Bowles story. Second: how the inhabitants of alien cultures regard the creatures of our civilized world, as in "Under the Sky." Bowles goes even further in a beautiful story called "The Circular Valley" where human life is depicted as it must appear to the anima of a place. This spirit inhabits at will those human beings who visit its valley; feeds on their emotions; alters them during its occupancy. Third: the stories of transference. In "You Are Not I" a madwoman becomes her sane sister. In "Allal," a boy exchanges personality with a snake. The intensity of these stories makes them more like waking dreams than so many words on a page. Identity is transferred in such a way that one wonders which, finally, is which? and what is what? The effect is rather like the Taoist story of the man who dreamed that he was a butterfly. When "he woke up with a start, he did not know whether he was Chuang Chou who had dreamed that he was a butterfly, or whether he was a butterfly dreaming that he was Chuang Chou. Between Chuang Chou and the butterfly there must be some distinction. This is what is called the transformation of things."

There are a number of more or less realistic stories that deal with the plain incomprehension of Americans in contact with the natives of Mexico, North Africa, Thailand. One of the most amusing is "You Have Left Your Lotus Pods on the Bus." An American goes on an excursion with some Buddhist priests. The day is filled with splendid misunderstandings. There is the man at the back of a crowded bus who never stops screaming. He is ignored by everyone except the American who wonders why no one shuts him up. At the end, the priests tell him that the "madman" is an employee of the bus company giving necessary warnings and advice to the driver.

In several stories white ladies respond not-so-ambiguously to dark-skinned youths. Bowles notes the sadism that sexual frustration can cause ("At Paso Rojo"). But where the ordinary writer would leave it at that, Bowles goes deeper into the human case and, paradoxically, he achieves his greatest effects when he concentrates entirely on surfaces. Although he seldom describes a human face, he examines landscape with the precision of a geologist. Bowles himself seems like one of those bright sharp-eyed birds that flit from story to story, staring with eyes that do not blink at desert, hills, sky. He records weather with all the solemnity of a meteorologist. He looks closely at food. As for his human characters, he simply lets them reveal themselves through what they say or do not say. Finally, he is a master of suggesting anxiety (Are all the traveler's checks lost or just mislaid?) and dread (Will this desert prove to be the setting for a very special death?). Story after story turns on flight. It is no accident that Bowles called his memoir (with pride?) *Without Stopping*.

Four stories were written to demonstrate that by using "kif-inspired motivations, the arbitrary would be made to seem natural, the diverse elements could be fused, and several people would automatically become one." These pieces strike me as entirely uninhabited, and of no interest. Yet in other stories (inspired perhaps by smaller doses of kif) he does demonstrate the essential oneness of the many as well as the interchangeability not only of personality but of all things. As Webster saw the skull beneath the skin, so Bowles has glimpsed what lies back of our sheltering sky . . . an endless flux of stars so like those atoms which make us up that in our apprehension of this terrible infinity, we experience not only horror but likeness.

INTRODUCTION TO COLLECTED STORIES
OF PAUL BOWLES
*(Santa Rosa, California: Black Sparrow Press, 1983)*

# CHAPTER 21

# CALVINO'S DEATH

On the morning of Friday, September 20, 1985, the first equinoctial storm of the year broke over the city of Rome. I awoke to thunder and lightning; and thought I was, yet again, in the Second World War. Shortly before noon, a car and driver arrived to take me up the Mediterranean coast to a small town on the sea called Castiglion della Pescáia where, at one o'clock, Italo Calvino, who had died the day before, would be buried in the village cemetery.

Calvino had had a cerebral hemorrhage two weeks earlier while sitting in the garden of his house at Pineta di Roccamare, where he had spent the summer working on the Charles Eliot Norton lectures that he planned to give during the fall and winter at Harvard. I last saw him in May. I commended him on his bravery: He planned to give the lectures in English, a language that he read easily but spoke hesitantly, unlike French and Spanish, which he spoke perfectly; but then he had been born in Cuba, son of two Italian agronomists; and had lived for many years in Paris.

It was night. We were on the terrace of my apartment in Rome; an overhead light made his deep-set eyes look even darker than usual. Italo gave me his either-this-or-that frown; then he smiled, and when he smiled, suddenly, the face would become like that of an enormously bright child who has just worked out the unified field theory. "At Harvard, I shall stammer," he said. "But then I stammer in every language."

=====

Unlike the United States, Italy has both an educational system (good or bad is immaterial) and a common culture, both good and bad. In recent years Calvino had become the central figure in Italy's culture. Italians were proud that they had produced a world writer whose American reputation began, if I may say so, since no one else will, when I described all of his novels as of May 30, 1974 in *The New York Review of Books.* By 1985, except for England, Calvino was read wherever books are read. I even found a Calvino coven in Moscow's literary bureaucracy, and I think that I may have convinced the state publishers to translate more of him. Curiously, the fact that he had slipped away from the Italian Communist party in 1957 disturbed no one.

Three weeks short of Calvino's sixty-second birthday, he died; and Italy went into mourning, as if a beloved prince had died. For an American, the contrast between them and us is striking. When an American writer dies, there will be, if he's a celebrity (fame is no longer possible for any of us), a picture below the fold on the front page; later, a short appreciation on the newspaper's book page (if there is one), usually the work of a journalist or other near-writer who has not actually read any of the dead author's work but is at home with the arcana of gossipy "Page Six"; and that would be that.

In Calvino's case, the American newspaper obituaries were perfunctory and incompetent: The circuits between the English departments, where our tablets of literary reputation are now kept, and the world of journalism are more than ever fragile and the reception is always bad. Surprisingly, *Time* and *Newsweek,* though each put him on the "book page," were not bad, though one thought him "surrealist" and the other a "master of fantasy"; he was, of course, a true realist, who believed "that only a certain prosaic solidity can give birth to creativity: fantasy is like jam; you have to spread it on a solid slice of bread. If not, it remains a shapeless thing, like jam, out of which you can't make anything." This homely analogy is from an Italian television interview, shown after his death.

*The New York Times,* to show how well regarded Calvino is in these parts, quoted John Updike, our literature's perennial apostle to the middle-brows* (this is not meant, entirely, unkindly), as well as Margaret Atwood (a name new to me), Ursula K. Le Guin (an estimable sci-fi writer, but what is she doing, giving, as it were, a last word on one of the most complex of modern writers?), Michael Wood, whose comment was pretty good, and, finally, the excellent Anthony Burgess, who was not up to his usual par on this occasion. Elsewhere, Mr. Herbert Mitgang again quoted Mr. Updike as well as John Gardner, late apostle to the lowbrows, a sort of Christian evangelical who saw Heaven as a paradigmatic American university.

Europe regarded Calvino's death as a calamity for culture. A literary critic, as opposed to theorist, wrote at length in *Le Monde,* while in Italy itself, each day for two weeks, bulletins from the hospital at Siena were published, and the whole country was suddenly united in its esteem not only for a great writer but for someone who reached not only primary schoolchildren through his collections of folk and fairy tales but, at one time or another, everyone else who reads.

===

After the first hemorrhage, there was a surgical intervention that lasted many hours. Calvino came out of coma. He was disoriented: He thought that one of the medical attendants was a policeman; then he wondered if he'd had open-heart surgery. Meanwhile, the surgeon had become optimistic, even garrulous. He told the press that he'd never seen a brain structure of such delicacy and complexity as that of Calvino. I thought immediately of the smallest brain ever recorded, that of Anatole France. The surgeon told the press that he had been obliged to do his very best. After all, he and his sons had read and argued over *Marcovaldo* last winter. The brain that could so puzzle them must be kept alive in all its rarity. One can

*Although the three estates, high-, middle-, and lowbrow, are as dead as Dwight Mac-donald, their most vigorous deployer, something about today's literary scene, combined with Calvino's death, impels me to resurrect the terms. Presently, I shall demonstrate.

imagine a comparable surgeon in America: Only last Saturday she had kept me and my sons in stitches; now I could hardly believe that I was actually gazing into the fabulous brain of Joan Rivers! On the other hand, the admirer of Joan Rivers might have saved Calvino; except that there was no real hope, ever. In June he had had what he thought was a bad headache; it was the first stroke. Also, he came from a family with a history of arterial weakness. Or so it was said in the newspapers. The press coverage of Calvino's final days resembled nothing so much as that of the recent operation on the ancient actor that our masters have hired to impersonate a president, the sort of subject that used to delight Calvino—the Acting President, that is.

==

As we drove north through the rain, I read Calvino's last novel, *Palomar*. He had given it to me on November 28, 1983. I was chilled—and guilty —to read for the first time the inscription: "For Gore, these last meditations about Nature, Italo." *Last* is a word artists should not easily use. What did this "last" mean? Latest? Or his last attempt to write about the phenomenal world? Or did he know, somehow, that he was in the process of "Learning to be dead," the title of the book's last chapter?

I read the book. It is very short. A number of meditations on different subjects by one Mr. Palomar, who is Calvino himself. The settings are, variously, the beach at Castiglion della Pescáia, the nearby house in the woods at Roccamare, the flat in Rome with its terrace, a food specialty shop in Paris. This is not the occasion to review the book. But I made some observations and marked certain passages that seemed to me to illuminate the prospect.

Palomar is on the beach at Castiglion: he is trying to figure out the nature of waves. Is it possible to follow just one? Or do they all become one? *E pluribus unum* and its reverse might well sum up Calvino's approach to our condition. Are we a part of the universe? Or is the universe, simply, us thinking that there is such a thing? Calvino often writes like the scientist that his parents were. He observes, precisely, the minutiae of nature: stars, waves, lizards, turtles, a woman's breast exposed on the beach. In the process, he vacillates between macro and micro. The whole and the part. Also, tricks of eye. The book is written in the present tense, like a scientist making reports on that ongoing experiment, the examined life.

The waves provide him with suggestions but no answers: Viewed in a certain way, they seem to come not from the horizon but from the shore itself. "Is this perhaps the real result that Mr. Palomar is about to achieve? To make the waves run in the opposite direction, to overturn time, to perceive the true substance of the world beyond sensory and mental habits?" But it doesn't quite work, and he cannot extend "this knowledge to the entire universe." He notes during his evening swim that "the sun's reflection becomes a shining sword on the water stretching from shore to him. Mr. Palomar swims in that sword . . ." But then so does everyone else at that time of day, each in the same sword which is everywhere and nowhere. "The sword is imposed equally on the eye of each swimmer; there is no avoiding it. 'Is what we have in common precisely what is given to each of us as something exclusively his?' " As Palomar floats he wonders if he exists. He drifts now toward solipsism: "If no eye except the glassy eye of the dead were to open again on the surface of the terraqueous globe, the sword would not gleam any more." He develops this, floating on his back. "Perhaps it was not the birth of the eye that caused the birth of the sword, but vice versa, because the sword had to have an eye to observe it at its climax." But the day is ending, the windsurfers are all beached, and Palomar comes back to land: "He has become convinced that the sword will exist even without him."

In the garden at Roccamare, Palomar observes the exotic mating of turtles; he ponders the blackbird's whistle, so like that of a human being that it might well be the same sort of communication. "Here a prospect that is very promising for Mr. Palomar's thinking opens out; for him the discrepancy between human behavior and the rest of the universe has always been a source of anguish. The equal whistle of man and blackbird now seems to him a bridge thrown over the abyss." But his attempts to communicate with them through a similar whistling leads to "puzzlement" on both sides. Then, contemplating the horrors of his lawn and its constituent parts, among them weeds, he precisely names and numbers what he sees until "he no longer thinks of the lawn: he thinks of the universe. He is trying to apply to the universe everything he has thought about the lawn. The universe as regular and ordered cosmos or as chaotic proliferation." The analogy, as always with Calvino, then takes off (the jam on the bread) and the answer is again the many within the one, or "collections of collections."

≡

Observations and meditations continue. He notes, "Nobody looks at the moon in the afternoon, and this is the moment when it would most require our attention, since its existence is still in doubt." As night comes on, he wonders if the moon's bright splendor is "due to the slow retreat of the sky, which, as it moves away, sinks deeper and deeper into darkness or whether, on the contrary it is the moon that is coming forward, collecting the previously scattered light and depriving the sky of it, concentrating it all in the round mouth of its funnel." One begins now to see the method of a Calvino meditation. He looks; he describes; he has a scientist's respect for data (the opposite of the surrealist or fantasist). He wants us to see not only what he sees but what we may have missed by not looking with sufficient attention. It is no wonder that Galileo crops up in his writing. The received opinion of mankind over the centuries (which is what middlebrow is all about) was certain that the sun moved around the earth but to a divergent highbrow's mind, Galileo's or Calvino's, it is plainly the other way around. Galileo applied the scientific methods of his day; Calvino used his imagination. Each either got it right or assembled the data so that others could understand the phenomenon.

In April 1982, while I was speaking to a Los Angeles audience with George McGovern, Eugene McCarthy, and the dread physical therapist Ms. Fonda-Hayden, "the three 'external' planets, visible to the naked eye . . . are all three 'in opposition' and therefore visible for the whole night." Needless to say, "Mr. Palomar rushes out on to the terrace." Between Calvino's stars and mine, he had the better of it; yet he wrote a good deal of political commentary for newspapers. But after he left the Communist party, he tended more to describe politics and its delusions than take up causes. "In a time and in a country where everyone goes out of his way to announce opinions or hand down judgments, Mr. Palomar has made a habit of biting his tongue three times before asserting anything. After the bite, if he is still convinced of what he was going to say, he says it." But then, "having had the correct view is nothing meritorious; statistically, it is almost inevitable that among the many cockeyed, confused or banal ideas that come into his mind, there should also be some perspicacious ideas, even ideas of genius; and as they occurred to him, they can surely have occurred also to somebody else." As he was a writer of literature and not a theorist, so he was an observer of politics and not a politician.

≡

Calvino was as inspired by the inhabitants of zoos as by those of cities. "At this point Mr. Palomar's little girl, who has long since tired of watching the giraffes, pulls him toward the penguins' cave. Mr. Palomar, in whom penguins inspire anguish, follows her reluctantly and asks himself why he is so interested in giraffes. Perhaps because the world around him moves in an unharmonious way, and he hopes always to find some pattern to it, a constant. Perhaps because he himself feels that his own advance is impelled by uncoordinated movements of the mind, which seem to have nothing to do with one another and are increasingly difficult to fit into any pattern of inner harmony."

Palomar is drawn to the evil-smelling reptile house. "Beyond the glass of every cage, there is the world as it was before man, or after, to show that the world of man is not eternal and is not unique." The crocodiles, in their stillness, horrify him. "What are they waiting for, or what have they given up waiting for? In what time are they immersed? . . . The thought of a time outside our existence is intolerable." Palomar flees to the albino gorilla, "sole exemplar in the world of a form not chosen, not loved." The gorilla, in his boredom, plays with a rubber tire; he presses it to his bosom by the hour. The image haunts Palomar. " 'Just as the gorilla has his tire, which serves as tangible support for a raving, wordless speech,' he thinks, 'so I have this image of a great white ape. We all turn in our hands an old, empty tire through which we would like to reach the final meaning, at which words do not arrive.' " This is the ultimate of writers' images; that indescribable state where words are absent not because they are stopped by the iron bars of a cage at the zoo but by the limitations of that bone-covered binary electrical system which, in Calvino's case, broke down on September 19, 1985.

≡

Suddenly, up ahead, on a hill overlooking the sea, is Castiglion della Pescáia. To my left is the beach where Palomar saw but sees no longer the sword of light. The sea has turned an odd disagreeable purple color, more suitable to the Caribbean of Calvino's birth than the Mediterranean. The sky is overcast. The air is hot, humid, windless (the headline of today's newspaper, which has devoted six pages to Calvino's life and work: CATA-CLISMA IN MESSICO). I am forty minutes early.

The cemetery is on a hill back of the town which is on a lower hill. We park next to a piece of medieval wall and a broken tower. I walk up to the cemetery which is surrounded by a high cement wall. I am reminded of Calvino's deep dislike of cement. In one of his early books, *La Speculazione Edilizia,* he described how the building trade had managed, in the 1950s, to bury the Italian Riviera, his native Liguria, under a sea of "horrible reinforced cement"; *"il boom,"* it was called. To the right of the cemetery entrance a large section of wall has been papered over with the same small funeral notice, repeated several hundred times. The name "Italo Calvino," the name of Castiglion della Pescáia, "the town of Palomar," the sign says proudly; then the homage of mayor and city council and populace.

Inside the cemetery there are several walled-off areas. The first is a sort of atrium, whose walls are filled with drawers containing the dead, stacked one above the other, each with a photograph of the occupant, taken rather too late in life to arouse much pity as opposed to awe. There are plastic flowers everywhere and a few real flowers. There are occasional small chapels, the final repository of wealthy or noble families. I have a sense of panic: They aren't going to put Italo in a drawer, are they? But then to the right, at the end of the atrium, in the open air, against a low wall, I see a row of vast floral wreaths, suitable for an American or Neapolitan gangster, and not a drawer but a new grave, the size of a bathtub in a moderately luxurious hotel. On one of the wreaths, I can make out the words *Senato* and *Communist* . . . , the homage of the Communist delegation in the Italian Senate. Parenthetically, since Italy is a country of many political parties and few ideologies, the level of the ordinary parliamentarian is apt to be higher than his American or English counterpart. Moravia sits in the European Parliament. Sciascia was in the chamber of deputies. Every party tries to put on its electoral list a number of celebrated intellectual names. The current mayor of Florence was, until recently, the head of the Paris Opéra: According to popular wisdom, anyone who could handle that can of worms can probably deal with Florence.

===

Over the wall, the purple sea and red-tiled whitewashed houses are visible. As I gaze, moderately melancholy, at Palomar country, I am recognized

by a journalist from Naples. I am a neighbor, after all; I live at nearby
Ravello. Among the tombs, I am interviewed. How had I met Calvino?
A few drops of warm rain fall. A cameraman appears from behind a family
chapel and takes my picture. The state television crew is arriving. Eleven
years ago, I say, I wrote a piece about his work. Had you met him *before*
that? Logrolling is even more noticeable in a small country like Italy than
it is in our own dear *New York Times*. No, I had not met him when I wrote
the piece. I had just read him, admired him; described (the critic's only
task) his work for those who were able to read me (the critic's single aim).
Did you meet him later? Yes, he wrote me a letter about the piece. In
Italian or English? Italian, I say. What did he say? What do you think he
said? I am getting irritable. He said he liked what I'd written.

Actually, Calvino's letter had been, characteristically, interesting and
tangential. I had ended my description with "Reading Calvino, I had the
unnerving sense that I was also writing what he had written; thus does his
art prove his case as writer and reader become one, or One." This caught
his attention. Politely, he began by saying that he had always been attracted by my "mordant irony," and so forth, but he particularly liked what
I had written about him for two reasons. The first, "One feels that you
have written this essay for the pleasure of writing it, alternating warm
praise and criticism and reserve with an absolute sincerity, with freedom,
and continuous humor, and this sensation of pleasure is irresistibly com-
municated to the reader. Second, I have always thought it would be
difficult to extract a unifying theme from my books, each so different from
the other. Now you—exploring my works as it should be done, that is, by
going at it in an unsystematic way, stopping here and there; sometimes
aimed directly without straying aside; other times, wandering like a vaga-
bond—have succeeded in giving a general sense to all I have written,
almost a philosophy—'the whole and the many,' etc.—and it makes me
very happy when someone is able to find a philosophy from the productions of my mind which has little philosophy." Then Calvino comes to the
point. "The ending of your essay contains an affirmation of what seems
to me important in an absolute sense. I don't know if it really refers to me,
but it is true of an ideal literature for each one of us: the end being that
every one of us must be, that the writer and reader become one, or One.
And to close all of my discourse and yours in a perfect circle, let us say
that this One is All." In a sense, the later Palomar was the gathering

together of the strands of a philosophy or philosophies; hence, the inscription "my last meditations on Nature."

I let slip not a word of this to the young journalist. But I do tell him that soon after the letter I had met Calvino and his wife, Chichita, at the house of an American publisher, and though assured that there would be no writers there but us, I found a room ablaze with American literary genius. Fearful of becoming prematurely One with them, I split into the night.

Two years ago, when I was made an honorary citizen of Ravello, Calvino accepted the town's invitation to participate in the ceremony, where he delivered a splendid discourse on my work in general and on *Duluth* in particular. Also, since Calvino's Roman flat was on the same street as mine (we were separated by—oh, the beauty of the random symbol!—the Pantheon), we saw each other occasionally.

$$\equiv$$

For the last year, Calvino had been looking forward to his fall and winter at Harvard. He even began to bone up on "literary theory." He knew perfectly well what a mephitic kindergarten our English departments have become, and I cannot wait to see what he has to say in the five lectures that he did write. I had planned to arm him with a wonderfully silly bit of lowbrow criticism (from *Partisan Review*) on why people just don't like to read much anymore. John Gardner is quoted with admiration: " 'In nearly all good fiction, the basic—all but inescapable—plot form is this: a central character wants something, goes after it despite opposition (perhaps including his own doubts), and so arrives at a win, lose or draw.' " For those still curious about high-, middle-, and lowbrow, this last is the Excelsior of lowbrow commercialites, written in letters of gold in the halls of the Thalberg Building at MGM but never to be found in, say, the original *Partisan Review* of Rahv and Dupee, Trilling and Chase. The *PR* "critic" then quotes "a reviewer" in *The New York Times* who is trying to figure out why Calvino is popular. "If love fails, they begin again; their lives are a series of new beginnings, where complications have not yet begun to show themselves. Unlike the great Russian and French novelists [this is pure middlebrow: *Which* novelists, dummy? Name names, make your case, *describe*], who follow their characters through the long and winding caverns [!] of their lives, Calvino just turns off the set after the easy beginning and switches to another channel." This sort of writing has given American bookchat (a word I coined, you will be eager to know) a permanently bad name. But our *PR* critic, a woman, this year's favored minority *(sic)*, states, sternly, that all this "indeterminacy" is not the kind of stuff real folks want to read. "And Calvino is popular, if at all, among theorists, consumers of 'texts' rather than of novels and stories." I shall now never have the chance to laugh with Calvino over this latest report from the land to which Bouvard and Pécuchet emigrated.

At the foot of cemetery hill, a van filled with police arrives. Crowds are anticipated. The day before, the president of the republic had come to the Siena hospital to say farewell. One can imagine a similar scene in the United States. High atop the Tulsa Tower Hospital, the Reverend Oral Roberts enters the hushed room. "Mr. President, it's all over. *He* has crossed the shining river." A tear gleams in the Acting President's eye. "The last roundup," he murmurs. The tiny figure at his side, huge lidless eyes aswim with tears, whispers, "Does this mean, no more Harlequin novels?" The Acting President holds her close. "There will always be Harlequins, Mommie," he says. 'But they won't be the same. Not without Louis L'Amour."

$$===$$

Now several hundred friends of Calvino, writers, editors, publishers, press, local dignitaries fill up the cemetery. I hold Chichita's hand a long moment; she has had, someone said, two weeks of coming to terms not so much with death as with the nightmare of dying.

The last chapter of *Palomar* begins, "Mr. Palomar decides that from now on he will act as if he were dead, to see how the world gets along without him." So far, not too good, I thought. Mexico City has fallen down and his daughter is late to the burial. On the plus side, there is no priest, no service, no words. Suddenly, as a dozen television cameras switch on, the dark shiny wooden box, containing Calvino, appears in the atrium. How small the box is, I think. Was he smaller than I remember? Or has he shrunk? Of course, he is dead but, as he wrote, "First of all, you must not confuse being dead with not being, a condition that occupies the vast expanse of time before birth, apparently symmetrical with the other, equally vast expanse that follows death. In fact, before birth we are part of the infinite possibilities that may or may not be fulfilled; whereas, once dead, we cannot fulfill ourselves either in the past (to which we now belong entirely but on which we can no longer have any influence) or in the future (which, even if influenced by us, remains forbidden to us)."

With a crash, the pallbearers drop the box into the shallow bathtub. Palomar's nose is now about four inches beneath the earth he used to examine so minutely. Then tiles are casually arranged over the coffin; and the box is seen no more. As we wait for the daughter to arrive, the heat is disagreeable. We look at one another as though we are at a party that has refused to take off. I recognize Natalia Ginzburg. I see someone who looks as if he ought to be Umberto Eco, and is. "A person's life consists of a collection of events, the last of which could also change the meaning of the whole . . ." I notice, in the crowd, several dozen young schoolchildren. They are fans of Calvino's fairy tales; plainly, precocious consumers of "texts" and proto-theorists. Then daughter and buckets of cement arrive simultaneously. One of the masons pours cement over the tiles; expertly, he smooths the viscous surface with a trowel. Horrible cement. "Therefore Palomar prepares to become a grouchy dead man, reluctant to submit to the sentence to remain exactly as he is; but he is unwilling to give up anything of himself, even if it is a burden." Finally, the cement is flush with the ground; and that's that.

I am standing behind Chichita, who is very still. Finally, I look up from the gray oblong of fresh cement and there, staring straight at me, is Calvino. He looks anguished, odd, not quite right. But it is unmistakably Mr. Palomar, witnessing his own funeral. For one brief mad moment we stare at each other; then he looks down at the coffin that contains not himself but Italo. The man I thought was Italo is his younger brother, Floriano.

I move away, before the others. On the drive back to Rome, the sun is bright and hot; yet rain starts to fall. Devil is beating his wife, as they say in the South. Then a rainbow covers the entire eastern sky. For the Romans and the Etruscans, earlier inhabitants of the countryside through which we are driving, the rainbow was an ominous herald of coming change in human affairs, death of kings, cities, world. I make a gesture to ward off the evil eye. Time can now end. But " 'If time has to end, it can be described, instant by instant,' Palomar thinks, 'and each instant, when described, expands so that its end can no longer be seen.' He decides that he will set himself to describing every instant of his life, and until he has described them all he will no longer think of being dead. At that moment he dies."* So end "my last meditations on Nature," and Calvino and Nature are now one, or One.

THE NEW YORK REVIEW OF BOOKS
*November 21, 1985*

*Now that Calvino's work is done, one must praise the faithful William Weaver for his elegant translations over many years.

# CHAPTER 22

# WHY I AM
# EIGHT YEARS YOUNGER THAN
# ANTHONY BURGESS

I saw them coming, an army of two with banners. He was tall, pale, eyes narrowed from cigarette smoke of his own making (an eighty-a-day man for years); she was small, round faced, somewhat bloated. In the gracious plywood-paneled room, the hard stuff was flowing, and the flower of British bookchat and publishing was on hand to drink it all up in honor, not quite the noun, of my return, after a decade's absence, to Literature, with a long reflection on the origins of Christianity, novelly disguised as a novel. The year, 1964.

She said in a loud clear voice, "You," and then I ceased to understand her, "chung cheers boog sightee Joyce yearsen roscoe conkling." I am certain that I heard the name of the nineteenth-century New York senator, and I turned to the man—the senator's biographer?—and saw, like infected buttonholes, eyes I dare not meet in dreams. "Tchess." He took up the refrain. "Boog Joyce venially blind, too, bolder." I had been drinking, but not that much, while the tall man appeared sober. Obviously, I was having my chronic problem with English voices: the low rapid mumble, the urgent wheeze, the imploding diphthong, vowels wrongly stressed, and consonants long since gone west with the thirteen colonies.

We were separated. I was told that I had been talking to Anthony Burgess and his wife, Lynne. Burgess had written some comic novels about life east of Maugham—or Suez; now there was a new book called *A Clockwork Orange.* I knew nothing of him except for one splendid anecdote. Under another name, he had reviewed one of his own books in a British paper. The Brits were horrified. I was delighted: Whitman had done the same. Besides, I was stern, shouldn't there be at least one review in all of England written by someone who had actually read the book?

Again the army approached, banners raised high. We worked out a common language. Lynne was pissed off that my novel *Julian* was a Book Society choice. She was even more annoyed when I wanted to know what the Book Society was. I had a vision of aged flappers reciting Dorothy Richardson over sugary tea. The society was like an American book club, she growled. I apologized. This was not enough. Truth crackled in the air. A novel by Burgess had finally been chosen, in 1961; yet *he was eight years my senior.* I was too young to be so honored. I mounted my high horse, tethered conveniently near. "I have written more books than Mr. Burgess," I said, settling myself into the saddle. "And over a greater length of time." Swift, suspicious adding and subtracting was done as we ate small but heavy sausages, diapered in a fried bread and speared with lethal plastic toothpicks. True, eighteen years had passed since my first book was published (at twenty) and a mere seven years since his first (at thirty-seven) but he was certain that he was well ahead in units of production. I was not. But before I could begin the long count, he said, "Anyway, I'm actually a composer." This was superb, and I ceded the high ground to him. Lynne did not. She rounded on him: You are *not* a composer. Pussy-whipped, he winced and muttered, "roscoe *g.* conkling." As I rode off into the night, no boyish treble sounded, "Shane!"

Four years later Lynne was dead of the drink (cirrhosis of the liver). In due course, Burgess married an Italian, lived in Rome, and from time to time our paths crossed, cross. Now, twenty-three years after our first meeting, he is suddenly, astonishingly, seventy years old (I remain, throughout eternity, eight years his junior), and the author of twenty-eight novels and dozens of odd volumes on this and that as well as a part-time laborer in television and films and the theater, where he recently distinguished himself with an adaptation of *Cyrano* that changed everyone's view of that familiar but not-so-high war horse.

===

Burgess has now published *Little Wilson and Big God,* "Being the First Part of the Autobiography," which, long as it is, takes him only to the age of forty-two in 1959 when he was told that he had an inoperable brain tumor, and a year to live. In order to provide for Lynne, he started turning out books at a prodigious rate, and now, twenty years after her death, he still, undead, goes on. Incomparable British medicine ("In point of fact, Dr. Butterfingers, that's *my* scalpel you're standing on") is responsible for the existence of easily the most interesting English writer of the last half century. Like Meredith, Burgess does the best things best; he also does the worst things pretty well, too. There is no other writer like him, a cause of some alarm to others—him, too. Now, in the sad—the vain, I fear—hope that once we've known the trouble he's seen we will forgive him his unfashionable originality and prodigiousness, he makes confession not to merciful God but to merciless us.

The subject of the first part of the autobiography bears, I should guess, very little resemblance to the man who wrote it, who, in turn, bears no resemblance at all to the John Wilson that he was born and continued to be until his relatively late blossoming as a novelist. It is not that he bears false witness; it is, simply, the problem of recalling past time as it occurs to someone in a present where "I have trouble with memory, especially of names." Also, this testament is not extravagantly and carefully shaped like one of his novels; rather, it is doggedly improvised (from diaries? There is a single reference to a diary).

Burgess tells us that in 1985, he was in New York's Plaza Hotel, waiting for a car to take him to the airport. Suddenly, like Gibbon on the steps of Santa Maria d'Aracoeli, he decided to tell this story. But when he started to write, I don't think that he had a clue where he was going or how he was going to get there. Fortunately, he has not the gift of boredom. He can make just about anything interesting except on those occasions when he seems to be writing an encoded message to N. Chomsky, in celebration not so much of linguistics as his own glossolalia, so triumphantly realized in his screenplay for *Quest for Fire.*

But the narrative itself is in order. Born John Wilson, February 25, 1917, in Manchester, England; father arrives home from the First World War to find wife and daughter dead of the influenza epidemic; in the same room as the corpses, young Wilson lies, giggling, in his crib. I am not sure if every detail is meant to stand up in court, but certainly Burgess, as artist always on oath (as opposed to defendant in the dock), is keeping close to the essential facts of the case. The father is musical; plays piano in silent movie houses; marries a second time to a woman of some means who becomes a tobacconist. Young Wilson is solidly lower middle class and might have made it up to mid-middle class were it not for the fact that Celtic blood flows in his veins and so, as a Roman Catholic, he was literally set apart from the Protestant majority and was sent to church schools where the good brothers, as is their wont, managed to detach him from his faith. When Burgess starts to question Holy Church, a priest remarks that this is plainly a case of Little Wilson and Big God; hence the book's title, the author's problem.

There is a great deal of carefully described sex. Although Burgess had had sex with girls at an early age, and once observed another boy masturbating, he himself did not know how to masturbate until late adolescence; even more traumatic and poignant, he was equally ignorant of lending libraries. For me, Burgess demonstrates, yet again, how uninteresting the sexual lives of others are when told by them. At one point, he remarks that most literature is about sex. If true, then, perhaps, that is why it is necessary for us to have literature. Once the imagination has, kinetically, translated the act from bed to page excitement begins. But nothing happens when a writer, or anyone, tells us what he himself has actually done in bed or on the floor or in the bushes, where Burgess was caught in the army. Nevertheless, from Frank Harris to Henry Miller to Tennessee Williams to Burgess, there is a weird desire to tell us all, and the rest of us (unless we lust for aged auctorial flesh) start to skip, looking for gossip, jokes, wisdom, or just a good sentence.

Of course, Burgess was brought up, as was I, before the Second World War. In those days, in most circles (not mine, happily) sex and guilt were one and the same, and a new religion was even based on the idea of universal sexual repression (the universe, as symbolized by a corner of bourgeois Vienna) which could only be raised through confession. It is not until mid-career that Burgess suspects that there may be other sources of joy if little guilt, like the perfect bowel movement, which his eponymous hero-poet, the costive Enderby, pursues like a mad surfer waiting upon the perfect wave.

═══

In youth, Burgess must have found bewildering the variety of his talents. He was, first, a musician entirely bewitched by that arithmetic muse. He could remember a thousand popular songs. Wistfully, he suggests that even to this day he could earn his living as a cocktail-bar pianist. But he was more ambitious than that. He set poems, wrote symphonies, attempted operas. He still does, he tells us, somewhat defensively because, parallel to his successful literary career, he has been a not-so-successful composer. Plainly, he is puzzled. Are they right? Is he any good? Currently, he is working on an opera about Freud ("Show Me Your Dream, I'll Show You Mine"?). So, perhaps, there is method to his recollections here of early sexual experiences.

Nevertheless, it is an article of faith (bad) in our dull categorizing time that no one may practice more than a single art; even worse, within the house of literature itself, the writer must keep to only one, preferably humble, room; yet a gift for any art is almost always accompanied by at least the ability to master one or more of the other arts. This is a secret of genius's lodge that is kept from every faculty room lest there be nervous breakdowns and losses of faith and transfers from English studies to physics. But where Goethe, say, was allowed his universality, today's artist is expected to remain cooped up in mediocrity's vast columbarium. The reputation of our best short-story writer, Paul Bowles, has suffered because he is, equally, a fine composer: For musicians, he is a writer; for writers, a composer.

Along with music, Burgess had a talent for drawing; fortunately, he is also color-blind; otherwise he might have been pecked to death by angry crows at the Tate. Finally, he could write, but it was a long time before he allowed that old shoe of an art to bemuse him. I suspect that Burgess has been severely shaken by those music critics who have put him in his place, high in the gallery of Albert Hall; as a result, he believes that they are probably right because one person cannot be more than one thing. To a born-again atheist like myself, it is clear that each of us has multiple selves, talents, perceptions. But to the Roman Catholic, unity is all. At birth, each is handed One Immortal Soul, and that's that. One god for each; one muse for each. Then, at the end, we all line up. Good to the right. Bad to the left. All right! Now let's hear those voices raised in praise of HIM. Because—Heee-res De Lawd! Burgess! Less vibrato. This isn't Heaven, you know.

＝

Three themes emerge in the course of the autobiography. The first, religion. What it means to be lower-middle-class Roman Catholic in the English mid-Midlands; what it means to lose—or lapse from—one's faith; what it means to be forever on the alert for another absolute system to provide one with certainty about everything. At one point, in Southeast Asia, Burgess was tempted to convert to Islam. But Islamic bigotry distressed him, and he backed away. Now,

in old age I look back on various attempts to cancel my apostasy and become reconciled to the Church again. This is because I have found no metaphysical substitute for it. Marxism will not do, nor will the kind of sceptical humanism that Montaigne taught. I know of no other organization that can both explain evil and, theoretically at least, brandish arms against it.

This is bewildering to an American of the Enlightenment; but as the twig was bent . . . Also, to the extent that Burgess has any political ideas at all, he's deeply reactionary and capable of such blimpisms as, "In February the Yalta Conference sold half of Europe to the Russians."

The second theme is sex. After the glut of the salacious sexy seventies, and the hysteria of the anxious AIDSy eighties, it is hard for those who grew up after the great divide—the Second World War—to realize that just about the only thing any of us ever thought about was getting laid. Burgess went into the British army at twenty-three in 1940. Three years later, at seventeen, I went into the American army. Each got out of the army in 1946; each with the neither-fish-nor-fowl rank of warrant officer. Although Burgess was for all practical purposes married to Lynne when he was scooped up by the army, he, too—like the rest of us—was introduced to a world of sex where every traditional barrier had fallen with a crash. There was a general availability unknown to previous generations of European—much less American—Christendom. Those of us who joined the orgy in our teens often failed, in later life, to acquire the gift of intimacy. Burgess himself had other problems; innocently—always innocently—he tells us about them, unaware that an autobiography is no place for truth as opposed to the true: Augustine's sententious nonsense about those pears should have taught him that.

Because Burgess had no mother, he writes,

> I was not encouraged to express tenderness. I was reared emotionally cold. . . . I regret the emotional coldness that was established then and which, apart from other faults, has marred my works.

At least one dull American bookchat writer thought that this was really insightful stuff and moved Burgess several rungs down the literary ladder. He cannot love; ergo, he cannot write. He is not warm; ergo, he is not good. He is cold; ergo, he is bad. Burgess is very conscious of his reviewers but I do not think that he has ever quite grasped the deep ignorance of the average American bookchat writer, who is in place to celebrate obedience and conformity to that deadly second-rateness which has characterized our garrison state for the last third of a century.

Recently a television documentary on one of our public schools was screened for the local school board. The board was near rapture. But when the public saw the film, the board realized that what they had admired, the successful attempt to destroy individuality in the young, did not play so well with the TV audience, hardly themselves naysayers. Since power not sex is true motor to human life, the powerless often prefer to die. That is why today's young do not eat goldfish. They kill themselves.

===

Burgess's thirty-year marriage is more harrowing to read about than, perhaps, to have lived. At first, he was obliged to share Lynne with a pair of well-off brothers, one of whom might bring her the money that he could not. Then Burgess attended the party that was the Second World War. Finally, Lynne and the brothers parted and the open marriage of the Burgesses gaped anew. Postwar, Burgess taught in Malaya and Brunei. He and she each drank a bottle of gin a day. She made love to a number of men; he to women. She fought with everyone; demanded a divorce; was reconciled by the publication of his first books. Fortunately, he enjoys being humiliated by women, a theme that runs through the novels, giving them their sexual edge (see the final Enderby volume). Fascinating but mysterious—like Grace. Anyway, he loved her, he tells us, for thirty years.

Religion, sex, art—three themes that, unlike the Trinity, never become one. Finally, despite the distractions of the first two, it is the third that matters because that is all that's ever left. Burgess himself does not seem quite to know what to make of his novels. Wistfully, he goes on about music and the structure of language but, in the end, he is a writer of prose, a novelist, a sometime movie and television writer. There was a time whenever a producer came to me for a script on Jesus or the Borgias, or even Jesus and the Borgias, I'd send them on to Burgess, who would oblige. Today, he is the best literary journalist alive, as V. S. Pritchett is the best literary critic. Pritchett, of course, modestly opts for the word *journalist,* aware that the high ground of criticism is currently occupied by academic literary theoreticians who have presided, during the last two decades, a 60 percent drop in English studies. Well, if you can't lick 'em, change the game.

This is not the place (nor does space afford, as Henry James would coyly note, having filled his review of some dim novel with a series of glittering false starts) to describe the twenty-eight novels of Anthony Burgess. So I shall stick to what he himself has to say about them in his memoir. One thing becomes clear: Like so many highly serious brilliant men, he has no natural humor or comic sense as opposed to verbal wit. Bewitched by *Finnegans Wake,* he dreamed of the marriage of high literature to high music. When he wrote his first novel, about wartime Gibraltar, he gave it to an editor at Heinemann. "It was, he said, funny. I had not, in fact, intended it to be funny, but I assumed the right posture of modesty on this revelation that I was a coming comic novelist." Dutifully—seriously? —he wrote several more novels set east of Suez and each turned out comic, even though he was writing of sad exotic places, and people; but, of course, he was writing about the painful untidy lives of Anthony and Lynne in far-off places where, as Horace (no, not Greeley) so pithily put it, "People change their skies, not their feelings, when they rush overseas." The *rush* is often funny while *overseas,* for the Brits, always is. Thus tragedy turns out comedy.

Of Burgess's fourth novel *(The Right to an Answer)* he writes, it "was almost entirely invention. That I could invent was the final proof, to me, that I had not mistaken my vocation." For the Burgess reader, the great breakthrough came after his death sentence, when he was furiously writing and inventing. In 1944, the pregnant Lynne had been robbed and beaten up in a London street by four American soldiers. She aborted. Burgess turned this true story into a novel that he has small regard for because the world at large has such a high regard for the film version, done by another, of *A Clockwork Orange*. Burgess hurls the story into a future London where four local louts have been Sovietized and speak a new vulgate, part London prole, part Russian. The result is chilling, and entirely other. When Burgess moves away from his own immediate life, his books come most startlingly alive, if ink markings on mute paper can ever be called a life form or even its surrogate.

═══

In the light of his three obsessions, Burgess wanted to bring God into the novel in a big way, with Berlioz-cum-Joyce symbolism, and resonating like a struck cymbal with atavistic Lorenzian blood myths. Happily, he failed. Of an early novel, he writes, "The realism overcame the symbolism. This usually happens when the novelist possesses, which Joyce did not, a genuine narrative urge." One detects a regret here, an acknowledgment that the Wilsonian passion for *Finnegans Wake* has no place in the Burgessian novel. But then, "I see that the novel, an essentially comic and Protestant art form, is no place for the naked posturing of religious guilt." He means of course the English novel in this century. A twentieth-century novel each of us admires, *Doctor Faustus,* has roots in the human bloodstream (spirochete-ridden as it is) in a way not allowed by our meager culture and overrich language.

If Burgess is obsessed with sex in his memoirs, he uses sex judiciously in his novels and in the best (he will not agree), The Enderby Four, as I call them—*Inside Mr. Enderby, Enderby Outside, The Clockwork Testament, or Enderby's End,* and *Enderby's Dark Lady*—he uses his obsession much as Nabokov did in *Lolita* to make a thousand and one points about literature and life and their last human sanctuary, the motels of America. On the showing of the fugitive poems in the autobiography, Burgess himself is not much of a poet but his invention, the poet Enderby, on the showing of *his* poems is one of the finest of contemporary poets and ought to be anthologized as himself, with symposia devoted to his art, and no reference to Wilson/Burgess as amanuensis. There is no invention quite so extraordinary as that which surpasses, at inventing, the original inventor. Baron Frankenstein's creation just hangs out. But Enderby's poems have the effect that only the best writing can have on a reader who also writes. They make him want to write poems, too; and surpass self.

The Burgess who doubts his comic sense or, rather, was slightly appalled that his "serious" works made others laugh must know by now that the highest art, which is comedy, is grounded in obsession. With a bit of luck (a Roman Catholic education?) Melville might have created a masterpiece in *Moby Dick*. As it is, we laugh—though not enough—at Captain Ahab (*Pierre* is funnier). But Burgess was wise enough to allow *his* obsessions with religion, sex, language, to work themselves out as comedy. Also, he has been able to put to good use his passion, rather than obsession, for language and its forms, and his lively restless inventions have considerably brightened the culturally flat last years of our century. How he managed to do this is implicit, if not always explicit, in the pages of *Little Wilson and Big God*, which might better be called *Little Wilson and Big Burgess*, who did it his, if not His, way.

# CHAPTER 23

# DAWN POWELL:
# THE AMERICAN WRITER

### 1

Once upon a time, New York City was as delightful a place to live in as to visit. There were many amenities, as they say in brochures. One was something called Broadway, where dozens of plays opened each season, and thousands of people came to see them in an area which today resembles downtown Calcutta without, alas, that subcontinental city's deltine charm and intellectual rigor.

One evening back there in once upon a time (February 7, 1957, to be exact) my first play opened at the Booth Theatre. Traditionally, the playwright was invisible to the audience: One hid out in a nearby bar, listening to the sweet nasalities of Pat Boone's rendering of "Love Letters in the Sand" from a glowing jukebox. But when the curtain fell on this particular night, I went into the crowded lobby to collect someone. Overcoat collar high about my face, I moved invisibly through the crowd, or so I thought. Suddenly a voice boomed-tolled across the lobby. *"Gore!"* I stopped; everyone stopped. From the cloakroom a small round figure, rather like a Civil War cannon ball, hurtled toward me and collided. As I looked down into that familiar round face with its snub nose and shining bloodshot eyes, I heard, the entire crowded lobby heard: *"How could you do this?* How could you *sell out* like this? To *Broadway!* To *Commercialism!* How could you give up *The Novel?* Give up the *security?* The security of knowing that every two years there will be—like clockwork—*that five-hundred-dollar advance!"* Thirty years later, the voice still echoes in my mind, and I think fondly of its owner, our best comic novelist. "The field," I can hear Dawn Powell snarl, "is not exactly overcrowded."

On the night that *Visit to a Small Planet* opened, Dawn Powell was fifty-nine years old. She had published fourteen novels, evenly divided between accounts of her native Midwest (and how the hell to get out of there and make it to New York) and the highly comic New York novels, centered on Greenwich Village, where she lived most of her adult life. Some twenty-three years earlier, the Theatre Guild had produced Powell's comedy *Jig Saw* (one of *her* many unsuccessful attempts to sell out to commercialism), but there was third-act trouble and, despite Spring Byington and Ernest Truex, the play closed after forty-nine performances.

For decades Dawn Powell was always just on the verge of ceasing to be a cult and becoming a major religion. But despite the work of such dedicated cultists as Edmund Wilson and Matthew Josephson, John Dos Passos and Ernest Hemingway, Dawn Powell never became the popular writer that she ought to have been. In those days, with a bit of luck, a good writer eventually attracted voluntary readers and became popular. Today, of course, "popular" means bad writing that is widely read while good writing is that which is taught to involuntary readers. Powell failed on both counts. She needs no interpretation and in her lifetime she should have been as widely read as, say, Hemingway or the early Fitzgerald or the mid O'Hara or even the late, far too late, Katherine Anne Porter. But Powell was that unthinkable monster, a witty woman who felt no obligation to make a single, much less a final, down payment on Love or The Family; she saw life with a bright Petronian neutrality, and every host at life's feast was a potential Trimalchio to be sent up.

In the few interviews that Powell gave, she often mentions as her favorite novel, surprisingly for an American, much less for a woman of her time and place, the *Satyricon*. This sort of thing was not acceptable then any more than it is now. Descriptions of warm, mature, heterosexual love were—and are—woman's writerly task, and the truly serious writers really, heartbreakingly, flunk the course while the pop ones pass with bright honors.

Although Powell received very little serious critical attention (to the extent that there has ever been much in our heavily moralizing culture), when she did get reviewed by a really serious person like Diana Trilling (*The Nation*, May 29, 1948), *la* Trilling warns us that the book at hand is no good because of "the discrepancy between the power of mind revealed on every page of her novel [*The Locusts Have No King*] and the insignificance of the human beings upon which she directs her excellent intelligence." Trilling does acknowledge the formidable intelligence but because Powell does not deal with morally complex people (full professors at Columbia in mid journey?), "the novel as a whole . . . fails to sustain the excitement promised by its best moments."

Apparently, a novel to be serious must be about very serious—even solemn—people rendered in a very solemn—even serious—manner. Wit? What is that? But then we all know that power of mind and intelligence count for as little in the American novel as they do in American life. Fortunately neither appears with sufficient regularity to distress our solemn middle-class middlebrows as they trudge ever onward to some Scarsdale of the mind, where the red light blinks and blinks at pier's end and the fields of the republic rush forward ever faster like a rug rolling up.

═══

Powell herself occasionally betrays bewilderment at the misreading of her work. She is aware, of course, that the American novel is a middlebrow middle-class affair and that the reader/writer must be as one in pompous self-regard. "There is so great a premium on dullness," she wrote sadly (Robert Van Gelder, *Writers and Writing*, New York: Scribner's, 1946), "that it seems stupid to pass it up." She also remarks that

it is considered jolly and good-humored to point out the oddities of the poor or of the rich. The frailties of millionaires or garbage collectors can be made to seem amusing to persons who are not millionaires or garbage collectors. Their ways of

speech, their personal habits, the peculiarities of their thinking are considered fair
game. I go outside the rules with my stuff because I can't help believing that the
middle class is funny, too.

Well, she was warned by four decades of bookchatterers.

My favorite was the considered judgment of one Frederic Morton (*The
New York Times*, September 12, 1954):

But what appears most fundamentally lacking is the sense of outrage which serves
as an engine to even the most sophisticated [*sic*] satirist. Miss Powell does not
possess the pure indignation that moves Evelyn Waugh to his absurdities and
forced Orwell into his haunting contortions. Her verbal equipment is probably
unsurpassed among writers of her genre—but she views the antics of humanity
with too surgical a calm.

It should be noted that Mr. Morton was the author of the powerful, purely
indignant, and phenomenally compassionate novel, *Asphalt and Desire.* In
general, Powell's books usually excited this sort of commentary. (Waugh
*indignant?* Orwell hauntingly *contorted?*) The fact is that Americans have
never been able to deal with wit. Wit gives away the scam. Wit blows the
cool of those who are forever expressing a sense of hoked-up outrage. Wit,
deployed by a woman with surgical calm, is a brutal assault upon nature
—that is, Man. Attis, take arms!

Finally, as the shadows lengthened across the greensward, Edmund
Wilson got around to his old friend in *The New Yorker* (November 17,
1962). One reason, he tells us, why Powell has so little appeal to those
Americans who read novels is that "she does nothing to stimulate feminine
day-dreams [sexist times!]. The woman reader can find no comfort in
identifying herself with Miss Powell's heroines. The women who appear
in her stories are likely to be as sordid and absurd as the men." This sexual
parity was—is—unusual. But now, closer to century's end than 1962,
Powell's sordid, absurd ladies seem like so many Mmes. de Staël compared
to our latter-day viragos.

Wilson also noted Powell's originality: "Love is not Miss Powell's
theme. Her real theme is the provincial in New York who has come on
from the Middle West and acclimatized himself (or herself) to the city and
made himself a permanent place there, without ever, however, losing his

fascinated sense of an alien and anarchic society." This is very much to the (very badly written) point. Wilson finds her novels "among the most amusing being written, and in this respect quite on a level with those of Anthony Powell, Evelyn Waugh, and Muriel Spark." Wilson's review was of her last book, *The Golden Spur;* three years later she was dead of breast cancer. "Thanks a lot, Bunny," one can hear her mutter as this belated floral wreath came flying through her transom.

≡

Summer. Sunday afternoon. Circa 1950. Dawn Powell's duplex living room at 35 East Ninth Street. The hostess presides over an elliptical aquarium filled with gin: a popular drink of the period known as the martini. In attendance, Coby—just Coby to me for years, her *cavaliere servente;* he is neatly turned out in a blue blazer, rosy faced, sleek silver hair combed straight back. Coby can talk with charm on any subject. The fact that he might be Dawn's lover has never crossed my mind. They are so old. A handsome, young poet lies on the floor, literally at the feet of E. E. Cummings and his wife, Marion, who ignore him. Dawn casts an occasional maternal eye in the boy's direction; but the eye is more that of the mother of a cat or a dog, apt to make a nuisance. Conversation flows. Gin flows. Marion Cummings is beautiful; so indeed is her husband, his eyes a faded denim blue. Coby is in great form. Though often his own subject, he records not boring triumphs but improbable disasters. He is always broke, and a once distinguished wardrobe is now in the hands of those gay receivers, his landladies. This afternoon, at home, Dawn is demure; thoughtful. "Why," she suddenly asks, eyes on the long body beside the coffee table, "do they never have floors of their own to sleep on?"

Cummings explains that since the poet lives in Philadelphia he is too far from his own floor to sleep on it. Not long after, the young poet and I paid a call on the Cummingses. We were greeted at the door by an edgy Marion. "I'm afraid you can't come in." Behind her an unearthly high scream sounded. "Dylan Thomas just died," she explained. "Is that Mr. Cummings screaming?" asked the poet politely, as the keening began on an even higher note. "No," said Marion. "That is not Mr. Cummings. That is Mrs. Thomas."

But for the moment, in my memory, the poet is forever asleep on the floor while on a balcony high up in the second story of Dawn's living room, a gray blurred figure appears and stares down at us. "Who," I ask, "is that?"

Dawn gently, lovingly, stirs the martinis, squints her eyes, says, "My husband, I think. It is Joe, isn't it, Coby?" She turns to Coby, who beams and waves at the gray man, who withdraws. "Of course it is," says Coby. "Looking very fit." I realize, at last, that this is a *ménage à trois* in Greenwich Village. My martini runs over.

2.

To date the only study of Dawn Powell is a doctoral dissertation by Judith Faye Pett (University of Iowa, 1981). Miss Pett has gathered together a great deal of biographical material for which one is grateful. I am happy to know, at last, that the amiable Coby's proper name was Coburn Gilman, and I am sad to learn that he survived Dawn by only two years. The husband on the balcony was Joseph Gousha, or Goushé, whom she married November 20, 1920. He was musical; she literary, with a talent for the theater. A son was born retarded. Over the years, a fortune was spent on schools and nurses. To earn the fortune, Powell did every sort of writing, from interviews in the press to stories for ladies' magazines to plays that tended not to be produced to a cycle of novels about the Midwest, followed by a cycle of New York novels, where she came into her own, dragging our drab literature screaming behind her. As doyenne of the Village, she held court in the grill of the Lafayette Hotel—for elegiasts the Lafayette was off Washington Square, at University Place and Ninth Street.

Powell also runs like a thread of purest brass through Edmund Wilson's *The Thirties:* "It was closing time in the Lafayette Grill, and Coby Gilman was being swept out from under the table. Niles Spencer had been stuttering for five minutes, and Dawn Powell gave him a crack on the jaw and said, '*Nuts* is the word you're groping for.' " Also, "[Peggy Bacon] told me about Joe Gousha's attacking her one night at a party and trying to tear her clothes off. . . . I suggested that Joe had perhaps simply thought that this was the thing to do in Dawn's set. She said, 'Yes: he thought it was a social obligation.' " Powell also "said that Dotsy's husband was very much excited because the Prince of Wales was wearing a zipper fly, a big thing in the advertising business." A footnote to this text says that "Dawn Powell (1897–1965)" and Wilson carried on a correspondence in which she was Mrs. Humphry Ward and he "a seedy literary man named Wigmore." Later, there is a very muddled passage in which, for reasons not quite clear, James Thurber tells Dawn Powell that she does not *deserve* to be in the men's room. That may well be what it was all about.

=

I have now read all of Powell's novels and one of the plays.* Miss Pett provides bits and pieces from correspondence and diaries, and fragments of bookchat. Like most writers, Powell wrote of what she knew. Therefore, certain themes recur, while the geography does not vary from that of her actual life. As a child, she and two sisters were shunted about from one midwestern farm or small town to another by a father who was a salesman on the road (her mother died when she was six). The maternal grandmother made a great impression on her and predisposed her toward boardinghouse life (as a subject not a residence). Indomitable old women, full of rage and good jokes, occur in both novel cycles. At twelve, Powell's father remarried, and Dawn and sisters went to live on the stepmother's farm. "My stepmother, one day, burned up all the stories I was writing, a form of discipline I could not endure. With thirty cents earned by picking berries I ran away, ending up in the home of a kind aunt in Shelby, Ohio." After graduation from the local high school, she worked her way through Lake Erie College for Women in Painesville, Ohio. I once gave a commencement address there and was struck by how red-brick New England Victorian the buildings were. I also found out all that I could about their famous alumna. I collected some good stories to tell her. But by the time I got back to New York she was dead.

Powell set out to be a playwright. One play ended up as a movie while another, *Big Night*, was done by the Group Theatre in 1933. But it was the First World War not the theater that got Powell out of Ohio and to New York in 1918, as a member of the Red Cross: The war ended before

*I have omitted an interesting short novel because it is not part of the New York cycle. Powell made one trip to Europe after the war. Although Paris was no match for the Village, Powell, ever thrifty, uses the city as a background for a young man and woman trapped in *A Cage for Lovers* (published the year that Dawn roared at me in the Booth Theatre). The girl is a secretary-companion to a monster-lady, and the young man her chauffeur. The writing is austere; there are few characters; the old lady, Lesley Patterson, keeper of the cage, is truly dreadful in her loving kindness. In a rather nice if not perhaps too neat ending, they cage *her* through her need to dominate. Thus, the weak sometimes prevail.

her uniform arrived. Powell wrote publicity. Married. Wrote advertising copy (at the time Goushé or Gousha was an account executive with an advertising agency). Failure in the theater and need for money at home led her to novel writing and the total security of that five-hundred-dollar advance each of us relied on for so many years. Powell's first novel, *Whither*, was published in 1925. In 1928 Powell published *She Walks in Beauty*, which she always maintained, mysteriously, was really her first novel. For one thing, the Ohio heroine of *Whither* is already in New York City, like Powell herself, working as a syndicated writer who must turn out thirty thousand words a week in order to live (in Powell's case to pay for her child's treatments). In a sense, this New York novel was premature; with her second book, Powell turns back to her origins in the Western Reserve, where New Englanders had re-created New England in Ohio; and the tone is dour Yankee, with a most un-Yankeeish wit.

The Ohio cycle begins with *She Walks in Beauty*, which is dedicated to her husband, Joe. The story is set in Powell's youth before the First World War. The book was written in 1927. Popular writers of the day: Thornton Wilder had published *The Bridge of San Luis Rey* in the same year as Powell's first but really second novel. Louis Bromfield received the Pulitzer Prize for *Early Autumn* (a favorite Bromfield phrase, "candy pink and poison green," occasionally surfaces in Powell) while Cather's *Death Comes for the Archbishop* was also published in 1927. The year 1925, of course, had been the most remarkable in our literary history. After satirizing life in the Midwest, Sinclair Lewis brought his hero Arrowsmith to New York City, a pattern Powell was to appropriate in her Ohio cycle. Also in that miraculous year alongside, as it were, *Whither:* Theodore Dreiser's *An American Tragedy*, Dos Passos's *Manhattan Transfer*, Fitzgerald's *The Great Gatsby*. It is interesting that Dreiser, Lewis, Hemingway, Fitzgerald, Dos Passos, and the popular Bromfield were all, like Powell, midwesterners with a dream of some other great good place, preferably Paris but Long Island Sound and social climbing would do.

Powell briskly shows us the town of Birchfield. Dorrie is the dreamy, plain, bright sister (always two contrasting sisters in these early novels); she stands in for Powell. Linda is the vain, chilly one. Aunt Jule keeps a boardinghouse. The Powell old lady makes her debut: "She pinned her muslin gown at the throat, dropped her teeth with a cheerful little click in the glass of water on the table, and turned out the gas." The "cheerful" launches us on the Powell style. The story is negligible: Who's going to make it out of the sticks first. In the boardinghouse there is an old man who reads Greek; his son has already made it to the big city, where he is writing a trilogy. Powell doesn't quite see the fun of this yet. But Dorrie falls for the young man, Dorrie "with that absurd infantile tilt to her nose" (Dawn to a T). Also Dorrie's tact is very like her creator's. A theatrical couple of a certain age are at the boardinghouse. The actress, Laura, tries on a hat. " 'It will look wonderful on Linda,' Dorrie vouchsafed pleasantly. 'It's too young for you, Aunt Laura.' " The adverb "pleasantly" helps make the joke, a point of contention between no-adverbs Graham Greene and myself. I look to the adverb for surprise. Greene thinks that the verb should do all the work.

Dorrie observes her fellow townspeople—nicely? "He had been such a shy little boy. But the shyness had settled into surliness, and the dreaminess was sheer stupidity. Phil Lancer was growing up to be a good Birchfield citizen." Points of view shift wildly in Powell's early books. We are in Linda's mind, as she is about to allow a yokel to marry her. "Later on, Linda thought, after they were married, she could tell him she didn't like to be kissed." The book ends with Dorrie still dreaming that the trilogist will come and take her off to New York.

=

In 1929 came *The Bride's House*. One suspects that Powell's own wit was the result of being obliged for so long to sing for her supper in so many strange surroundings: "Lotta's children arrived, . . . three gray, horrid-looking little creatures and their names were Lois and Vera and Custer. . . . 'We've come to stay!' they shouted. . . . 'We've come to stay on the farm with Uncle Stephen and Aunt Cecily. Aren't you glad?' " No one is, alas. But these children are well-armored egotists. " 'She tells lies,' Lois hissed in George's ear. 'I'm the pretty one and she's the bright one. She told the conductor we lived in the White House. She's a very bad girl and mother and I can't do a thing with her. . . . Everything she says is a lie, Cousin Sophie, except when it hurts your feelings then it's true.' " A child after absolutely no one's heart.

Unfortunately, Powell loses interest in the children; instead we are told the story of Sophie's love for two men. The grandmother character makes a dutiful appearance, and the Powell stock company go rather mechanically through their paces. Powell wants to say something original about love but cannot get the focus right: "A woman needed two lovers, she

finally decides, one to comfort her for the torment the other caused her."
This is to be a recurring theme throughout Powell's work and, presumably,
life: Coby versus Joe? or was it Coby *and* Joe?

≡

*Dance Night* (1930) is the grittiest, most proletarian of the novels. There
are no artists or would-be artists in Lamptown. Instead there is a railroad
junction, a factory, the Bon Ton Hat Shop, where the protagonists, a
mother and son, live close to Bill Delaney's Saloon and Billiard Parlor. Like
the country, the town has undergone the glorious 1920s boom; now the
Depression has begun to hit. Powell charts the fortunes of the mother-
milliner, Elsinore Abbott, and her adolescent son, Morry. Elsinore's husband is a traveling salesman; he affects jealousy of his wife, who has made
a go of her shop but given up on her life.

Morry gets caught up in the local real estate boom. He also gets involved
with a waif, Jen, from an orphanage, who has been adopted by the saloon-
keeper as a sort of indentured slave. Jen dreams of liberating her younger
sister, Lil, from the home where their mother had deposited them. Jen is
not much of an optimist: "People last such a little while with me. There's
no way to keep them, I guess, that's why I've got to go back for Lil because
I know how terrible it is to be left always—never see people again." It took
Powell a long time to work all this out of her system. Happily, farce
intrudes. A young swain in a romantic moment "slid his hand along her
arm biceps and pressed a knuckle in her arm-pit. 'That's the vein to tap
when you embalm people,' he said, for he was going to be an undertaker."

The highest work for a Lamptown girl is telephone operator, then
waitress, then factory hand. Powell has a Balzacian precision about these
things; and she remembers to put the price tag on everything. Money is
always a character in her novels, as it was in Balzac's. In fact, Powell makes
several references to Balzac in her early books as well as to his Eugénie
Grandet.

Morry grows up, and his mother hardly notices him: "She had moved
over for Morry as you would move over for someone on a street car, certain
that the intimacy was only for a few minutes, but now it was eighteen years
and she thought, why Morry was hers, hers more than anything else in the
world was." This revelation shatters no earth for her or for him; and one
can see how distressing such realism must have been—as it still is—for
American worshipers of the family, Love, too.

Morry gets involved with a builder who indulges him in his dreams to create handsome houses for a public that only wants small lookalike boxes jammed together. Meanwhile, he loves Jen's sister, Lil, while Jen loves him: a usual state of affairs. The only bit of drama, indeed melodrama, is the return of Morry's father; there is a drunken fight between father and son, then a row between father and Elsinore, whom he accuses, wrongly, of philandering. Finally, "wearing down her barriers," she reaches for a pistol: "This was one way to shut out words. . . . She raised the gun, closed her eyes and fired." Although everyone knows that she killed her husband, the town chooses to believe it was suicide, and life goes on. So does Morry, who now realizes that he must go away: "There'd be no place that trains went that he wouldn't go."

In 1932, Powell published *The Tenth Moon*. This is a somewhat Catheresque novel composed with a fuguelike series of short themes (the influence of her ex-music-critic husband?). Connie Benjamin is a village Bovary, married to a cobbler, with two daughters; she once dreamed of being a singer. Connie lives now without friends or indeed a life of any kind in a family that has not the art of communication with one another. Connie daydreams through life while her daughters fret ("They went to bed at ten but whispered until twelve, remembering through all their confidences to tell each other nothing for they were sisters"). The husband works in amiable silence. Finally, Connie decides to have a social life. She invites to supper her daughter's English teacher; she also invites the music teacher, Blaine Decker, an exquisite bachelor, as adrift as Connie in dreams of a career in music that might have been.

Powell now introduces one of her major themes: the failed artist who, with luck, might have been—what? In dreams, these characters are always on stage; in life, they are always in the audience. But Blaine has actually been to Paris with his friend, a glamorous one-shot novelist, Starr Donnell (Glenway Wescott?). Blaine and Connie complement and compliment each other. Connie realizes that she has been "utterly, completely, hideously unhappy" for fifteen years of marriage. Yet each pretends there are compensations to village life and poverty. " 'Isn't it better, I've often thought,' she said, 'for me to be here keeping up with my interests in music, keeping my ideals, than to have failed as an opera singer and been trapped into cheap musical comedy work?' " To hear them tell it, they are as one in the contentment of failure.

But Blaine still hears his mother's voice from offstage, a Powellesque killer: "I sometimes wonder, Blaine, if I didn't emphasize the artistic too much in your childhood, encouraging you and perhaps forcing you beyond your real capacity in music. It was only because you did so poorly in school, dear. . . ." Powell always knows just how much salt a wound requires.

Although the dreamers "talked of music until the careers they once planned were the careers they actually had but given up for the simple joys of living," knowing "success would have destroyed us," Connie goes too far. First, she tries indeed to sing and, for an instant, captures whatever it was she thought that she had and promptly hemorrhages—tuberculosis. Second, she confides to Blaine that she lost a career, home, virginity to Tony the Daredevil, a circus acrobat, who abandoned her in Atlantic City, where the kindly cobbler met and married her. He needed a wife; she could not go home. Blaine is made furious by the truth.

Then daughter Helen runs off with a boy, and the dying Connie pursues her. She finds that Helen has not only managed to get herself a job with a theatrical stock company but she is about to drop the boy; and Connie "knew almost for a certainty that Helen would climb the heights she herself had only glimpsed." Connie goes home to die, and Powell shifts to the dying woman's point of view:

When Dr. Arnold's face flashed on the mirror she thought, "This must be the way one dies. People collect on a mirror like dust and something rushes through your mind emptying all the drawers and shelves to see if you're leaving anything behind." . . . What a pity, she thought, no one will ever know these are my last thoughts—that Dr. Arnold's mouth was so small.

At the end Connie is spared nothing, including the knowledge that her husband never believed that she came of a good family and studied music and only fell once from grace with an acrobat. Blaine goes off to Paris as a tour guide.

 =

With *The Story of a Country Boy* (1934) she ends the Ohio cycle. This is the most invented of the novels. There is no pretty sister, no would-be artist, no flight from village to city. Instead Powell tells the story of a conventional young man, a country boy, who becomes a great success in business; then he fails and goes home to the country, no wiser than before. Ironically, Powell was doing the exact reverse in her own life, putting down deep lifelong roots in that village called Greenwich, far from her own origins. In a sense, this book is a good-bye to all that.

Again, one gets the boom and bust of the twenties and early thirties. Chris Bennett is the all-American boy who makes good. He is entirely self-confident and sublimely unaware of any limitations. Yet, in due course, he fails, largely because he lacks imagination. There is a good deal of Warren Harding, Ohio's favorite son, in his makeup. He is more striking-appearance than reality. Also, Powell was becoming more and more fascinated by the element of chance in life, as demonstrated by Harding's incredible election (those were simple times) to the presidency. "Chris could not remember ever being unsure of himself except in little details of social life where his defects were a source of pride rather than chagrin." He also wonders "if pure luck had brought him his success." He is right to wonder: It has. When he finally looks down from the heights he falls. No fatal flaw—just vertigo.

A splendid new character has joined the stock company, a former U.S. senator who sees in Chris the sort of handsome mediocrity that, properly exploited, could be presidential. John J. Habbiman's drunken soliloquies are glorious:

"Tell them I died for Graustark," said the Senator in a faraway voice. He somberly cracked peanuts and ate them, casting the shells lightly aside with infinite grace. "What wondrous life is this I lead. Ripe apples drop about my head."

Powell also developed an essayistic technique to frame her scenes. A chapter will begin with a diversion:

In the utter stillness before dawn a rat carpentered the rafters, a nest of field mice seduced by unknown applause into coloratura ambitions, squeaked and squealed with amateur intensity. . . . Here, at daybreak, a host of blackbirds were now meeting to decide upon a sun, and also to blackball from membership in the committee a red-winged blackbird.

Unfortunately, her main character is too schematic to interest her or the reader. In any case, except for one final experiment, she has got Ohio out of her system; she has also begun to write more carefully, and the essays make nice point counterpoint to the theatricality of her scene writing.

The theater is indeed the place for her first New York invention, *Jig Saw* (1934), a comedy. The gags are generally very good but the plotting is a bit frantic. Claire is a charming lady, whose eighteen-year-old daughter, Julie, comes to stay with her in a Manhattan flat. Claire has a lover; and a best woman friend to make the sharper jokes. Julie "is a very well brought up young lady—easy to see she has not been exposed to home life." Again it takes two to make a mate: "It takes two women to make your marriage a success." To which Claire's lover, Del, responds, "Have it your way— then Claire and I have made a success of my marriage to Margaret."

A young man, Nathan, enters the story. Both mother and daughter want him. Julie proves to be more ruthless than Claire. Julie moves in on Nathan and announces their coming marriage to the press. He is appalled; he prefers her mother. But Julie is steel: "I can make something of you, Nate. Something marvelous." When he tried to talk her out of marriage, she declares, "I expect to go through life making sacrifices for you, dear, giving up my career for you." When he points out that she has never had a career, she rises to even greater heights: "I know. That's what makes it all the more of a sacrifice. I've never had a career. I never will have. Because I love you so much." Nate is trapped. Claire wonders if she should now marry Del, but he advises against it: "You're the triangular type. . . ." With a bit of the sort of luck that so fascinated Powell by its absence in most lives, she might have had a successful commercial career in the theater. But that luck never came her way in life, as opposed to imagination. Finally, Powell's bad luck on Broadway was to be our literature's gain.

3.

The New York cycle begins with *Turn, Magic Wheel* (1936), dedicated to Dwight Fiske, a sub-Coward nightclub performer for whom Powell wrote special material. Powell now writes about a writer, always an edgy business. Dennis Orphen is a male surrogate for Powell herself. He is involved with two women, of course. He is also on the scene for good: He reappears in almost all her books, and it is he who writes finis to *The Golden Spur*, some twenty years later, as the Lafayette Hotel is being torn down and he realizes that his world has gone for good. But in 1936 Dennis is eager, on the make, fascinated by others: "his urgent need to know what they were knowing, see, hear, feel what they were sensing, for a brief moment to *be* them." He is consumed by a curiosity about others which time has a pleasant way of entirely sating.

Corinne is the profane love, a married woman; Effie is the sacred love, the abandoned wife of a famous writer called Andrew Callingham, Hemingway's first appearance in Powell's work. Effie is a keeper of the flame; she pretends that Andrew will come back: "Why must she be noble, frail shoulders squared to defeat, gaily confessing that life was difficult but that was the way things were?" Dennis publishes a *roman à clef*, whose key unlocks the Callingham/Hemingway story, and he worries that Effie may feel herself betrayed because Dennis completely dispels her illusion that the great man will return to her. As Dennis makes his New York rounds, the Brevoort Café, Longchamps, Luchow's, he encounters Okie, the ubiquitous man about town who will reappear in the New York novels, a part of their Balzacian detail. Okie edits an entertainment guide magazine, writes a column, knows everyone, and brings everyone together. A party is going on at all hours in different parts of the town, and Powell's characters are always on the move, and the lines of their extramarital affairs cross and recross. The essays now grow thoughtful and there are inner soliloquies:

Walter missed Bee now but sometimes he thought it was more fun talking to Corinne about how he loved Bee than really being with Bee, for Bee never seemed to want to be alone with him, she was always asking everyone else to join them. In fact the affair from her point of view was just loads of fun and that was all. She never cried or talked about divorce or any of the normal things, she just had a fine time as if it wasn't serious at all.

Powell is much concerned with how people probably ought to behave but somehow never do. The drinking is copious: "Corinne went into the ladies room and made up again. It was always fun making up after a few pernods because they made your face freeze so it was like painting a statue." Of course, "Walter was as mad as could be, watching the cunning little figure in the leopard coat and green beret patter out of the room." Whenever "cunning" or "gaily" or "tinkling" is used, Powell is stalking dinner, with the precision of a saber-toothed tiger. She also notes those "long patient talks, the patient civilized talks that, if one knew it, are the end of love."

There are amusing incidents rather than a plot of the sort that popular novels required in those days: Effie is hurt by Orphen's portrayal of her marriage in his book; Corinne vacillates between husband and lover; the current Mrs. Callingham goes into the hospital to die of cancer. There are publishers who live in awe of book reviewers with names like Gannett, Hansen, Paterson. One young publisher "was so brilliant that he could tell in advance that in the years 1934–35 and -36 a book would be called exquisitely well-written if it began: 'The boxcar swung out of the yards. Pip rolled over in the straw. He scratched himself where the straw itched him.'" Finally, the book's real protagonist is the city:

In the quiet of three o'clock the Forties looked dingy, deserted, incredibly nine-teenth century with the dim lamps in dreary doorways; in these midnight hours the streets were possessed by their ancient parasites, low tumble-down frame rooming houses with cheap little shops, though by day such remnants of another decade retreated obscurely between flamboyant hotels.

*That* city is now well and truly gone.

"Fleetingly, Effie thought of a new system of obituaries in which the lives recorded were criticized, mistaken steps pointed out, structure con-demned, better paths suggested." This is the essence of Dawn Powell: The fantastic flight from the mundane that can then lead to a thousand conver-sational variations, and the best of her prose is like the best conversation where no *escalier* is ever wit's receptacle. As a result, she is at her best with the Party; but then most novels of this epoch were assembled around The Party, where the characters proceed to interact and the unsayable gets said. Powell has a continuing hostess who is a variation on Peggy Guggenheim, collecting artists for gallery and bed. There is also a minor hostess, inter-ested only in celebrities and meaningful conversation. She quizzes Dennis: "'Now let's talk,' she commanded playfully [Powell's adverbs are often anesthetic preparatory for surgery]. 'We've never really had a nice talk, have we, Dennis? Tell me how you came to write? I suppose you had to make money so you just started writing, didn't you?'" Callingham himself comes to The Party. Powell's affection for the real Hemingway did not entirely obscure his defects, particularly as viewed by an ex-wife, Effie, who discovers to her relief "there was no Andy left, he had been wiped out by Callingham the Success as so many men before him had been wiped out by the thing they represented." Effie frees herself from him and settles back into contented triangularity with Dennis and Corinne. Cake had; ingested, too.

═

In 1938, with *The Happy Island,* the Powell novel grows more crowded and The Party is bigger and wilder. This time the rustic who arrives in the city is not a young woman but a young man. Powell is often more at home with crude masculine protagonists, suspecting, perhaps, that her kind of tough realism might cause resentment among those who think of women as the fair sex.

A would-be playwright, Jeff Abbott (related to Morry?), arrives on the bus from Silver City; a manager has accepted his play with the ominous telegram, CASTING COMPLETE THIRD ACT NEEDS REWRITING [like that of *Jig Saw*] COME IMMEDIATELY. Jeff has two friends in the city. One is Prudence Bly, a successful nightclub singer; the other is Dol, a gentleman party giver and fancier of young men. At the book's end, Dol gives great offense by dying, seated in a chair, at his own party. How like him! the guests mutter.

Prudence is the most carefully examined of Powell's women. She is successful; she drinks too much; she is seldom involved with fewer than two men. But it is the relationships between women that make Powell's novels so funny and original. Jean Nelson, a beautiful dummy, is Prudence's best friend; each needs the other to dislike. At the novel's beginning, Jean has acquired Prudence's lover Steve. The two girls meet for a serious drunken chat over lunch. "You aren't jealous of me, are you, Prudence?" "*Jealous?* Jealous? Good God, Jean, you must think this is the Middle Ages!" Prudence then broods to herself:

Why do I lunch with women anyway? . . . We always end up sniveling over men and life and we always tell something that makes us afraid of each other for weeks to come. . . . Women take too much out of you, they drink too much and too earnestly. They drink the way they used to do china painting, and crewel work and wood burning.

In the restaurant things grow blurred: " 'You're so good to everyone,' sighed Jean. 'You really are.' Nothing could have enraged Prudence more or been more untrue." Finally, Jean goes: "Prudence looked meditatively after Jean as she wove her way earnestly through tables and knees. The girl did look like a goddess but the trouble was she walked like one, too, as if her legs had been too long wound in a flag."

Prudence's forebears include, yet again, the eccentric grandmother. This one is rich, and "Prudence was always glad her grandmother had been neither kind nor affectionate." The escape from Silver City had been easy. The grandmother was indifferent to everyone, including "her surly young Swedish chauffeur." A great traveler, Mrs. Bly "always wanted to buy one dinner with two plates, as if he were a Pekinese, and, more alarming still, to take one room in the hotels where they stayed. . . . After all, she explained, she always slept with her clothes on so there was nothing indecent in it." In addition, Mrs. Bly is a sincere liar, who believes that she was on the *Titanic* when it was sunk; and was courted by the czar.

Jeff Abbott and Prudence meet. They have an affair. Jeff is sublimely humorless, which intrigues Prudence. He is also a man of destiny, doomed to greatness in the theater. " 'I never yet found anything to laugh at in this world,' said Jeff. 'You never heard of a great man with a sense of humor, did you? Humor's an anesthetic, that's all, laughing gas while your guts are jerked out.' " Since they are not made for each other, marriage is a real possibility. Prudence is growing unsure of herself:

She could not find the place where the little girl from Ohio, the ambitious, industrious little village girl, merged into the *Evening Journal* Prudence Bly, *The Town and Country* Bly. There were queer moments between personalities, moments such as the hermit crab must have scuttling from one stolen shell to the next one. . . . Prudence Bly was not so much a person as a conspiracy.

Then Powell, in a quick scuttle, briefly inhabits her own shell:

Prudence slew with a neat epithet, crippled with a true word, then, seeing the devastation about her and her enemies growing, grew frightened of revenge, backed desperately, and eventually found the white flag of Sentimentality as her salvation. For every ruinous *mot* she had a tear for motherhood.

The failure of Jeff's powerful play does not disturb him, and Prudence is somewhat awed since worldly success is the only thing that makes the island happy. But "he belongs to the baffling group of confident writers who need no applause. For them a success is not a surprise but cause for wonder that it is less than international. . . . A failure proves that a man is too good for his times." When he says he wants to buy a farm in the Midwest and settle down and write, Prudence is astonished. When he does exactly that, she goes with him. Intergrity at last. No more glamour. No more happy island. Only fields, a man, a woman. In no time at all, she is climbing the walls and heading back to New York where she belongs. Since Jean has let go of Steve, he receives her amiably (but then hardly anyone has noticed her departure). The book ends with: "Prudence's looks, [Steve] reflected with some surprise, were quite gone. She really looked as hard as nails, but then so did most women eventually." That excellent worldly novelist Thackeray never made it to so high a ground.

═══

*Angels on Toast* (1940); war has begun to darken the skyline. But the turning wheel's magic is undiminished for Ebie, a commercial artist, whose mother is in the great line of Powell eccentrics. Ebie lives with another working woman, Honey, who "was a virgin (at least you couldn't prove she wasn't), and was as proud as punch of it. You would have thought that it was something that had been in the family for generations." But Ebie and Honey need each other to talk at, and in a tavern

where O. Henry used to go . . . they'd sit in the dark smoked-wood booth drinking old-fashioneds and telling each other things they certainly wished later they had never told and bragging about their families, sometimes making them hot-stuff socially back home, the next time making them romantically on the wrong side of the tracks. The family must have been on wheels back in the Middle West, whizzing back and forth across tracks at a mere word from the New York daughters.

Brooding over the novel is the downtown Hotel Ellery. For seventeen dollars a week Ebie's mother, Mrs. Vane, lives in contented genteel squalor.

BAR and GRILL: it was the tavern entrance to a somewhat medieval looking hotel, whose time-and-soot-blackened façade was frittered with fire-escapes, . . . its dark oak-wainscotting rising high to meet grimy black walls, its ship windows covered with heavy pumpkin chintz. . . . Once in you were in for no mere moment.

. . . The elderly lady residents of the hotel were without too much obvious haste taking their places in the grill-room, nodding and smiling to the waitresses, carrying their knitting and a slender volume of some English bard, anything to prop against their first Manhattan . . . as they sipped their drinks and dipped into literature. It was sip and dip, sip and dip until cocktail time was proclaimed by the arrival of the little cocktail sausage wagon.

In its remoteness, this world before television could just as easily be that of *St. Ronan's Well.*

It is also satisfying that in these New York novels the city that was plays so pervasive a role. This sort of hotel, meticulously described, evokes lost time in a way that the novel's bumptious contemporary, early talking movies, don't.

Another curious thing about these small, venerable, respectable hotels, there seemed no appeal here to the average newcomer. BAR and GRILL, for instance, appealed to seemingly genteel widows and spinsters of small incomes. . . . Then there were those tired flashes-in-the-pan, the one-shot celebrities, and, on the other hand, there was a gay younger group whose loyalty to the BAR and GRILL was based on the cheapness of its martinis. Over their simple dollar lunches (four martinis and a sandwich) this livelier set snickered at the older residents.

Ebie wants to take her mother away from all this so that they can live together in Connecticut. Mrs. Vane would rather die. She prefers to lecture the bar on poetry. There is also a plot: two men in business, with wives. One has an affair with Ebie. There is a boom in real estate; then a bust. By now, Powell has mastered her own method. The essay-beginnings to chapters work smartly:

In the dead of night wives talked to their husbands, in the dark they talked and talked while the clock on the bureau ticked sleep away, and the last street cars clanged off on distant streets to remoter suburbs, where in new houses bursting with mortgages and the latest conveniences, wives talked in the dark, and talked and talked.

The prose is now less easygoing; and there is a conscious tightening of the language although, to the end, Powell thought one thing was different *than* another while always proving not her mettle but metal.

===

Powell is generally happiest in the BAR and GRILL or at the Lafayette or Brevoort. But in *A Time to Be Born* (1942) she takes a sudden social leap, and lands atop the town's social Rockies. Class is the most difficult subject for American writers to deal with as it is the most difficult for the English to avoid. There are many reasons. First, since the Depression, the owners of the Great Republic prefer not to be known to the public at large. Celebrities, of the sort that delight Powell, fill the newspapers while the great personages are seldom, if ever, mentioned; they are also rarely to be seen in those places where public and celebrities go to mingle. "Where," I asked the oldest of my waiter-acquaintances at the Plaza (we've known each other forty years), "have the nobles gone?" He looked sad. "I'm told they have their own islands now. Things"—he was vague—"like that."

As I read my way through Powell I noted how few names she actually does drop. There is a single reference to the late Helen Astor, which comes as a mild shock. Otherwise the references are no more arcane than Rockefeller equals money (but then John D. had hired the first press agent). In a sense, midwesterners were the least class-conscious of Americans during the first half of the twentieth century and those who came from the small towns (Hemingway, Dreiser, Powell herself) ignore those drawing rooms where Henry James was at home amongst pure essences, whose source of wealth is never known but whose knowledge of what others know is all that matters. Powell, agreeably, knows exactly how much money everyone makes (not enough) and what everything costs (too much). As for value, she does her best with love, but suspects the times are permanently inflationary for that overhyped commodity. Powell never gets to Newport, Rhode Island, in her books but she manages Cape Cod nicely. She inclines to the boozy meritocracy of theater and publishing and the art world both commercial and whatever it is that Fifty-seventh Street was and is.

But in *A Time to Be Born*, she takes on the highest level of the meritocracy (the almost-nobles) in the form of a powerful publisher and his high-powered wife, based, rather casually, on Mr. and Mrs. Henry Luce. At last Powell will have a fling at those seriously important people Diana Trilling felt that she was not up to writing about. But since one person is pretty much like another, all are as one in art, which alone makes the difference. Humble Ebie is neither more nor less meaningful than famous Amanda. It's what's made of them in art. Powell does have a good deal of fun with Julian and Amanda Evans, and the self-important grandeur of their lives. But Powell has no real interest in power or, more to this particular point, in those whose lives are devoted to power over others. Powell is with the victims. The result is that the marginal characters work rather better than the principals. One never quite believes that Julian owns and operates sixteen newspapers. One does believe Vicki Haven, who comes from the same Ohio town as Amanda, authoress of a *Forever Amber* best seller that has been written for her by the best pen-persons and scholar-squirrels that Julian's money can buy. Ken Saunders, a reasonably failed hack, gets Powell's full attention: he is a friend of Dennis Orphen, who makes an obligatory appearance or two as does the great novelist, Andrew Callingham, still hugely at large.

Powell sets *A Time* (magazine?) *to Be Born* in that time *not* to be born, the rising war in the West:

This was a time when the true signs of war were the lavish plumage of the women; Fifth Avenue dress shops and the finer restaurants were filled with these vanguards of war. Look at the jewels, the rare pelts, the gaudy birds on elaborate hair-dress and know that war was here; already the women had inherited the earth. The ominous smell of gunpowder was matched by a rising cloud of Schiaparelli's *Shocking.* The women were once more armed, and their happy voices sang of destruction to come. . . . This was a time when the artists, the intellectuals, sat in cafés and in country homes and accused each other over their brandies or their California vintages of traitorous tendencies. This was a time for them to band together in mutual antagonism, a time to bury the professional hatchet, if possible in each other. . . . On Fifth Avenue and Fifty-fifth Street hundreds waited for a man on a hotel window ledge to jump; hundreds waited with craning necks and thirsty faces as if this single person's final gesture would solve the riddle of the world. Civilization stood on a ledge, and in the tension of waiting it was a relief to have one little man jump.

I know of no one else who has got so well the essence of that first war-year before we all went away to the best years of no one's life.

=

Again the lines of love and power cross and recross as they do in novels and often, too, in life. Since Julian publishes newspapers and magazines and now propaganda for England, much of it written in his wife's name, there is a Sarrautesque suspicion of language in Powell's reflections. A publisher remarks, "A fact changes into a lie the instant it hits print." But he does not stop there. "It's not print, it's the word," he declares. "The Spoken Word, too. The lie forms as soon as the breath of thought hits air. You hear your own words and say—'That's not what I mean. . . .' " Powell is drawing close to the mystery of literature, life's quirky—quarkish— reflection.

Amanda's power world does not convince quite as much as the Village life of Vicki and Ken and Dennis Orphen. Earlier readers will be happy to know that cute Corinne "had considered leaving her husband for Dennis Orphen for two or three years, and during her delay" the husband had divorced her "with Corinne still confused by this turn of events. . . . She wanted a little more time to consider marrying Dennis." When in doubt, do nothing, is the Powellesque strategy for life. Ken goes back and forth between Amanda and Vicki. For a time Amanda is all-conquering:

She knew exactly what she wanted from life, which was, in a word, everything. She had a genuine distaste for sexual intimacy . . . but there were so many things to be gained by trading on sex and she thought so little of the process that she itched to use it as currency once again.

This time with the great writer-hunter Callingham. As it is, ironically, she gets knocked up by Ken and falls out with Julian. But she is never not practical: On the subject of writing, she believes that "the tragedy of the Attic poets, Keats, Shelley, Burns was not that they died young but that they were obliged by poverty to do all their own writing." Amanda's descendants are still very much with us: sweet lassies still saddened at the thought of those too poor to hire someone who will burn with a bright clear flame, as he writes their books for them.

It is plain that Powell was never entirely pleased with the Ohio cycle. She had a tendency to tell the same story over and over again, trying out new angles, new points of view, even—very occasionally—new characters. Finally, in mid-war, she made one last attempt to get Ohio (and herself) right. *My Home Is Far Away* (1944) is lapidary—at least compared to the loose early works. New York has polished her style; the essays glitter convincingly. The rural family is called Willard. A Civil War veteran for a grandfather; missing the odd eye, limb. Two sisters again: Lena the pretty one, Marcia the bright one. Powell again holds up the mirror to her past: "The uncanniness of [Marcia's] memory was not an endearing trait; invariably guests drew respectfully away from the little freak and warmed all the more to the pretty unaffected normalcy of little Lena." The book begins when father, mother, daughters leave a contented home. Suddenly, there is a nightmare vision: A man in a balloon floats across a starry sky. Home is now forever faraway.

Too clever by more than half and too much obliged throughout a peripatetic childhood to sing for a supper prepared by tone-deaf strangers, Powell hammered on the comic mask and wore it to the end. But when the dying mother has a horrendous vision of the man in the balloon, the mask blinks—for the last time.

Aunt Lois has a boardinghouse. The girls work. The old ladies are more than ever devastating. " 'A grandmother doesn't like children any more than a mother does,' she declared. 'Sometimes she's just too old to get out of tending them, that's all, but I'm not.' " Lena goes first. Then Marcia leaves town, as Powell left town, and catches that train "which will go everywhere on earth that is not home." On a foggy pane of glass, she writes, with her finger, *Marcia Willard*. Dawn Powell.

4.

After the war, Powell returned to the New York cycle for good. She published a book of short stories, *Sunday, Monday and Always* (1952). There are occasional ill-omened visits back home but no longer does she describe the escape; she has escaped for good. There are some nice comic moments. Edna, a successful actress, comes home to find her rustic family absorbed in radio soap operas. Although she is quite willing to describe her exciting life, the family outmaneuvers her. " 'Well, Edna,' cackled Aunt Meg, hugging her. 'I declare I wouldn't have known you. Well, you can't live that life and not have it show, they tell me.' " The "they tell me" is masterful. Powell's ear for the cadences of real-life talk only improved with time.

The final New York novels, *The Locusts Have No King* (1948), *The WickedPavilion* (1954), and *The Golden Spur* (1962), demonstrate Powell's ultimate mastery of subject, art, self. Where the last two are near-perfect in execution, *The Locusts Have No King* ("yet they, all of them, go forth by bands": Proverbs) shares some of the helter-skelterness of the early books. It is as if before Powell enters her almost-benign Prospero phase, she wants to cut loose once more at The Party.

===

This time the literary scene of the forties gets it. The protagonist, Frederick Olliver, is a young man of integrity (a five-hundred-dollar-advance man) and literary distinction and not much will. He has been having an affair with Lyle, part of a married team of writers: Lyle is all taste and charm. But Frederick Olliver meets Dodo in a bar. Dodo is deeply, unrepentantly vulgar and self-absorbed. She says, "Pooh on you," and talks baby talk, always a sign for Powell of Lilithian evil. They meet in one of Powell's best bars downtown, off Rubberleg Square, as she calls it. The habitués all know one another in that context and, often, no other: parallel lives that are contiguous only in the confines of a cozy bar.

Frederick takes Dodo to a publisher's party (our friend Dennis is there) and Dodo manages to appall. Lyle is hurt. Everyone is slightly fraudulent. A publisher who respects Frederick's integrity offers him the editorship of *Haw,* a low publication which of course Frederick makes a success of. Lyle writes her husband's plays. There is a literary man who talks constantly of Jane Austen, whom he may not have read, and teaches at the League for Cultural Foundations (a.k.a. The New School), where "classes bulged with middle-aged students anxious to get an idea of what it would be like to have an idea." But under the usual bright mendacities of happy island life, certain relationships work themselves out. The most Powellesque is between two commercial artists, Caroline and Lorna:

Ever since their marriages had exploded Caroline and Lorna had been in each other's confidence, sharing a bottle of an evening in Lorna's studio or Caroline's penthouse. In fact they had been telling each other everything for so many years over their cups that they'd never heard a word each other had said.

In an ecstasy of female bonding, they discuss their lost husbands:

They told each other of their years of fidelity—and each lamented the curse of being a one-man woman. Men always took advantage of their virtue and Caroline agreed with Lorna that, honestly, if it could be done over again, she'd sleep with every man who came along instead of wasting loyalty on one undeserving male. After a few drinks, Caroline finally said she had slept with maybe forty or fifty men but only because she was so desperately unhappy. Lorna said she didn't blame anyone in Caroline's domestic situation for doing just that, and many times wished she had not been such a loyal sap about George, but except for a few vacation trips and sometimes being betrayed by alcohol she had really never—well, anyway, she didn't blame anyone.

Revelations bombard deaf ears. "Frequently they lost interest in dinner once they had descended below the bottle's label and then a remarkable inspiration would come to open a second bottle and repeat the revelations they had been repeating for years to glazed eyes and deaf ears." Finally, "Both ladies talked in confidence of their frustrations in the quest for love, but the truth was they had gotten all they wanted of the commodity and had no intention of making sacrifice of comfort for a few Cupid feathers." Powell was a marvelous sharp antidote for the deep-warm-sincere love novels of that period. Today she is, at the least, a bright counterpoint to our lost-and-found literary ladies.

Powell deals again with the, always to her, mysterious element of luck in people's careers. When one thinks of her own bad luck, the puzzlement has a certain poignancy. But she can be very funny indeed about the admiration that mediocrity evokes on that happy island where it has never been possible to be too phony. Yet when Frederick, free of his bondage to Dodo, returns to Lyle, the note is elegiac: "In a world of destruction one must hold fast to whatever fragments of love are left, for sometimes a mosaic can be more beautiful than an unbroken pattern." We all tended to write this sort of thing immediately after Hiroshima, *mon assassin*.

=

*The Wicked Pavilion* (1954) is the Café Julien is the Lafayette Hotel of real life. The title is from *The Creevey Papers*, and refers to the Prince Regent's Brighton Pavilion, where the glamorous and louche wait upon a mad royal. Dennis Orphen opens and closes the book in his by now familiarly mysterious way. He takes no real part in the plot. He is simply still there, watching the not-so-magic wheel turn as the happy island grows sad. For him, as for Powell, the café is central to his life. Here he writes; sees friends; observes the vanity fair. Powell has now become masterful in her setting of scenes. The essays—preludes, overtures—are both witty and sadly wise. She has also got the number to Eisenhower's American, as she brings together in this penultimate rout all sorts of earlier figures, now grown old: Okie is still a knowing man about town and author of the definitive works on the painter Marius; Andy Callingham is still a world-famous novelist, serene in his uncontagious self-love; and the Peggy Guggenheim figure is back again as Cynthia, an art gallery owner and party giver. One plot is young love: Rick and Ellenora who met at the Café Julien in wartime and never got enough of it or of each other or of the happy island.

A secondary plot gives considerable pleasure even though Powell lifted it from a movie of the day called *Holy Matrimony* (1943) with Monty Woolley and Gracie Fields, from Arnold Bennett's novel *Buried Alive*. The plot that Powell took is an old one: A painter, bored with life or whatever, decides to play dead. The value of his pictures promptly goes so high that he is tempted to keep on painting after "death." Naturally, sooner or later, he will give himself away: Marius paints a building that had not been built before his "death." But only two old painter friends have noticed this, and they keep his secret for the excellent reason that one of them is busy turning out "Marius" pictures, too. Marius continues happily as a sacred presence, enjoying in death the success that he never had in life: "Being dead has spoiled me," he observes. It should be noted that the painting for this novel's cover was done by Powell's old friend, Reginald Marsh.

A new variation on the Powell young woman is Jerry: clean-cut, straight-forward, and on the make. But her peculiar wholesomeness does not inspire men to give her presents; yet "the simple truth was that with her increasingly expensive tastes she really could not afford to work. . . . As for settling for the safety of marriage, that seemed the final defeat, synony-mous in Jerry's mind with asking for the last rites." An aristocratic lady, Elsie, tries unsuccessfully to launch her. Elsie's brother, Wharton, and sister-in-law, Nita, are fine comic emblems of respectable marriage. In fact, Wharton is one of Powell's truly great and original monsters, quite able to hold his own with Pecksniff:

Wharton had such a terrific reputation for efficiency that many friends swore that the reason his nose changed colors before your very eyes was because of an

elaborate Rimbaud color code, indicating varied reactions to his surroundings.
. . . Ah, what a stroke of genius it had been for him to have found Nita! How happy
he had been on his honeymoon and for years afterward basking in the safety of
Nita's childish innocence where his intellectual shortcomings, sexual coldness and
caprices—indeed his basic ignorance—would not be discovered. . . . He was well
aware that many men of his quixotic moods preferred young boys, but he dreaded
to expose his inexperience to one of his own sex, and after certain cautious
experiments realized that his anemic lusts were canceled by his overpowering fear
of gossip. . . . Against the flattering background of Nita's delectable purity, he
blossomed forth as the all-round He-man, the Husband who knows everything.
. . . He soon taught her that snuggling, hand-holding, and similar affectionate
demonstrations were kittenish and vulgar. He had read somewhere, however, that
breathing into a woman's ear or scratching her at the nape of the neck drove her
into complete ecstasy. . . . In due course Nita bore him four daughters, a sort of
door prize for each time he attended.

The Party is given by Cynthia now, and it rather resembles Proust's last
roundup: "There are people here who have been dead twenty years,"
someone observes, including "the bore that walks like a man." There is
a sense of closing time; people settle for what they can get. "We get sick
of our clinging vines, he thought, but the day comes when we suspect that
the vines are all that hold our rotting branches together." Dennis Orphen
at the end records in his journal the last moments of the wicked pavilion
as it falls to the wrecker's ball:

It must be that the Julien was all that these people really liked about each other
for now when they chance across each other in the street they look through each
other, unrecognizing, or cross the street quickly with the vague feeling that here
was someone identified with unhappy memories—as if the other was responsible
for the fall of the Julien.

What had been a stage for more than half a century to a world is gone
and "those who had been bound by it fell apart like straws when the baling
cord is cut and remembered each other's name and face as part of a dream
that would never come back."

=

In 1962, Powell published her last and, perhaps, most appealing novel,
*The Golden Spur*. Again, the protagonist is male. In this case a young man

from Silver City, Ohio (again), called Jonathan Jaimison. He has come to the city to find his father. Apparently twenty-six years earlier his mother, Connie, had had a brief fling with a famous man in the Village; pregnant, she came home and married a Mr. Jaimison. The book opens with a vigorous description of Wanamaker's department store being torn down. Powell is now rather exuberant about the physical destruction of her city (she wrote this last book in her mid-sixties, when time was doing the same to her). There is no longer a Dennis Orphen on the scene; presumably, he lies buried beneath whatever glass-and-cement horror replaced the Lafayette. But there are still a few watering holes from the twenties, and one of them is The Golden Spur, where Connie mingled with the bohemians.

Jonathan stays at the Hotel De Long, which sounds like the Vanderbilt, a star of many of Powell's narratives. Jonathan, armed with Connie's cryptic diary, has a number of names that might be helpful. One is that of Claire van Orphen (related to Dennis?), a moderately successful writer, for whom Connie did some typing. Claire now lives embalmed in past time. She vaguely recalls Connie, who had been recommended to her by the one love of her life, Major Wedburn, whose funeral occurs the day Jonathan arrives at the De Long. Claire gives Jonathan possible leads; meanwhile, his presence has rejuvenated her. She proposes to her twin sister, Bea, that they live together and gets a firm no. The old nostalgia burned down long ago for the worldly Bea. On the other hand, Claire's career is revived, with the help of a professionally failed writer who gets "eight bucks for fifteen hundred words of new criticism in a little magazine or forty for six hundred words of old criticism in the Sunday book section." He studies all of Claire's ladies' magazine short stories of yesteryear; he then reverses the moral angle:

"In the old days the career girl who supported the family was the heroine, and the idle wife was the baddie," Claire said gleefully. "And now it's the other way round. In the soap operas, the career girl is the baddie, the wife is the goodie because she's better for *business*. . . . Well, you were right. CBS has bought the two [stories] you fixed, and Hollywood is interested."

Powell herself was writing television plays in the age of Eisenhower and no doubt had made this astonishing discovery on her own.

Jonathan is promptly picked up by two girls at The Golden Spur; he moves in with them. Since he is more domestic than they, he works around the house. He is occasionally put to work in bed until he decides that he doesn't want to keep on being "a diaphragm-tester." Among his possible fathers is Alvine Harshawe alias Andrew Callingham alias Ernest Hemingway. Alvine is lonely; "You lost one set of friends with each marriage, another when it dissolved, gaining smaller and smaller batches each time you traded in a wife." Alvine has no clear memory of Connie but toys with the idea of having a grown son, as does a famous painter named Hugow. Another candidate is a distinguished lawyer, George Terrence, whose actress daughter, unknown to him, is having an affair with Jonathan. Terrence is very much school of the awful Wharton of *The Wicked Pavilion*, only Terrence has made the mistake of picking up a young actor in the King Cole Bar of the St. Regis Hotel; the actor is now blithely blackmailing him in a series of letters worthy of his contemporary Pal Joey. Terrence welcomes the idea of a son but Jonathan shies away: He does not want his affair with the daughter to be incestuous.

$$=$$

Finally, Cassie, the Peggy Guggenheim character, makes her appearance, and The Party assembles for the last time. There are nice period touches: girls from Bennington are everywhere. While Cassie herself "was forty-three—well, all right, forty-eight, if you're going to count every lost weekend—and Hugow's betrayal had happened at birthday time, when she was frightened enough by the half-century mark reaching out for her before she'd even begun to have her proper quota of love." Cassie takes a fancy to Jonathan and hires him to work at her gallery. He has now figured out not only his paternity but his maternity and, best of all, himself. The father was Major Wedburn, who was, of course, exactly like the bore that his mother, Connie, married. The foster father appears on the scene, and there is recognition of this if not resolution. As for Connie, she had slept with everyone who asked her because "she wanted to be whatever anybody expected her to be, because she never knew what she was herself." Jonathan concludes, "That's the way I am." At an art gallery, he says, "I have a career of other people's talents."

The quest is over. Identity fixed. The Party over, Jonathan joins Hugow in his cab. "He was very glad that Hugow had turned back downtown, perhaps to the Spur, where they could begin all over." On that blithe note, Powell's life and lifework end; and the wheel stops; the magic's gone— except for the novels of Dawn Powell, all of them long since out of print, just as her name has been erased from that perpetually foggy pane, "American Literature."

THE NEW YORK REVIEW OF BOOKS
*November 5, 1987*

# CHAPTER 24

# How I Do What I Do
# If Not Why

In the beginning, there was the spoken word. The first narrations concerned the doings of gods and kings, and these stories were passed on from generation to generation, usually as verse in order to make memorizing easier. Then, mysteriously, in the fifth century B.C. all the narratives were written down, and literature began. From Greece to Persia to India to China, there was a great controversy. Could a narrative be possessed that had been committed to writing rather than to memory? Traditionalists said no; modernists said yes. The traditionalists lost. Now, twenty-five hundred years later, there is a similar crisis. Modernists believe that any form of narration and of learning can be transmitted through audiovisual means rather than through the, now, traditional written word. In this controversy I am, for once, a conservative to the point of furious reaction.

In any case, we are now obliged to ask radical questions. What is the point to writing things down other than to give directions on how to operate a machine? Why tell stories about gods and kings or, even, men and women?

Very early, the idea of fame—eternal fame—afflicted our race. But fame for the individual was less intense at the beginning than for one's tribe. Thucydides is often read as a sort of biographer of Pericles when, indeed, he was writing the biography, to misuse the word, of their city, Athens. It is the idea of the city that the writer wants us to understand not the domestic affairs of Pericles, which he mentions only as civic illustrations. Love had not yet been discovered as opposed to lust. Marriage was not yet a subject except for comedy (Sophocles did not care who got custody of the children, unless Medea killed them; or they were baked in a pie). For more than two millennia, from Homer to Aeschylus to Dante to Shakespeare to Tolstoy, the great line of our literature has concerned itself with gods, heroes, kings, in conflict with one another and with inexorable fate. Simultaneously, all 'round each story, whether it be that of Prometheus or of a Plantagenet prince, there is a people who need fire from heaven or land beyond the sea. Of arms and of the man, I sing, means just that. Of the people then and now, of the hero then and his image now, as created or re-created by the poet. From the beginning, the bard, the poet, the writer was a most high priest to his people, the custodian of their common memory, the interpreter of their history, the voice of their current yearnings.

All this stopped in the last two centuries when the rulers decided to teach the workers to read and write so that they could handle machinery. Traditionalists thought this a dangerous experiment. If the common people knew too much might they not overthrow their masters? But the modernists, like John Stuart Mill, won. And, in due course, the people— proudly literate—overthrew their masters. We got rid of the English while the French and the Russians—ardent readers—shredded their ancient monarchies. In fact, the French—who read and theorize the most— became so addicted to political experiment that in the two centuries since our own rather drab revolution they have exuberantly produced one Directory, one Consulate, two empires, three restorations of the monarchy, and five republics. That's what happens when you take writing too seriously.

Happily, Americans have never liked reading all that much. Politically ignorant, we keep sputtering along in our old Model T, looking wistfully every four years for a good mechanic.

Along with political change—the result of general literacy and the printing press—the nature of narrative began to fragment. High literature concerned itself, most democratically, with the doings of common folk. Although a George Eliot or a Hardy could make art out of these simple domestic tales, in most hands crude mirrors of life tend to be duller than Dumas, say, and, paradoxically, less popular. Today's serious novel is apt to be a carefully written teacherly text about people who teach school and write teacherly texts to dwindling classes. Today's popular novel, carelessly, recklessly composed on—or by—a machine, paradoxically has taken over the heroes and kings and gods, and places them in modern designer clothes amongst consumer dreams beyond the dreams of Sheherazade.

This is a strange reversal. The best writers tend to write, in a highly minimal way, of the simple and the dull, while the worst give us whirlwind tours of the house—I mean home—of Atreus, ripping every skeleton from its closet, and throwing back every Porthault sheet. The fact that this kind of bad writing is popular is not because the reading public—an endangered minority—cherishes bad writing for its own sake but because the good writers fail to interest them. As a result, everything is now so totally out of whack that the high academic bureaucrats have dropped literature, with some relief, and replaced it with literary theory, something that one needs no talent to whip up. As a result, in twenty years, enrollment in American English departments has been cut by more than half. Writers and writing no longer matter much anywhere in freedom's land. Mistuh Emerson, he dead. Our writers are just entertainers, and not all that entertaining either. We have lost the traditional explainer, examiner, prophet.

So what am I up to? If nothing else, I continue, endlessly, to explain, to examine, to prophesy, particularly in the five novels* where I deal with the history of the United States from the beginning to now. The fact that there is still a public eager to find out who we are and what we did ought to encourage others to join me but, by and large, the universities have made that impossible. They have established an hegemony over every aspect of literature—except the ability to make any. They have also come to believe that a serious novelist deals only with what he knows and since

---

*Burr; Lincoln; 1876; Empire; Washington, D.C.

our educational system is what it is he is not apt to know much about anything; and since our class system is uncommonly rigid he is not going to have much chance to find out about any world other than the one he was born into—and the school he went to. Certainly, he will never, like his predecessors, be able to deal with his nation's rulers. They prefer the shadows. Mary McCarthy recently listed all the things that cannot be put into a serious novel—from sunsets to a hanging to a cabinet meeting. Also, to be fair, though our political life is entirely devoid of politics, it is so vivid with personalities and the stuff of bad fiction that one can hardly expect the novelist to compete with the journalist.

One of the absolutes of bookchat land is that the historical novel is neither history nor a novel. On the other hand, a literal record of a contemporary murder is, triumphantly, a novel. This is what I call "the Capote confusion," his monument. Actually, there is no such thing as The Novel as opposed to novels. No one can say what a novel ought to be. But history is something else. Although I try to make the agreed-upon facts as accurate as possible, I always use the phrase "agreed upon" because what we know of a figure as recent, say, as Theodore Roosevelt is not only not the whole truth—an impossibility anyway—but the so-called facts are often contradicted by other facts. So one must select; and it is in selection that literature begins. After all, with *whose* facts do you agree? Also, in a novel, as opposed to a literal history, one can introduce made-up characters who can speculate on the motives of the real people. How real are the real people? Do I have them say what they really said, or am I, like Shakespeare, reinventing them? For those of you ablaze with curiosity regarding the difference between Shakespeare and me, I'll give you an example.

There is in Washington, D.C., my native city and often subject, a South Korean newspaper called the *Washington Times*. This paper is owned by the Moonies and its political line is, baroquely, fascist. Now let's watch one of their employees in action. The first scene of a recent book of mine, *Empire,* takes place in England, at a country house that has been rented for the summer of 1898 by Henry Adams and Senator Don Cameron for the use of their friend John Hay, our ambassador. All those present at a lunch that I describe were actually there, including Henry James, an old friend of Hay and of Adams, who was living at nearby Rye. Confronted with such a scene, the hostile reviewer—who writes only of what *he* knows —often shouts name-dropper. But how is it possible to tell the story of

John Hay without mentioning the fact that as Lincoln's secretary, he got to meet Lincoln? The South Korean reviewer does the ritual attack on me: I hate my native land because I deplore the National Security State. Because I deplore our imperial adventures, I am an *isolationist.* He tells us, "Henry James and Henry Adams figure in *Empire,* neither of them believably, alas . . . for their main function is to serve as spokesmen for Mr. Vidal's isolationism. 'You speak of the laws of history and I am no lawyer,' says the Vidalized James. 'But I confess to misgivings. How can we, who honestly cannot govern ourselves, take up the task of governing others? Are we to govern the Philippines from Tammany Hall?' Neither in style nor in substance does this mini-editorial sound even remotely like the Master." That is very magisterial indeed. Plainly, a James scholar. But let's look at what the Master actually wrote apropos the Spanish-American war. In a letter, he remarks on his "deep embarrassment of thought—of imagination. I have hated, I have almost loathed it." James also spoke most sardonically of the exportation of Tammany and King Caucus to the newly acquired Philippines, "remote countries run by bosses." My South Korean critic did not quote easily the harshest of the Vidalized Henry James's remarks: "The acquisition of an empire civilized the English. That may not be a law but it is a fact. . . . But what civilized them might very well demoralize us even further." That's about as anti-imperial—or "isolationist"—as you can get. Now did the real Henry James ever say so un-American a thing? Yes, he did, when he confided to his nephew Harry: "Expansion has so made the English what they are—for good or for ill, but on the whole for good—that one doesn't quite feel one's way to say for one's country 'No—I'll have none of it.' Empire has educated the English. Will it only demoralize us?" Now you see how I have "my" James say, in substance, precisely what the original said. I do condense and rearrange, something a biographer must never do but a novelist must do. If the James of *Empire* is not credible then he himself would not be credible to a jingo on a Washington newspaper, who also tells us, basking in his ignorance, that no young woman—like my invented Caroline— could have taken over a Washington newspaper and made a success of it. But less than twenty years later one Eleanor Patterson, whom I knew very well, did just that and published the earlier *Washington Times-Herald.* As for America's perennially venal press, the *Washington Times* reviewer will be stunned to hear Henry James, in real life, blame the newspapers for the despicable war with Spain because of "the horrible way in which they envenomize all dangers and reverberate all lies." Like Mark Twain and William Dean Howells he was, incredibly, an "isolationist" with a contempt for the popular press. So, as you can see, I do not invent my literary ancestors. If anything, they invented me.

I have mentioned agreed-upon facts as the stuff of history. But if it is impossible to take seriously the press of one's own time, why should the historian treat old newspaper cuttings as unimpeachable primary sources? For instance, I am now writing about Warren Harding. One of the few quotations of Harding that I have known all my life was what he said, after his unlikely nomination for president, "We drew to a pair of deuces, and filled." This strikes absolutely the right note for the agreed-upon Harding that our canting society requires: a sleazy poker-playing, hard-drinking, womanizing nonentity put in office by cynical Republican bosses. Yet the journalist Mark Sullivan was with Harding before, during, and after the 1920 convention. In *Our Times* he quotes the poker phrase; then, in a footnote, he says this sort of phrase was not characteristic of Harding, who had a considerable sense of his own dignity. Apparently, Sullivan, who could have asked Harding at any time during the next three years if he had made this remark, never did. Instead he tells us that maybe Harding said it when he was "off balance" from excitement. "Or he may never have said it—it may have been some reporter's conception of what he ought to say." There we have it. In effect, the press invents us all; and the later biographer or historian can only select from the mass of crude fictions and part-truths those "facts" that his contemporaries are willing to agree upon.

Where many English Department hustlers now favor literary theory over literature, the workaday bureaucrats of the History Departments are solemnly aware that *their* agreed-upon facts must constitute—at least in the short term—a view of the republic that will please their trustees. Since all great Americans are uniquely great, even saints, those who record the lives of these saints are hagiographers. This is quite a big solemn business, not unlike the bureaucracy of some huge advertising firm, handling a hallowed account like Ivory soap. A major bureaucrat is Comar Vann Woodward, Sterling Professor of History Emeritus at Yale. A southerner, he noticed, many years ago, that blacks were people. This Newtonian revelation brought him tenure; and landed him many important accounts.

Like so many academic bureaucrats the Sterling Professor is highly protective of his turf; he does not want the untenured loose in the field. Sadly, he noted in the *New York Review*, regarding my novel *Lincoln*, that the "book was extravagantly praised by both novelists and historians—a few of the latter at least. Some of the foremost Lincoln scholars do not share these views. After listing numerous historical blunders and errors of the novel, Richard N. Current, a leading Lincoln biographer, declares that " 'Vidal is wrong on big as well as little matters. He grossly distorts Lincoln's character and role in history.' " Woodward gives no examples of these distortions. He does tell us that "Roy P. Basler, editor of *The Collected Works of Abraham Lincoln,* estimates that 'more than half of the book could never have happened as told by Vidal.' " Apparently, Woodward believes that it is sufficient merely to assert. He does not demonstrate, doubtless because he is innocent of the text in question; so he cites, vaguely, other assertions.

The late Vladimir Nabokov said that when anyone criticized his art, he was indifferent. That was their problem. But if anyone attacked his scholarship, he reached for his dictionary. After reading Woodward, I took the trouble to read the two very curious little essays that he cites. What case do they make? Is half the book all wrong; and Lincoln himself grossly distorted? Although I do my own research, unlike so many professors whose hagiographies are usually the work of those indentured servants, the graduate students, when it comes to checking a finished manuscript, I turn to Academe. In this case professor David Herbert Donald of Harvard, who has written a great deal about the period which the Sterling Professor, as far as I recall, has not written about at all. Once the book was written, I employed a professional researcher to correct dates, names, and even agreed-upon facts.

Professor Richard N. Current fusses, not irrelevantly, about the propriety of fictionalizing actual political figures. I also fuss about this. But he has fallen prey to the scholar-squirrels' delusion that there is a final Truth revealed only to the tenured few in their footnote maze; in this he is simply naïve. All we have is a mass of more or less agreed-upon facts about the illustrious dead, and each generation tends to rearrange those facts according to what the times require. Current's text seethes with resentment, and I can see why. "Indeed, Vidal claims to be a better historian than any of the academic writers on Lincoln ('hagiographers' he calls them)." Current's source for my unseemly boasting is, God help us, the Larry King radio show, which lasts several hours from midnight on, and no one is under oath for what he says during—in my case—two hours. On the other hand, Larry King, as a source, is about as primary as you can get.

Now it is true that I have been amazed that there has never been a first-rate biography of Lincoln, as opposed to many very good and—yes, scholarly—studies of various aspects of his career. I think one reason for this lack is that too often the bureaucrats of Academe have taken over the writing of history and most of them neither write well nor, worse, understand the nature of the men they are required to make saints of. In the past, history was the province of literary masters—of Gibbon, Macaulay, Burke, Locke, Carlyle and, in our time and nation, Academe's bête noire, Edmund Wilson. In principle, it would be better if English teachers did not write novels and history teachers did not write history. After all, teaching is a great and essential profession, marvelously ill-practiced in our country as was recently demonstrated when half of today's college freshmen could not locate on an unmarked map of the world, the United States. Obviously, there are fine academic historians (to whom I am indebted) but the Donalds, McPhersons, and Foners are greatly outnumbered by—the others.

Then, zeroing in on my chat with Larry King, Current writes that

by denying there is any real basis for Vidal's intimation that Lincoln had syphilis, [Stephen] Oates "shows," according to Vidal, "that, . . . Mr. Oates is not as good a historian as Mr. Vidal."

First, I like Current's slippery "any real basis" for Lincoln's syphilis. No, there is no existing Wassermann report or its equivalent. But there is the well-known testimony of William Herndon, Lincoln's law partner, that Lincoln told him that he had contracted syphilis in his youth and that it had "clung to him." This is a primary source not to be dismissed lightly; yet Mr. Oates was quoted in the press as saying that there was never any evidence that Lincoln had had syphilis, ignoring Lincoln's own words to Herndon. It was *Newsweek*, not I, who said that Mr. Vidal is a better historian than Mr. Oates. I have no opinion in the matter as I've never read Oates except on the subject of me, where he is bold and inaccurate.

Current finds my trust in Herndon naïve; and quotes Professor Donald on Herndon as being important largely because of "the errors that he spread." But Donald was referring to Herndon's haphazard researches into Lincoln's family and early life, conducted after Lincoln's death. I am not aware that Donald or anyone—except a professional hagiographer—could doubt Herndon when he says that Lincoln himself told him something.

For the record, Donald's actual words: "Herndon stands in the backward glance of history, mythmaker and truthteller."

═══

Current has literary longings; he frets over my prose. I spell "jewelry" and "practice" in the English manner and speak of a house *in* Fourteenth Street instead of *on* Fourteenth Street. It was not until H. L. Mencken, in 1919, that an attempt was made to separate the American language from the English; and even then, many writers ignored and still ignore the Sage of Baltimore. Since *Burr* and *1876* were written in the first person, as if by an American early in the last century, I used those locutions that were then common to agreed-upon American speech. For consistency's sake, I continued them in *Lincoln.* As for myself, neither in prose nor in life would I say that someone lived on Fourteenth Street, though in the age of Reagan I have detected quite a few people living on rather than in streets. I also note that two novels I've been rereading follow my usage: *The Great Gatsby,* 1925, *The Last Puritan,* 1936. Current wins only one small victory: I use the word *trolley* in 1864 when the word did not surface until the 1890s. But his other objections are not only trivial but wrong. He says Charles Sumner was struck with a "cane" not, as I say, a "stick"; then and now the words are interchangeable, at least in Senator Sumner's circles. He also trots out the tired quibble over the origin of "hooker." For the purposes of a Civil War novel it is enough to give General Hooker the credit because the whores in Marble Alley, back of, what is now the Washington Post Office, were commonly known as Hooker's Division. According to Partridge's *Dictionary of Slang,* the only British meaning we have for the word at that time is a watch-stealer or pickpocket.

Current then fires off a series of statements that I have written such and such. And such and such is not true. This is dizzy even by contemporary American university standards. For instance, "Ulysses S. Grant had not failed in 'the saddlery business.' " That he had failed is an offhand remark I attribute (without footnote) to a contemporary. The truth? At thirty-seven Grant had failed at every civilian job he had put his hand to, obliging him to become a clerk in his father's firm, Grant & Perkins, which "sold harnesses and other leather goods . . . providing new straps for old saddles" (William McFeely's *Grant*), and the business was run not by failure Grant but by his younger brother Orvil. Current is also outraged by a reference to Lincoln's bowels, whose "frequency," he tells us, "cannot be documented." But, of course, they can. "Truth-teller" Herndon tells us that Lincoln was chronically constipated and depended on a laxative called blue-mass. Since saints do not have bowels, Current finds all this sacrilegious; hence "wrong."

=

Now there is no reason why Current, master of our language though he is, should understand how a novel—even one that incorporates actual events and dialogue—is made. The historian-scholar, of course, plays god. He has his footnotes, his citations, his press clippings, his fellow scholar-squirrels to quote from. If he lacks literary talent, he then simply serves up the agreed-upon facts as if they were the Truth, and should he have a political slant—and any American schoolteacher is bound to, and most predictable it is—the result will emerge as a plaster saint, like that dead effigy of Jefferson by Dumas Malone and his legion of graduate students.

Although a novel *can* be told as if the author is God, often a novel is told from the point of view of one or more characters. For those of us inclined to the Jamesian stricture, a given scene ought to be observed by a single character, who can only know what he knows, which is often less than the reader. For someone with no special knowledge of—or as yet interest in—Grant, the fact that harnesses and *other* leather goods were sold along with saddles by the failure Grant is a matter of no interest. The true scholar-squirrel, of course, must itemize everything sold in the shop. This is the real difference between a novel and a biography. But though I tend in these books more to history than to the invented, I am still obliged to dramatize my story through someone's consciousness. But when it comes to a great mysterious figure like Lincoln, I do not enter his mind. I only show him as those around him saw him at specific times. This rules out hindsight, which is all that a historian, by definition, has; and which people in real life, or in its imitation the novel, can never have.

Current is a master of the one-line unproved assertion. Here are some of what he calls my false "contentions." "As early as April 1861 Lincoln was thinking of emancipation as possibly justifiable as 'a military necessity.'" I looked up the scene in the novel and found that it was not Lincoln but the abolitionist Sumner who was thinking along those lines; Lincoln himself was noncommittal. Then "Vidal pictures Lincoln as an ignoramus in regard to public finance. He makes him so stupid as to think Secretary of the Treasury Chase personally signed every greenback, and so uninformed as to have 'no idea what the greenbacks actually represented.' " This is nicely—deliberately?—garbled. It is not Chase that Lincoln thinks signs the greenbacks but the treasurer, Lucius Crittenden; this provided a famous scene in Carl Sandburg's hagiography, on which I do an ironical variation.

Current tells us that I go along with the "innuendo" that Stanton "masterminded the assassination." If he had actually read the whole book, he would have been able to follow almost every turn to Booth's assassination plot, in which Stanton figures not at all; had he got to the end of the book, he would have heard Hay make fun of those who believed that Stanton had any connection with the murder of the man to whom he owed everything. Next I "intimate" that there was a second plot afoot, involving "Radical Republicans in Congress." There was indeed a second plot, to be found in Pinkerton's Secret Service files. But no one knows who masterminded it.

Next, I propose the following outrage: that "Lincoln excluded Union-held areas from the Emancipation Proclamation" as a favor to "pro-Union slaveholders." Yet it is a fact that seven counties in and around Norfolk, Virginia, and several Louisiana parishes were allowed to maintain slavery while slavery was banned in the rest of the South. Why did Lincoln do this? He needed Unionist votes in Congress, and one belonged to a Louisiana congressman. After all, Lincoln was never an abolitionist; he was a Unionist, and as he most famously said, if he could preserve the Union only by maintaining slavery, he would do so. Apparently, saints don't make deals.

＝

By and large, Current's complaints range from the trivial to the pointless. Does he find me wrong on anything of consequence? Yes, he does. And I think it is the whole point to his weird enterprise. Current tells us that "there is no convincing evidence" for Vidal's contention that "as late as April 1865 [Lincoln] was still planning to colonize freed slaves outside the United States." This is a delicate point in the 1980s, when no national saint can be suspected of racism. I turned to one of my authorities for this statement; and realized that I may have relied on suspect scholarship. Here is the passage I used:

Lincoln to the last seemed to have a lingering preference for another kind of amendment, another kind of plan. He still clung to his old ideas of postponing final emancipation, compensating slaveholders, and colonizing freedmen. Or so it would appear. As late as March of 1865, if the somewhat dubious Ben Butler is to be believed, Lincoln summoned him to the White House to discuss with him the feasibility of removing the colored population of the United States.

This is from a book called *The Lincoln Nobody Knows* (p. 230) by Richard N. Current. So either Current is as wrong about this as he is about me, or he is right and between March and April 15, 1865, when Lincoln departed this vale of tears, the President changed his mind on the colonizing of slaves. If he did, there is no record known to me—or, I suspect, to anyone else.

What is going on here is a deliberate revision by Current not only of Lincoln but of himself in order to serve the saint in the 1980s as opposed to the saint at earlier times when blacks were still colored, having only just stopped being Negroes. In colored and Negro days the saint might have wanted them out of the country, as he did. But in the age of Martin Luther King even the most covertly racist of school boards must agree that a saint like Abraham Lincoln could never have wanted a single black person to leave freedom's land much less bravery's home. So all the hagiographers are redoing their plaster images and anyone who draws attention to the discrepancy between their own past crudities and their current falsities is a very bad person indeed, and not a scholar, and probably a communist as well.

===

Roy P. Basler, Woodward's other "authority," is given to frantic hyperbole. He declares Sandburg's *Lincoln* a "monumental achievement." Well, it's a monument all right—to a plaster saint, of the sort that these two professional hagiographers are paid to keep dusted. Basler finds my *Lincoln* the "phoniest historical novel I have ever had the pleasure of reading." Well, there may be *one* phony bit, the Crittenden signature story, which I got from Basler's monumental biographer Sandburg. Basler should have at least liked that. Also, "more than half the book could never have happened as told." Unfortunately, he doesn't say which half. If I knew, we could then cut it free from the phony half and publish the result as Basler's Vidal's *Lincoln.*

Like Current, Basler gets all tangled up in misread or misunderstood trivia. He goes on at great length that it was not the Reverend James Smith whom Lincoln appointed consul in Scotland but his son Hugh. Well, the son, Hugh, was appointed consul on June 10, 1861; then died; and the father was appointed, later, in his place. Basler says that Mary Todd's scene with General Ord's wife "is histrionically exaggerated out of all proportion to the recorded facts." But it conforms with those recorded facts given by Justin G. and Linda Levitt Turner's standard *Mary Todd Lincoln: Her Life and Letters.* He is also most protective of the saint. For instance, every saint is a kind and indulgent yet gently stern father, devoted to his children who worship him. But Lincoln's oldest son, Robert, did not much like his father.

Basler gets all trembly as he writes,

When Vidal has Robert Lincoln say to Hay about his father, "He hates his past. He hates having been a scrub. . . . He wanted me to be what he couldn't be," I find no excuse. Robert did admit that he and his father had never been close after he was grown, and he may have felt neglected, but for him to speak thus is beyond comprehension.

But he did speak thus, to Senator Thomas Pryor Gore of Oklahoma, my grandfather, who often talked to me about Robert's bleak attitude toward his father, who, having sent his son to Exeter and Harvard in order to move him up in the world, then found that he had a son with whom he had not much in common. I myself attended Exeter four score years after Robert, and memories of Lincoln were still vivid; and well-described not long ago in the alumni bulletin: how Lincoln spoke at the Academy shortly after Cooper Union, and enthralled the boys. But not Robert.

Basler is also protective of the only recently beatified, by Academe, Walt Whitman. (This miracle was accomplished by making Walt Whitman homoerotic rather than homosexual.) "Consider," he rails, "the three pages [actually one and a half] that he devotes to a fictional interview with Secretary of the Treasury, Salmon P. Chase, looking for a job." Basler correctly notes that a Mr. Trowbridge presented a letter to Chase from Emerson, asking that Whitman be given a job. I have Whitman delivering the letter. Basler is stern. "Anyone who knows about Whitman would recognize that presenting the letter in person . . . is wholly false to Whitman's character at this time of his life, and his conversation with Chase is entirely what Vidal might have said, but not Whitman." If Whitman had thought a meeting with Chase would have got him a job he would have done so because, as he wrote of himself then, "I was pulling eminent wires in those days."

As for Whitman's dialogue with Chase, I quite fancied it. He describes the decorations of the Capitol and how "not in one's flightiest dreams has there been so much marble and china, gold and bronze, so many painted gods and goddesses." Whitman compares the Capitol—favorably—but fatally for the teetotaler Chase—to Taylor's saloon in New York. I took this particular passage from Whitman's *Democratic Vistas,* as anyone immersed in the Whitman style—or mine for that matter—would know. Literary criticism is not, perhaps, Basler's strong suit. Actually, I needed the encounter to fill in my portrait of Chase, who, exactly as I described, detested Whitman as the author of a "very bad book," which he had not read; then, being an autograph collector, Chase kept the Emerson letter; then, being a jittery man on the subject of public rectitude, he turned the letter over to the Treasury archive. This is not too bad for a page and a half—of agreed-upon facts, used to illuminate the character not of Whitman but of Chase.

═══

Basler like Current is eager to bring the saint into the mainstream of today's political superstition. Both are appalled whenever I mention his scheme for colonizing the ex-slaves. Both deny that he ever had anything but love and admiration for blacks, who were, he believed, in every way his equals, once slavery was past. "The one thing I most resented," writes Basler, "is the perpetuation of 'Lincoln's unshaken belief that the colored race was inferior to the white. . . .' I have never found any such categorical avowal in anything Lincoln wrote or was reported to have said." The slippery adjective here is "categorical." Yet Basler himself wrote in *The Lincoln Legend* (pp. 210–211), "[Lincoln] never contemplated with any degree of satisfaction the prospect of a free negro race living in the same country with a free white race." Not even I have dared go so far as to suggest that I have ever had any way of knowing what Lincoln may or may not have *contemplated*! In any case, Basler, like Current, is revising himself.

Actually, Lincoln's views of blacks were common to his time and place but, as he was an uncommon man, he tried to transcend them, as he did in a speech in Peoria, in 1854: "My first impulse," he said rather daringly for that year, "would be to free all slaves and send them to Liberia." He then lists all the objections that others would later make to him. He finally throws in the towel when he asks: "Free them and make them politically and socially our equals? Our own feelings would not admit of it, and if mine would, we well know that those of the great mass of whites will not."

It is my radical view that Americans are now sufficiently mature to be shown a Lincoln as close to the original as it is possible for us so much later in time to get. Since the race war goes on as fiercely as ever in this country, I think candor about blacks and whites and racism is necessary. It was part of Lincoln's greatness that, unlike those absolute abolitionists, the Radical Republicans, he foresaw the long ugly confrontation, and tried to spare future generations by geographically separating the races. The fact that his plan was not only impractical but inadvertently cruel is beside the point. He wanted to *do* something; and he never let go the subject, unless of course he had a vision in the last two weeks of his life, known only to Current, who has chosen not to share it.

Recently, an excellent academic historian, Theodore S. Hamerow, published a book called *Reflections on History and Historians.* It was reviewed in *The New York Times* by an English history don, Neil McKendrick. Here is what two professionals have to say of the average American history teacher. As presented by Hamerow, he is "cynical." I quote now from McKendrick: "He is also mean-minded, provincial and envious. We hear verdict after verdict condemning, in the words of one academic, 'the wretched pedantry, the meanness of motive, the petty rancors of rivalry, the stultifying provincialism.' " But then "most professors of history do little research and less publishing and there are statistical tables to prove it. What little is produced is seen as 'coerced productivity,' mainly a parade of second-hand learning and third-rate opinions." Thus, the high professional academics view their run-of-the-mill colleagues.

Recently in *The New York Times* Herbert Mitgang took me to task, indirectly, when he wrote: "Several revisionist academics have advanced the incredible theory that Lincoln really wanted the Civil War, with its 600,-000 casualties, in order to eclipse the Founding Fathers and insure his own place in the pantheon of great presidents." Now there is no single motive driving anyone but, yes, that is pretty much what I came to believe, as Lincoln himself got more and more mystical about the Union, and less and less logical in his defense of it, and more and more appalled at all the blood and at those changes in his country, which, he confessed—with pride?—were "fundamental and astounding." The Lincoln portrayed by me is based on a speech he made in 1838 at the Young Men's Lyceum in Springfield. He began by praising the Founding Fathers and their republic; then he went on:

This field of glory is harvested, and the crop is already appropriated. But new reapers will arise, and they too will seek a field. It is to deny what the history of the world tells us is true to suppose that men of ambitions and talents will not continue to spring up amongst us. And when they do, they will as naturally seek the gratification of their ruling passions as others have done before them. The question, then, is can that gratification be found in supporting and maintaining an edifice that has been erected by others? Most certainly it cannot.

Thus Lincoln warns us against Lincoln.

Towering genius disdains a beaten path. It seeks regions unexplored. . . . It denies that it is glory enough to serve under any chief. It scorns to tread in the path of any predecessor however illustrious. It thirsts and burns for distinction; and, if possible, it will have it, whether at the expense of emancipating slaves or enslaving free men.

Nothing that Shakespeare ever invented was to equal Lincoln's invention of himself and, in the process, us. What the Trojan War was to the Greeks, the Civil War is to us. What the wily Ulysses was to the Greeks, the wily Lincoln is to us—not plaster saint but towering genius, our nation's haunted and haunting re-creator.

THE NEW YORK REVIEW OF BOOKS
*April 28, 1988*

GORE VIDAL REPLIES

It's savory scholar-squirrel stew time again! Or, to be precise, one scholar-squirrel and one plump publicist-pigeon for the pot. So, as the pot boils and I chop this pile of footnotes fine, let me explain to both pigeon and the no doubt bemused readers of these pages why it was that *The New York Times,* the Typhoid Mary of American journalism, should have wanted to discredit, one week before airing, the television dramatization of my book on Abraham Lincoln. The publicist (a caption-*and*-text writer for two Civil War picture books that he shrewdly guesses I've never looked at) tells us that "the *Times* did not assign me to 'bloody' the mini-series . . . but to measure its faithfulness to history," etc. This begs the question: Why, if the *Times* were so uncharacteristically concerned with faithfulness to fact of any kind, should they select him, a nonhistorian, whose current job, he told me, disarmingly, is that of publicist for the admirable Mario Cuomo? I suspect that he was chosen because a publicist will give an editor exactly what he wants. In any case, my own long history with *The New York Times* does, in a curious way, illuminate not only this peculiar dispute but the rather more interesting nature of history itself.

In 1946 my first novel was published. A war novel, it was praised by the daily book reviewer of the *Times,* one Orville Prescott, whose power to "make or break" a book was then unique; and now unimaginable. I was made. Then, in 1948, two books were published within weeks of each other. First, *The City and the Pillar* by me; then *Sexual Behavior in the Human Male* by Dr. Alfred C. Kinsey, et al. In my novel, I found the love affair between two ordinary American youths to be a matter-of-fact and normal business. Dr. Kinsey then confirmed, statistically, that more than a third of the American male population had performed, at least once, a vile and abominable act against nature. Since the generation of American males that he was studying had just won the last great war that our sissy republic ever was to win (as R. M. Nixon would say, I mean "sissy" in the very best sense of that word), it was unthinkable that . . . The polemic began; and goes on.

At the time, Orville Prescott told my publisher, Nicholas Wreden of E.P. Dutton, that he would never again read much less review a book by me. The *Times* then refused to advertise either my book or the Kinsey report. True to Prescott's word, my next five novels were not reviewed in the daily *Times* or, indeed, in *Time* or *Newsweek*. In freedom's land what ought not to be is not and must be blacked out. I was unmade. For ten years I did television, theater, movies; then returned to the novel.

The war goes on, though with less spirit than in the old days when the Sunday editor of the *Times*, Lester Markel, canvassed five writers, among them my friend Richard Rovere, to see if one would "bloody" *The Best Man*, a play that their autonomous daily reviewer had liked. Finally, Douglass Cater wrote a mildly dissenting piece, which was duly published. Simultaneously, a writer was assigned to "bloody" my campaign for Congress in New York's Twenty-ninth District, a polity usually unnoticed by *The New York Times;* and then . . . and then . . . Anyway, we need not believe the publicist when he says that he was not engaged to "bloody" the television *Lincoln.* Of course he was; and I fell into the trap.

The publicist wrote to tell me that he was writing about the television *Lincoln* and the problems of dramatized history. Since I had nothing to do with the production, I thought that the *Times* might be playing it straight. Plainly, I had lost my cunning. I was interviewed on the telephone. He asked me if I read historical novels. I said, almost never. I'm obliged to read history. A few moments later he said, "As you never read history . . ." I realized then that I'd been had yet again by the foxy old *New York Times.* I remarked upon the mysteriousness of history. Quoted Henry Adams's famous summing up on the "why" and the "what." The publicist got the quotation right but attributed it to Thoreau.

The headline of *The New York Times* story:

A FILTERED PORTRAIT OF LINCOLN
COMES TO THE SMALL SCREEN.

Filtered is meant to indicate some sort of bias. A second headline was set up in type reminiscent of the *National Enquirer:*

THE PRODUCERS OF THE MINISERIES
ADAPTED IT FROM GORE VIDAL'S NOVEL,
A WORK ALREADY FAULTED BY HISTORIANS.

That was the best—and pretty good, too—that the *Times* could do to scare off viewers. The publicist's story was dim. There was no mention of those historians who had praised *Lincoln*. The caption writer found many things "troubling"; none of any consequence, except Lincoln's attitude toward blacks.

===

The publicist tells us that "Lincoln hardly made" a shady bargain with Salmon P. Chase "to win his support for his 1864 reelection campaign, by offering him in return the job of chief justice." I don't recollect the phrase *shady bargain* in either book or drama. But if the publicist does not understand Lincoln's devious game with Chase then he doesn't understand politics in general or Lincoln in particular. Although Lincoln had ended Chase's dream of being the Republican nominee that year, Chase could still have made trouble. Chase was also one of the few men in public life whom Lincoln genuinely disliked. In the summer of 1864, Chase, who had resigned as Lincoln's secretary of the treasury, was making overtures to the Democratic party: "This . . . might mean much," he wrote, "if the Democrats would only cut loose from slavery and go for freedom. . . . *If they would do that, I would cheerfully go for any man they might nominate.* "* Aware of Chase's conniving, Lincoln confided to his secretary, John Hay, "What Chase ought to do is to help his successor through his installation . . .; go home without making any fight and wait for a good thing hereafter, such as a vacancy on the Supreme Bench or some such matter."†

Lincoln played a lovely game with Chase; he even got him to stump Indiana and Ohio for him. He hinted to Chase's friends that Chase was under serious consideration for the chief justiceship, which my publicist-critic thinks impossible because the chief justice was still alive. Unknown to the caption writer, the chief justice, Roger B. Taney, was eighty-seven years old that summer and poorly. The new president was bound to make the appointment. So there was a lot of maneuvering, by the dark of the moon, on Lincoln's part to put Chase, in his daughter's phrase, "on the shelf." In exchange for not rocking the boat (supporting McClellan, say)

*See Robert B. Warden, *An Account of the Private Life and Public Services of Salmon Portland Chase* (Cincinnati, 1874), p. 627.

†Tyler Dennett, ed., *Lincoln and the Civil War in the Diaries and Letters of John Hay* (New York: Dodd, Mead, 1939), p. 203.

Chase became chief justice after Taney's death, which was after the election. Was Chase chosen because he was the best man for the job? No, he was not. Politics is bargains and their shadiness depends entirely on which side of the street you happen to be standing.

The publicist's confusions about Lincoln and slavery and what I am supposed to have written are simply hortatory. He seems to think that I think that Lincoln was "desperately seeking a way to renege on Emancipation while at the same time spearheading the Thirteenth Amendment that abolished slavery." This is OK for *The New York Times* but not for a responsible paper. Neither I nor the dramatizers ever suggested that he wanted to renege, desperately or not, on Emancipation. It will also come as news to any Lincoln scholars that the saint "spearheaded" the Thirteenth Amendment. He favored it. The spear-carriers were abolitionists, Radical Republicans. But Lincoln and the blacks is the crux of all this nonsense, and I shall address the question in due course.

≡

From the tone of Professor Richard N. Current's letter I fear that I may have hurt his feelings. In a covering letter to the editors of *The New York Review of Books*, he refers to my "personal attack" on him. As Current is as unknown to me as Lincoln was to him in his book *The Lincoln Nobody Knows*, I could hardly have been personal. I thought my tone in the last exchange sweetly reasonable if necessarily disciplinary. I am sorry he finds "hysterical" my "diatribe." What I was obliged to do in his case was to take, one by one, his flat assertions that such-and-such as written by me (often it wasn't) was untrue; and so great does he feel his emeritus weight that that was that.

Finally, about halfway through I gave up answering him. Now he is at it again. He tells us that I have "pretended" to be a scholar-squirrel; I give the impression (false it would seem) that I have visited libraries and looked at old newspapers, etc. Now, in the case of *Lincoln*, I have relied heavily on the diaries of John Hay and Salmon P. Chase since I observe Lincoln from the viewpoint of each. Current seems to think that I could not possibly have read these diaries despite internal evidence to the contrary. As for old newspapers, I used a reporter's shorthand version of the Gettysburg Address, which differs somewhat from the official text. But, by and large, I have always relied heavily on the work of *scholars* in my reflections on American history and, in a way, I have become their ideal reader because I have no professional ax to grind, no tenure to seek, no prizes or fellowships to win.

How does a scholar differ from a scholar-squirrel? The squirrel is a careerist who mindlessly gathers little facts for professional reasons. I don't in the least mind this sort of welfare for the "educated" middle class. They must live, too. But when they start working in concert to revise history to suit new political necessities, I reach for my ancient Winchester.

Current tells us that "[Vidal] implied that he was a greater Lincoln authority than Stephen B. Oates or any other academic historian except David Herbert Donald." As I pointed out in the last exchange, it was *Newsweek* that found me to be (in reference to Lincoln's alleged syphilis) a better historian than Mr. Oates, whom I have never read. I do not "imply" (Current has a guardhouse lawyer's way with weasel-words) that I am a better historian than anyone. This is the sort of thing that obsesses academic careerists. Scholar-squirrels spend their lives trying to be noted and listed and graded and seeded because such rankings determine their careers. Those of us engaged in literature and, perhaps, in history as well don't think in such terms. We also don't go on Pulitzer Prize committees to give a friend a prize which, in due course, when he is on the committee, he will give us for our squirrelings.

Current feels that I "grossly distort" Lincoln by showing him "as ignorant of economics, disregardful of the Constitution, and unconcerned with the rights of blacks." Even a casual reading of *Lincoln* shows that I spend quite a lot of time demonstrating the President's concern with the rights of blacks, and where and how they should be exercised. Disregardful of the Constitution? No other president until recent years has shown so perfect a disregard for that document in the guise of "military necessity." The chief justice himself thought the president so disregardful that he hurled the Constitution at his head. Lincoln just ducked; and the corpus of one Mr. Merryman of Baltimore was not delivered up for trial, as the chief justice had ordered. I should like Current to demonstrate (elsewhere, please) Lincoln's mastery of economics. Meanwhile, I highly recommend *Lincoln's Preparation for Greatness by Paul Simon* (yes, the Illinois senator),* where he records Lincoln's activities in the state House of Representatives. During four terms, Lincoln and eight other school-of-Clay

---

*Paul Simon, *Lincoln's Preparation for Greatness: The Illinois Legislative Years* (University of Oklahoma Press, 1965).

legislators, known as "the long Nine," nearly bankrupted the state with a "Big Improvements" bill that took Illinois forty-five years to pay off. The story about Lincoln's confusions over who signed the greenbacks occurs in Sandburg; and is public domain.* I'm sorry if Current finds my last "screed" somewhat "maundering" but there are a limited number of ways of saying "false" without actually using the word.

═══

Current, lord of language, wants Lincoln to be Will Rogers, all folksy and homey. But Lincoln's own language resounds with what Current calls "Briticisms." Lincoln's prose was drenched in Shakespeare. Of course, H.L. Mencken was not the first to try to separate American English from English. But in our country, he has been the prime instigator. Finally, prose is all a matter of ear. A word like *screed*, for instance, is now used only by the semiliterate when they want to sound highfalutin, usually in the course of a powerful letter to the editor.

We shall go no further into the word *hooker* other than to observe that a word, in different contexts, picks up additional meanings. A copperhead is a snake is a traitor is a Democrat, depending on the year the word is used and the user. One authority gives a New York origin for *hooker*. In Washington, in the Civil War, General Hooker's name added new resonance. Another authority says the word comes from the verb *to hook*, as the whores in London hooked arms with potential customers as a means of introduction.

Current affects not to understand what I mean by "agreed-upon facts" as the stuff of history. He would like the reader to think that I invent something and get someone to agree to it. The point to my long disquisition on *The New York Times* is to show that one cannot trust *any* primary source. If the *Times* says that I said Thoreau wrote something that Henry Adams actually wrote, my "error" becomes a fact because the *Times* is a primary source for scholar-squirrels—scholars, too. To take at face value any newspaper story is to be dangerously innocent. But one can't challenge everything that has ever been printed. So, through weariness and ignorance, there is a general consensus, which then becomes what I call an "agreed-upon" fact. We all decide not to worry it. Yet in two standard

*Carl Sandburg, *Abraham Lincoln: The War Years* (New York: Harcourt, Brace, 1939), Volume I.

biographies of John Hay, though the writers agree upon the year of his birth, each gives a different natal month. I have also found that whenever I do make a mistake in writing about history, it is usually because I have followed an acknowledged authority who turns out wrong.

On Emancipation and the exemption of certain areas for political reasons: Lincoln maintained slavery in the slave states within the Union and freed those in the Confederacy. Current is more than usually confused here. He thinks Lincoln maintained slavery in "liberated" or "restored" sections of Louisiana because the Union controlled these counties and no political necessity was involved. Like so many hagiographers, Current refuses to face the fact that before Lincoln became a saint he was a superb politician. He did nothing without political calculation. He was also a master of telling different people different things, causing no end of trouble for later worshipers who can't deal with all the contradictions. Emancipation was as much a political as a military necessity for Lincoln. For instance, when Lincoln appointed the proslavery Edward Stanly governor of occupied North Carolina, it was with the understanding that Lincoln would *not* interfere with slavery in the states. When the Emancipation Proclamation was issued, according to one professor of history,

Stanly went to Washington intending to resign. After several talks with Lincoln, however, Stanly was satisfied. He returned to his job, but first he called at the office of James C. Welling, editor of the *National Intelligencer.* Welling wrote in his diary: "Mr. Stanly said that the President had stated to him that the proclamation had become a civil necessity to prevent the Radicals from openly embarrassing the government in the conduct of the war."

So Lincoln speaks with forked tongue in this passage from Richard N. Current's *The Lincoln Nobody Knows.* * Personally, I'd not have let this agreed-upon fact sail so easily by. Wouldn't Stanly lie to Welling, to explain his behavior? Or might Welling have misunderstood what Stanly said Lincoln said? Or, unthinkable thought, could Lincoln have lied to Stanly? Current accepts too readily a story highly discreditable to the Great Emancipator he would now have us worship in all his seamless integrity.

*New York: McGraw-Hill (1958), p. 227.

≡

Here comes Grant again. One thing about Current, he knows not defeat. I "asserted that Ulysses S. Grant 'had gone into the saddlery business, where he had attractively failed.' " The "assertion" in the novel was John Hay's, in an idle moment, about a man he knew nothing much of in 1862. Triumphantly, Current now writes, "The point is that Grant had never gone into the saddlery, harness, or leather-goods business and therefore could not have failed at it. He was only an employee." This is the sort of thing that gives mindless pedantry a bad name. Even in Current's super American English, it is possible to fail at a job by being fired or being carried if your father owns the place. "At thirty-seven Grant had to go back [home] and admit that he was still a failure: the boy who could not bargain for a horse had become a man who could not bring in a crop of potatoes or collect a batch of bills. It was humiliating."* After a year as a clerk, under the managership of his younger brother, Grant was saved by the war and, as he himself wrote, "I never went into our leather store after the meeting" (where he got his command), "to put up a package or do other business."

But note the Current technique throughout this supremely unimportant business. He zeroes in on an idle remark by someone who knows nothing about Grant other than his failure in civilian life, most recently in leather goods. The man who said it is a character living in history not looking back on it. Current seems to think that I should supply the indifferent Hay with the full and absolute knowledge of Grant's affairs that a scholar-squirrel could find out but a contemporary stranger could hardly have known. Owing to Current's uneasy grasp of any kind of English he seems to think that to fail at a business means you must own the business and go broke. That's one meaning. But you can also fail by losing your job or by being tolerated as a hopeless employee by your family. Current wonders why I don't answer more of his charges. They are almost all of them as specious as this.

One of the signs of obsession is an inability to tell the difference between what matters and what does not. The obsessed gives everything the same weight. Current juggles words this way and that to try to "prove" what is often pointless and unprovable. There *is* an issue here but he can't focus

---

*William S. McFeely, *Grant: A Biography* (New York: Norton, 1981), p. 64.

on it. The issue is Lincoln and the blacks. The United States was then and is now a profoundly racist society that pretends not to be and so requires the likes of Current to disguise the American reality from the people, while menacing the society's critics, most successfully, it should be noted, within the academy where the squirrels predominate. I shall indulge Current on two minor points and then get to what matters.

Lincoln's bowels. This occupies a few lines in my book. It is necessary to mention the subject because one of Booth's conspirators tried to poison Lincoln's laxative, which was made up at Thompson's drugstore; whether or not prescription clerk David Herold actually poisoned the medicine is not agreed upon.* Current thinks that constipation is a central theme to the book, the Emancipator as Martin Luther. Herndon tells us: "Mr. Lincoln had an evacuation, a passage, about once a week, ate blue mass. Were you to read his early speeches thoroughly and well, you could see his, then, coarse nature, his materialism, etc." That's all. Since Herndon shared an office with Lincoln for seventeen years there is no reason for this subject not to have been mentioned. After all, many of Lincoln's famed funny stories concerned the outhouse. Current should read them. Also, Current might have given some thought to the sentence after constipation—Lincoln's early "coarse nature, his materialism"; this is provocative.

But Current is now prey to obsession: "Vidal would have us believe that every time Lincoln defecated he reported it to Herndon." I would not have anyone believe such a thing since Herndon in my book makes no mention of Lincoln's bowels, a subject of interest only to the putative poisoners. I fear Current is now sailing right round the bend. He claims that I said on NBC's *Today* show (he seems to be watching rather too much TV) that Lincoln definitely gave Mary Todd syphilis and that she had died of paresis that had affected the brain. He quotes me as saying that one is not "under oath" on television so that one can presumably tell lies. When I say I'm not under oath, I mean that I'm free to speculate on matters that cannot be proven. I would not write that Lincoln gave his wife syphilis, but I can certainly, in conversation, give an opinion. Since my book stops in 1865 and Mary Todd didn't die until 1882, I never tried to "prove" the subject. But years ago a doctor friend in Chicago told me that an autopsy had been

---

*Louis J. Weichmann, *A True History of the Assassination* (New York: Vintage, 1977), p. 44.

performed on Mrs. Lincoln (but only on the head, an odd procedure even then) and that the brain was found to have physically deteriorated, ruling out mere neurosis, the usual explanation for her behavior. I didn't write about this and have never followed it up. If Current can tear himself away from the Larry King show, he might have a go at it.

As for Lincoln's syphilis, I use the words Herndon himself used: "About the year 1835–36 Mr. Lincoln went to Beardstown and during a devilish passion had connection with a girl and caught the disease [syphilis]. Lincoln told me this. . . . About the year 1836–37 Lincoln moved to Springfield. . . . At this time I suppose that the disease hung to him and, not wishing to trust our physicians, he wrote a note to Doctor Drake." Since there is no reason for Herndon to lie about this, I suppose we should all agree upon it as a fact. But since no saint has ever had syphilis, Herndon is a liar and so the consensus finds against him. I don't much admire this sort of thing. Current, historian and master of the American language, now reveals another facet to a protean nature that nobody knows: Current, diagnostician:

If Vidal had the slightest concern for truth, he could easily have learned from such a reference as *The Merck Manual of Diagnosis and Therapy* that Mrs. Lincoln's symptoms and those of a paretic do not correspond.

This is a brave leap in the dark and, once again, Current, the Mr. Magoo of the History Department, lands on his face. From the *Merck Manual:*

General paresis or demential paralytica generally affects patients in their 40s and 50s. The onset is usually insidious and manifested by behavior changes. It also may be present with convulsions or epileptic attacks and there may be aphasia or a transient hemiparesis. Changes in the patient include irritability, difficulty in concentration, memory deterioration, and defective judgment. Headaches and insomnia are associated with fatigue and lethargy. The patient's appearance becomes shabby, unkempt, and dirty; emotional instability leads to frequent weeping and temper tantrums; neurasthenia, depression, and delusions of grandeur with lack of insight may be present.

This exactly describes Mrs. Lincoln's behavior as reported by contemporaries and by such sympathetic biographers as Ruth Painter Randall and the

Turners.* I am in Current's debt for leading me to this smoking, as it were, gun. But where, I wonder, is the autopsy report? Could Robert Lincoln have destroyed all copies? Has Walter Reed collected it in its great presidential net?

≡

Current admits to changing his mind about Lincoln in the course of many years of squirreling. But although he no longer holds to his views on Lincoln and the blacks as presented in *The Lincoln Nobody Knows* (a book, he'll be relieved to know, I never took very seriously, largely because of the megalomaniacal title in which he has inserted himself), he does find, as do I, disconcerting the way that Lincoln lovers (no hater would be allowed tenure anywhere in bravery's home) keep changing the image to conform to new policies. When the civil rights movement took off in the sixties, uppity blacks toyed with the notion that Lincoln was a honkie (Julius Lester, in *Look Out, Whitey!*, etc.). Immediately the agreed-upon facts of earlier times (colonize the freed slaves, reimburse the slave owners, etc.) had to be papered over and a new set of agreed-upon facts were hurried into place, so that LaWanda Cox could deliver a new verdict: "There is no mistaking the fact that by 1865 Lincoln's concern for the future of the freed people was directed to their condition and rights at home, rather than abroad."†

This is the new line, and I have no particular quarrel with it. But certain hagiographers are now pretending that Lincoln was *never* serious about colonization, which is a falsification of the record. In Lincoln's second annual message to Congress (December 1, 1862) he said: "I cannot make it better known than it is, that I strongly favor colonization." Certainly for the first two years of his administration Lincoln was mad on the subject. Gradually, he *seems* to have let the notion go because of the logistical impossibility of shipping out three or four million people who were less than enthusiastic about a long sea voyage to the respective wilds of Haiti, Panama, Liberia.

*Ruth Painter Randall, *Mary Lincoln: Biography of a Marriage* (New York: Little, Brown, 1953); Justin G. Turner and Linda Levitt Turner, eds., *Mary Todd Lincoln: Her Life and Letters* (New York: Knopf, 1972).

†LaWanda Cox, *Lincoln and Black Freedom: A Study in Presidential Leadership* (University of South Carolina Press, 1981), p. 23.

Current says that he "did not . . . state it as my opinion . . . that Lincoln remained a colonizationist." That was wise, because no one knows. I don't give my personal view either though I did note (but did not write) that usually when Lincoln started in on the necessity of reimbursing the slave owners, colonization was seldom far behind: the two seemed twinned in his head. The revisionists now admired by Current maintain that the only evidence that Lincoln at the end was still pondering colonization is Ben Butler's testimony that the president mentioned it to him some time after February 3, 1865. I found most intriguing Mark E. Neely, Jr.'s case that Lincoln could not have talked to Butler at the time that Butler says he did, because Butler had written Secretary of War Stanton a letter assuring him that he had stayed in New York until March 23, in conformance with War Department policy that forbade officers from visiting the capital without permission.* This is a scholarly not squirrelly finding. But if one is to factor out Butler as a crucial witness because he is a liar, why believe the letter to Stanton? If Dan Sickles and other general officers slipped into town without permission, why not the irrepressible Butler? My point is that when one decides a source is apt to be untrue (Herndon, Butler, *The New York Times*), how does one choose what to believe—if anything—from the discredited source?

I understand the politics behind the current (no pun) revisionists but I think they rather overdo it. One dizzy squirrel claims that after 1862, Lincoln discarded the idea of colonization with indecent haste. Yet July 1, 1864, John Hay writes, "I am glad the President has sloughed off that idea of colonization."† For obvious reasons, the revisionists never quote the next sentence. "I have always thought it a hideous & barbarous humbug & the thievery of Pomeroy and Kock have about converted him to the same belief." This sounds a lot more tentative than the revisionists would like us to believe. Perhaps they will now have to establish that Hay is untrustworthy.

In any event, when the black separatist movement starts up in the next decade, new revisionists will supersede the present lot, and Butler's probity will be rehabilitated and Lincoln the colonizer reestablished.

---

*Mark E. Neely, Jr., "Abraham Lincoln and Black Colonization: Benjamin Butler's Spurious Testimony," *Civil War History*, Vol. XXV (March 1979), pp. 77–83.
†*Diaries and Letters of John Hay*, p. 203.

===

On the dust jacket, between the title *Lincoln* and my name there is a one-inch-high caveat: *A Novel.* I tell the story of Lincoln's presidency from the imagined points of view of his wife, of E. B. Washburne, John Hay, Salmon P. Chase, and, marginally, David Herold, one of the conspirators. I never enter Lincoln's mind and, unlike the historian or biographer, I do not make magisterial judgments or quibble with others in the field. The five points of view were dictated, in the case of Hay and Chase, because they kept diaries, skimpily I fear, and many of their letters are available. What I aimed to achieve was balance. Hay admired Lincoln, Chase hated him, Mary Todd loved him, and so on. Each sees him in a different way, under different circumstances.

I am also reflecting upon the nature of fact as observed in fiction, and, indeed, fiction in fact. That is why the scholar-squirrels fascinate me much more than the scholars because they are like barometers, ever responsive to any change in the national weather. This bad period in American history has been, paradoxically, a good period for American history writing. There have never been so many intelligent biographies (yes, they are often written in academe but not by the squirrels) and interesting historians. But pure history, if such a thing could be, is flawed because "history will never reveal to us what connections there are, and at what times, between . . ." For the novelist it is the imagining of connections that brings life to what was. Finally, "History," as Tolstoy also observed, "would be an excellent thing if only it were true." Perhaps, in the end, truth is best imagined, particularly if it is firmly grounded in the disagreed- as well as agreed-upon facts.

My side of these exchanges is now complete. Let others argue elsewhere.

THE NEW YORK REVIEW OF BOOKS
*August 18, 1988*

# APPENDIX

Shortly before I gave this talk to the National Press Club, I spoke to the American-Arab Anti-Discrimination League in Washington (March 13, 1988). I used the same text, giving the history of the National Security State. Then instead of suggesting some things that might be done to help free ourselves from our masters, I addressed the thousand Arab-Americans on problems of specific interest to them. In the audience was the most dreaded of *The New Republic*'s secret agents, code name: Weasel, who, despite a shoulder-length gray fright wig, was easily identified by his tiny ruby-red rabid eyes. Later he characterized my remarks on the National Security State as "cheap patrician rant"—whatever that is; I've never heard a patrician rant the way I do, and at such cost: He characterized what follows not, surprisingly, as "anti-Semitic" but as "nativist," and accused me of now cheating the Arabs as I had once cheated the Jews. This is plainly code, meant to be understood only by the initiate. The Weasel knows:

It has been my fate—or, perhaps, function—to give warnings long before the politicians and the press are able to absorb them. After all, they are in place to give a rosy view of the National Security State, and they give good value for their salaries. Since I'm not paid, I can ruminate; and share my findings.

I am here today because I said much of what I've said just now in New York City at the Royale Theatre, on January 11, 1986. I also passed on the news that the American empire had officially died the previous year when we became, after seventy-one years, a debtor nation, and the money power had gone from New York to Tokyo. I was predictably attacked by the press that serves the National Security State. I was also attacked by those simple Jesus Christers who have been taught all their lives to fear and loathe communism, whatever it may be, and I was also attacked by that not-so-simple Israel lobby which never ceases to demonize the Soviet Union in order to make sure that half the federal revenue goes to defense, out of which the state of Israel, the lobby's sole preoccupation, is financed. I was promptly attacked by that small group of Israel Firsters, who call themselves neoconservatives. I hated my country, they said, because I had criticized that National Security State in which, like a prison, we have all been obliged to live —and go broke—for forty years.

I responded to my critics with characteristic sweetness, turning the other fist as is my wont. I said that as much as I hated what our rulers have done to my country, it was not us, the country, who were at fault. I then added, while we're on the subject of our respective homelands, I'm not so keen about yours, which is Israel. Until then, no one had really challenged the lobby in so public a way. Congress and president and press are all more or less bought or otherwise in-timidated by this self-described "sexy" lobby. While the sins and errors of Israel are openly debated in Israel itself, there has been only fearful silence in bravery's home and freedom's land. Well, I lanced the boil. Naturally, I was called an anti-Semite, usually with the adjective "frenzied" or "virulent" attached.

Now, at the risk of hurting more feelings, I must tell you that I regard monothe-ism as the greatest disaster ever to befall the human race. I see no good in Judaism, Christianity, or Islam—good people, yes, but any religion based on a single . . . well, frenzied and virulent god, is not as useful to the human race as, say, Confucianism, which is not a religion but an ethical and educational system that has worked pretty well for twenty-five hundred years. So you see I am ecumenical in my dislike for the Book. But, like it or not, the Book is there; and because of it people die; and the world is in danger.

Israel had the bad luck to be invented at a moment in history when the nation-state was going out of style. These two clumsy empires, the Soviet Union and the United States are now becoming unstuck. Only by force can the Soviets control their Armenians and Moslems and Mongols, and only by force can we try to control a whole series of escalating race wars here at home, as well as the brisk occupation of the southern tier of the United States by those Hispanics from whom we stole land in 1847. The world, if we survive, will be one not of nations but of *inter*national cartels, of computerized money hurtling between capitals, of countries making what contributions they can to a more or less homogeneous world economy. Simultaneously, armies and flags and centralized administrations will give way to a regionalism that is interdependent with everyone else on earth.

Is this possible? Well, Switzerland is a splendid small-scale model of what the world could be. Four languages, four races, four sets of superstitions about one another—all live most harmoniously in a small area where they make a fortune out of those of us who haven't learned that we are living in a post–national security world. When we finally stop giving to Israel the money that Japan so reluctantly lends us, peace will have to be made. If a cantonal system is set up, some areas of Palestine will be Orthodox Jewish; others Shiite Moslem; others secular Jewish and/or Moslem and/or Christian. In any event, the Great Bronze Age realtor in the sky will finally have to accept that none of those desirable rental properties between the Nile and the Euphrates can ever again include in the lease a discrimination clause.

So what shall we celebrate this joyous Sunday? The slow but highly visible collapse, due to bankruptcy, of the National Security Council-68 state and its ramshackle empire. Once we Americans are free of this dangerous state and its imperial burden we may not have heaven on earth, but we will certainly have lessened the current hell, and got *our* country back.

GORE VIDAL wrote his first novel, *Williwaw* (1946), at the age of nineteen while overseas in World War II.

During four decades as a writer, Vidal has written novels, plays, short stories, and essays. He has also been a political activist. As a Democratic candidate for Congress from upstate New York, he received the most votes of any Democrat in a half century. From 1970 to 1972 he was co-chairman of the People's Party. In California's 1982 Democratic primary for U.S. Senate, he polled a half million votes, and came in second in a field of nine.

In 1948 Vidal wrote the highly praised international best seller *The City and the Pillar*. This was followed by *The Judgment of Paris* and the prophetic *Messiah*. In the fifties Vidal wrote plays for live television and films for Metro-Goldwyn-Mayer. One of the television plays became the successful Broadway play *Visit to a Small Planet* (1957). Directly for the theater he wrote the prize-winning hit *The Best Man* (1960).

In 1964 Vidal returned to the novel. In succession, he created three remarkable works: *Julian, Washington, D.C., Myra Breckinridge*. Each was a number-one best seller in the United States and England. In 1973 Vidal published the popular novel, *Burr*, as well as a volume of collected essays, *Homage to Daniel Shays*. In 1976 he published yet another number-one best seller, *1876*, a part of his on-going American chronicle, which now consists of—in chronological order—*Burr, Lincoln, 1876, Empire*, and *Washington, D.C.*

In 1981 Vidal published *Creation*, "his best novel," according to *The New York Times*. In 1982 Vidal won the American Book Critics Circle Award for criticism for his collection of essays, *The Second American Revolution*. In 1984 Vidal published his most popular novel, *Lincoln*. A propos *Duluth* (1983), Italo Calvino wrote (*La Repubblica*, Rome): "Vidal's development . . . along that line from *Myra Breckinridge* to *Duluth* is crowned with great success, not only for the density of comic effects, each one filled with meaning, not only for the craftsmanship in construction, put together like a clock-work which fears no word processor, but because this latest book holds its own built-in theory, that which the author calls his 'après-poststructuralism.' I consider Vidal to be a master of that new form which is taking shape in world literature and which we may call the hyper-novel or the novel elevated to the square or to the cube."